ALL THE WAY TO THE USA

Australian WWII War Brides

ROBYN ARROWSMITH

Published in 2013 by Robyn Arrowsmith

National Library of Australia Cataloguing-in-Publication entry

Author: Arrowsmith, Robyn

Title: All the way to the USA : Australian WWII war brides
             / Robyn Arrowsmith.

ISBN: 9780987565105 (paperback)

Notes: Includes bibliographical references and index.

Subjects: War brides--Australia.
             War brides--United States.
             Australians--United States.
             Wives--United States--History.
             Women immigrants--United States.
             World War, 1939-1945--Women--Australia.
             World War, 1939-1945--Social aspects--Australia.
             Intercountry marriage--United States.
             Australia--Emigration and immigration--History--
             20th century.
             United States--Emigration and immigration--History--
             20th century.

Dewey Number: 306.8450973

Cover and book layout design
by Publicious Pty Ltd
www.publicious.com.au

Dedication

This book is dedicated to 15,000 Australian WWII war brides of American servicemen, especially those who generously shared their stories and made this book possible.

Also in memory of my sister
Shirley Evelyn Wyndham
6 April 1929 – 16 August 2011

ACKNOWLEDGEMENTS

So many people have made this book possible through their guidance, enthusiasm, encouragement and helpful advice. Firstly, I'd like to thank Professor Emerita Jill Roe, AO, and Professor Mary Spongberg who supervised my PhD thesis at Macquarie University, which was the beginning of my journey with the war brides and became the inspiration for this book.

My thanks also goes to the WWII War Brides Association in America for allowing me to contact members in order to record their stories, and for their faith in me to produce this book although it has taken so long. I am honoured to be an Honorary Member of this Association and to have been welcomed at some of the Association's annual reunions.

To all the Australian WWII war brides across America who shared their stories with me, my thanks is unbounded, as without their enthusiasm and generosity to share their individual experiences, there would be no book. I specially want to thank these remarkable women – and their families – for friendship and hospitality, and for their patience in waiting for the book's publication!

My gratitude also goes to my all my friends, new and old – too many to mention by name – (you'll know who you are!) for showing interest in my book and sustaining enthusiasm for its production, as well as providing me with necessary distractions from time to time.

Last but not least, to all my family – particularly my daughter Katherine Arrowsmith, my niece Susan Wyndham, and my late sister Shirley Wyndham – I owe a deep debt of gratitude for their interest, encouragement, patience, wise advice and always loving support.

Contents

PREFACE

I first became involved with researching the experiences of Australian WWII War Brides in 1999. This was the start of a 12-year period devoted to researching, recording and chronicling the stories of these remarkable women.

My obvious connections with wartime Australia are: my birthdate, which falls in March 1942, just one month after the Japanese bombed Darwin in northern Australia; memories of a young Australian airman brought home by my older sister, Kathy, to share a family dinner; and my sister Shirley's 1948 wedding, at which I was flower girl, where she married a returned sailor in the Royal Australian Navy.

Also, years later, I married my adventurous, English-born husband (many years my senior), who had worked as a young man on his uncle's copra plantation in New Guinea at the outbreak of WWII. Because of his knowledge of native 'pidgin-English', he was seconded by the Australian and New Guinea Administrative Unit (ANGAU) of the Australian Army to work with the Coast Guards to locate Japanese soldiers who had infiltrated the dense jungles in the north. He served in the army for four years and was mentioned in dispatches for his bravery after being shot by a lone Japanese sniper hidden in the treetops. He was lucky to survive, unlike his companion, who was shot and drowned. My husband spoke little of his wartime experiences, as was the custom of returned veterans in those days, but for the rest of his life he bore a three-inch scar under his chin where he had been shot. In one of his rare discussions of his wartime activities, my husband told me of the camaraderie between the Australian and American troops serving in the Pacific theatre of war and how he used to swap 'bully beef' for cigarettes, which the Americans had in good supply, and of his envy of the American troops' access to the luxury of frozen ice-cream in the tropics.

These associations with wartime, however, were not directly linked to my fateful entrance into the world of the Australian WWII war brides of American servicemen. In fact, my future destiny with these women and America was purely serendipitous.

At the age of 37, I was suddenly widowed and my life changed completely. I had a four-year-old daughter and kept busy working part-time, to fit in with school hours.

About five years later, when driving my boss's dog to the dog parlour, I suddenly had a 'light-bulb' moment and asked myself, 'What on earth am I doing? There has to be more to life than this!' It was opportune that on this very day I bumped into an old friend who suggested that I should go to university. I had a mortgage and school fees to pay, but university entrance was free in the mid-80s and there was a special entry program for Mature-Aged Students. So, after much thought and with little to lose, I applied, and was thrilled to be accepted at the University of New South Wales at the age of 42. It took four years to complete my BA (Hons) degree, majoring in Australian and American History, and for the next 15 years I did research work for various academics. During this time, I developed a love of fossicking in archives, digging up treasures from the past, and conducting oral history interviews.

Then, early in 1999, Professor Jill Roe at Macquarie University wanted me to locate some Australian women living in the United States for a project she was setting up. She suggested that since there were a large number of Australian women who had married US servicemen, this might be a good group to target.

Initially, it seemed a daunting task, but I wrote to 'RSVP' sections of major newspapers in each Australian state, seeking Australian WWII war brides living in America. Letters soon arrived from people all over Australia who had an aunt, sister, girlfriend, etc.

who matched the description. I wrote to each of these women in America, and soon, this initial random selection 'snowballed', with one war bride knowing others who also wanted to take part in the study. In no time, I had a database of 200 names of people from all across the United States.

In September of 1999, Professor Roe heard of a reunion of WWII war brides to be held in Reno, Nevada and asked if I could go to interview some of the Australian women who would be attending. Two weeks later, I found myself in Reno's high desert valley, staying in a huge hotel that was lit up like a Christmas tree, with clinking poker machines filling the ground floor. In the lift (elevator), I travelled with John Wayne 'look-alikes' – cowboys dressed in white fringed jackets and wearing wide-brimmed Stetsons and silver spurs! It was quite a culture shock!

There were war brides from many countries at the reunion, but only a small number of Australians. I recorded interviews with these 'salt-of-the-earth' women who were most eager to share their experiences, both in Australia and in America, and were grateful to be able to record their stories for the first time.

It was a rewarding exercise for me and my enthusiasm to interview more war brides prompted Professor Roe to suggest that I conduct my own study, offering to find some paid work for me at Macquarie University. Before I knew it, I was working at three part-time jobs on campus and was accepted as a Masters Candidate as well. Over the next few years, this candidacy was upgraded to a PhD.

During the course of my studies, I attended a war bride reunion in Denver, Colorado, in September 2001 (at the time of the 9/11 tragedy in New York) and visited a number of war brides living on the West Coast between San Francisco and San Diego. Not only did these women insist on my staying in their homes, but they organized luncheon gatherings of Australian war brides living nearby for me to interview. Their efforts really kept me on my toes. At one luncheon, there were 16 people to interview – my tape recorder actually overheated!

Some of these group get-togethers were regular occasions and the war brides looked forward to meeting in different homes each month. They would celebrate their 'Australian-ness' by serving foods remembered from Australia in the 1940s and by singing along to Australian music such as 'Kookaburra Sits in an Old Gum Tree', or jingles, such as 'I Love Aeroplane Jelly', as well as popular wartime songs.

They told me their stories, some more poignant than others, but each one had an underlying shadow of homesickness and longing for the families that had been left behind.

Contrary to my expectations, I returned to the USA a number of times to attend war bride reunions–in 2004 at Washington DC, in 2009 at San Francisco, CA, and last year at Boston, MA.

In 2007, I was honoured to be asked to speak at a special tribute to Australian WWII War Brides on the eve of ANZAC Day at the Australian Embassy in Washington DC. At the end of my talk, to an audience of about 200 people, one lady in the front row stood up, and then stated her name, the name of the ship and the date on which she had sailed to America.

Immediately, at the back of the large auditorium, another woman stood up and called out that she had sailed on the same ship. The two women recognized each other almost instantly and ran to embrace, remembering that shared journey of so long ago. It was a magic moment!

Almost one hundred Australian war brides and their families had come from all parts of the USA to celebrate this event held in their honour. It was very special for these women, now in their eighties and early nineties, to be officially recognized, after sixty years, as good ambassadors for Australian-American relations.

The transcription of approximately sixty in-depth taped interviews proved to be an onerous task, as each one-hour interview took five to six hours to transcribe. However, it was well worth the time spent, as these stories, told in the war brides' own words, were the basis of my research findings and the accuracy of their words was important.

My three part-time jobs at the University became more time-consuming and in 2006 I decided to stop work, sell my house in Sydney and move to the Southern Highlands to finish my thesis. Even after the move, it still took me another four years to complete it! However, the day finally arrived in March, 2010, when my thesis was submitted for examination, and seven months later, I was the proud recipient of my Doctorate.

The whole experience was very rewarding; and at times, when I felt despondent or that I couldn't keep going, I drew on the war brides' stories of strength and courage in the face of adversity. They have been great role models and their stories will inspire not only their children and grandchildren, but also future generations.

Sadly, over the last few years, some of the women I interviewed have died, one very recently. I am forever grateful to them for sharing their experiences and giving their consent for me to tell their stories and bring forward a forgotten part of women's social history.

It is with joy and satisfaction that I publish this book as a culmination of a project which has enriched my life and will hopefully be enjoyed by those who read it.

INTRODUCTION

The early 1940s was a time of great uncertainty for many in Australia, but it was also a time of excitement, especially when Allied troops visited by the thousands. Many young Australian women were quite taken with those handsome young men in uniform from so far away, especially when thousands of US military were stationed there, and inevitably, many relationships were formed.

So it was that WWII saw an unprecedented and worldwide mass movement of more than one million war brides and fiancées who left their homes to join their partners in new lands. 'Bride ships' transported more than 100,000 wives and fiancées of American servicemen alone, from over 50 countries, including the United Kingdom, Europe, Australia, New Zealand, Scandinavia, Africa, China, Japan, and others.[1] A significant portion of the female migration to the United States in the 1940s was the nearly 15,000 Australian war brides and fiancées of American servicemen.[2] Despite this being the largest contingent of Australian women ever to migrate, there has been no in-depth study of their experiences and little has been written about them, leaving their stories untold. In interviews from 1999 to 2008 with sixty Australian WWII war brides of American servicemen, now in their 80s and 90s, their stories were heard for the first time.

This unique source, originally part of the author's research for a doctoral degree at Macquarie University, reveals the particular circumstances encountered by the Australian women who married American servicemen during the social upheaval of WWII. The war brides tell of meeting their future husbands in the 1940s, the manner of their courtships and weddings, and the hardships and obstacles they encountered. Each story presents a more complex understanding of the mythology surrounding wartime romance. They tell about leaving their families and friends, more than sixty years ago, for a new life in an unknown land. Their stories highlight the challenges they faced in travelling to their newly adopted country. Their recorded narratives demonstrate the significance of their protracted voyages to the US; the way in which they adjusted to living in America; how they dealt with decisions regarding citizenship; and how they have nurtured and valued their continuing links with Australia over six decades.

As well as complementing previous studies of women on Australia's home front during WWII, this book adds to our understanding of the impact of the war on Australian women through a detailed analysis of their experiences.[3]

The War Brides

All the women who participated in this study grew up in the aftermath of WWI and most were young children during the difficult years of the Great Depression.[4] Yet in spite of this shared experience, the composition of the group was complex and diverse. The ages of the war brides, for example, cover a wide range. The youngest, Colleen Halter (née Moore), was born in Cairns, Queensland, in May 1927, and was only 12 years old at the outbreak of war. She met her future husband, Jerry Lydle, when she was 17 and married a year later in November, 1945 at the age of 18. Some girls were barely out of school, as in the case of young Ivy Diers (née Willis) from Rockhampton, Queensland, who was 16 when she first met Paul from Omaha, Nebraska, and the couple married three and a half years later in 1945 when Ivy was 19. Ten older women in this group, born between 1913 and 1919, were children during WWI and had reached their mid- to late-20s when the war came to Australia in 1942, their ages ranging from 24 to 32 when they married. However, most women interviewed were born in the early to mid-1920s and at the outbreak of war, their ages ranged from 12 to 25. By 1942, when thousands of American troops arrived in Australia to be welcomed and initially hailed as 'saviours' and 'heroes', their ages ranged from 15 to 29, with most being around the age of 19.[5] Their ages when married ranged from 17 to 32, with most being around the ages of 20 and 21.[6] These figures indicate that the women who married American servicemen did so at a slightly younger age than other women in the general population. Official statistics show that in 1940 the median age at first marriage in Australia was 23.7 for brides, with this figure steadily declining in the post-war years, falling to 20.9 as late as 1974.[7]

Marriage between an Australian girl and an American serviceman was problematic. Once a couple had decided to marry, the ceremony was usually delayed by a mandatory waiting period of six months, after permission was granted by the groom's commanding officer. In many cases, it was a much longer time before the couples could marry due to the re-deployment of the groom to the war zone, his return to America for further training or at the end of his war service.

Given these conditions, the time lapse between meeting and being married varied significantly for this group of women, the shortest periods being two months in one case and three months in another. Both weddings took place before the mandatory six month's waiting period was introduced. The longest period between meeting and marriage was six years. Most of the women, however, married within three years of meeting their future husbands. These figures indicate that marriages between Australian women and American servicemen were not generally made in haste and challenge contemporary stereotypes which categorised these women as 'good-time girls' and 'one-night stands'.

These young women came from suburban and rural locations, as well as cities, across Australia and from diverse socio-economic backgrounds. Their fathers' occupations ranged from 'shearer', 'tram conductor', 'carpenter', and 'goldminer' to 'teacher', 'journalist', 'banker', engineer' and 'chamber magistrate'.[8] Their origins clearly crossed class boundaries, but all were affected in some way by the years of the Great Depression. Some of these women were the only children in the family, while some had one or two siblings. However, many came from large families, despite the plummeting marriage and fertility rates of the 1920s.[9] While most grew up at home, some were sent away as children to live with grandparents or aunts to ease financial stress or to be closer to schools. Aware of the hardships their parents experienced during the 1930s, this particular generation of young women grew up in households that generally practised frugality out of necessity, where it was a matter of course to wear home-made clothes, to help look after younger children, and to be delighted with the smallest gifts at Christmas.[10]

Three-quarters of this group left school at the junior level, when they were around 14 or 15 years of age, to earn a living.[11] Some then took courses to prepare for office work. A very small number enrolled at university or embarked on a professional career, and few had ever travelled interstate, let alone outside Australia.

The waiting time for transportation by ship to the US also varied from six to eighteen months, but for most brides who sailed at the end of the war, during 'Operation War Bride', it had been two to four years since they had seen their husbands. Those who were engaged to be married waited even longer. In the case of Sydney war bride, Patricia Law, who met her future husband in 1942, it was five years before the couple was married in America, six weeks after her arrival in 1947.[12]

Once settled in America, very few war brides returned to live permanently in Australia. Despite evidence of strong pangs of homesickness and difficulties with cultural adjustment, most marriages survived and divorces were well in the minority. Among those women interviewed, the longevity of their marriages was remarkable, given the circumstances of their wartime liaisons. Only six of the sixty war brides interviewed finally divorced their husbands, but not for some years and not before their children were teenagers or older. Most of the women in this study took up US citizenship within the first ten years of living in America and their stories highlight the reasons which motivated them to do so. Dual citizenship was not available for these women and a very small number (3 in a sample of 60) chose not to take up US citizenship in order to avoid the necessary forfeiture of their cherished Australian citizenship.

Migration

The special legislative provisions of the *War Brides Act* of December, 1945, followed by the *G.I. Fiancées Act* of June 29, 1946, facilitated the reunion of US servicemen to their foreign wives, fiancées, and children. This allowed for the generation of statistics regarding the numbers of war brides immigrating to the US, but not specifically for numbers of Australian wives. Between January 1946 and December 1948, there were 112,882 wives of US servicemen admitted to the US, almost 25 per cent of all US immigration during that period. Female immigrants to the US peaked (at 61.2%) during the 1940s, a decade of exceptionally large US military presence abroad.[13] The Australian war brides and fiancées of American servicemen who migrated to the US, based on a maximum figure of 15,000, made up a significant part (13.3%) of the total number of war brides admitted to the US during the same period.

Although it is a common experience for all migrants to suffer feelings of loss, separation, and severance, the immigration experience for Australian war brides differed in many respects from that of war brides coming from Britain, Europe, and Japan desperate to escape the appalling conditions of destruction and loss in their own war-torn countries. For the 40,000 British wives of American servicemen, this was made worse by their processing through bleak Tidworth Barracks before sailing to America.[14] European war brides often found it difficult to assimilate and to be accepted into the American way of life. French war brides found that the reality of adapting to a new culture without the support of family and friends was fraught with difficulties, and the cross-cultural adjustments for these women were complex and challenging, causing friction and a lack of understanding in their exogamous marriages, many of which ended in divorce.[15] A study of German war brides in America in 2005 highlights the 'cultural baggage' they brought with them from their Old World background.[16] It reveals their struggle to free themselves from negative stereotypes and popular assumptions of collective guilt for Nazi atrocities and taboo topics such as post-war rape and survival prostitution. Even after fifty years, many of these women were wary of being interviewed, fearful of continuing stereotyping.[17] Similarly, Italian brides of US servicemen found it difficult to acculturate to the American way of life and missed their traditional customs.[18] The European war brides did not have English as their first language, which restricted their ability to communicate and made it more difficult for them to adjust to living in their new country.

Memory and Oral History

Over the past sixty years, oral history has transformed the practice of contemporary history in many countries, its most distinctive contribution being to uncover 'the experiences and perspectives of groups of people who might otherwise have been "hidden from history"'.[19] Conventional history, drawn from archives, books, and other paper sources, is both challenged and complemented by oral history, which is drawn from the narratives of living memories and offers valuable insights from new perspectives with subjective interpretations of history. These are mostly omitted from official documentary sources. Through the process of remembering and re-interpreting the past, oral history has empowered individuals or social groups who have previously not had the opportunity to tell of their experiences.[20]

The Australian WWII war brides of American servicemen are an example of such a group, and for the first time, are able to record their experiences from their own perspectives.

Diversity is central to an interpretation of the Australian war brides' experiences, as these women originated from different socio-economic backgrounds and from a variety of geographic locations across Australia, before settling in disparate locations scattered across North America. Their encounters with other women in shared circumstances during the sea voyage, where they were commonly identified as 'war brides', was a bonding experience–if only temporarily–for many of these women. Even then, depending on their individual temperament and outlook on life, as well as their health and emotional state at the time, their experiences were differently self-interpreted. How they perceived their own experiences, as well as their expectations of what their future might hold, was influenced by various factors revealed in their recorded interviews. Despite the differences of self-interpretation, however, it is unmistakably clear that a common thread of events involuntarily bound these women together into the shared identity of 'war brides'.

During the period of my research, with numerous visits to America, I have been invited to visit war brides in their homes and some have visited me in Australia. It is inevitable that with such interaction, over an extended period, a personal relationship grows between the participants and the researcher, as well as the women becoming more aware of their war bride 'sisters' in other parts of America. The war brides are now either octogenarians or nonagenarians, and in writing their stories, I fully appreciate the inherent responsibilities resulting from the special relationship which has developed.

The war brides' migration to a new country and the impact of that migration was not publicly recognised until forty years later, when the first nationwide reunion of war brides in America was organised in April, 1985. The event took place on the Queen Mary in Long Beach, California and was recognized by dignitaries of the United States and of many countries abroad who sent congratulations to the war brides. Ronald Reagan, President of the United States at the time, sent a letter of greeting from the White House which read:

> The approximately one million European women who married American servicemen and came to the United States after the Second World War have played a significant role in the life and history of our nation. They have contributed to many fields and developments since that time and made a great impact on their adopted homeland. America has indeed been fortunate to have had the benefit of the strength and ability of these citizens and I proudly join with so many others in saluting their impact and their continuing gift to this great land.
>
> Nancy joins me in sending best wishes for this occasion and for the future. God bless you.
> (signed) Ronald Reagan.[21]

Australian war brides, however, were overlooked, and not specifically addressed in this or in the other letters and speeches which congratulated the war brides on their accomplishments. Although Australian women were present at the reunion, the focus was on 'European' war brides from countries where they had experienced 'the ravages of war first hand' and on the role they played in the 'peace and reconstruction of new relationships between countries'.[22]

It would be another twenty-two years before a special tribute was given specifically to the Australian WWII war brides at a reception at the Australian Embassy in Washington DC, in May 2007, in conjunction with ANZAC Day celebrations. These women had waited sixty years for recognition and were proud to be, at last, officially acknowledged and honoured as ambassadors for good relations between Australia and America for over six decades.

The principal aim of this book, as well as to chronicle the stories for the war brides and their families, is to document the experiences of Australian WWII war brides, previously overlooked in official histories of World War II, and to enable these accounts to take their rightful place in the larger national wartime arena.

CHAPTER ONE

MEETING AND FALLING IN LOVE

A shy young girl from W.A.
A worldly man from the U.S.A
They met at a party, ignited a spark,
Then walked next day in a wooded park,
She already betrothed to a Navy man,
He a C.P.O. in the U.S.N.
(Betty Kane, 'The War Bride', November 2001)[1]

Irene Vickers lived in Perth, Western Australia in the early 1940s, not far from the US naval base at Crawley Bay, now known as Matilda Bay. She was a pretty, vivacious 17-year-old when she met her future husband in a whirlwind courtship she clearly recalls as if it were yesterday:

When the Americans came, I went absolutely wild, and I was running with five or seven men at the time! I was at a dance. It was a big hall and I was with this young man and a sailor came up to me – a darling looking sailor – and asked me to dance, and so we did. Then, he asked me for a date. I was living in the home of a very nice woman who had rented a room to me. Of course, I was living on practically nothing then, I think £1.0.5d. a week, and that was all I could afford. But she said: "Have your friend come to dinner", which was very nice, and she was a very good cook.[2]

Now in her late 70s, Irene has an unlined face softly framed by shoulder-length brown hair. Her dark eyes dance as she recalls her life, 60 years ago, in wartime Australia.

> *So, the night he was supposed to come, there was a big storm and the squadron was tied up in Crawley Bay. There was a knock at the door and this big, blonde, gorgeous man in a sailor uniform said: "I'm Herb Franck". There were no phones of course, so my date couldn't call, and it seemed that he had 'the duty' that night, because the boats, planes, whatever, had to be tied down. So, Herb came by to give me the message. Of course, he says – and he still claims – that the moment he saw me, 'that was it!' So, we started dating from then. We couldn't get married right away; we had about six months' waiting period, so it wasn't until 1943, I guess, that we got married.*[3]

Irene and Herbert Franck, 15th April, 1943,
Perth, Western Australia.

Irene Franck (née Vickers), daughter of a Jewish-Russian mother and a Portuguese father, was born on 17 February, 1923, in Shanghai. There were no Jewish influences in her upbringing or that of her siblings, as her mother was not religious, but her father was a Catholic, and the son and two daughters began their education at parochial schools. Irene moved on to an English Public School for Girls before enrolling at Business College, by which time her mother had married an Englishman from Liverpool. In 1940, when Irene's stepfather had retired from the Fire Department in Shanghai, the family escaped the Japanese occupation when they immigrated to live on a small farm at Margaret River in Western Australia. The two girls moved to Perth, where they could find work.

Soon after they were married, Herb Franck was shipped back to the US and Irene stayed in Perth for three months. Not realising she was pregnant, Irene then took the 5-day train trip across the dry heartland of Australia to Melbourne, where she embarked on the sea voyage to America.

Irene sailed on a Swedish freighter, which carried the first batch of eight Australian brides from Melbourne and took 28 days to reach San Francisco. Although Irene made this long and perilous journey across the Pacific during the turmoil of WWII, she remembers not thinking about the treacherous conditions:

> *I was too sick. I was pregnant and I had morning sickness and sea sickness.*[4]

*   *   *

The War Brides

The Australian WWII war brides, mostly born in the 1920s, grew up in the aftermath of World War I and the years of the Great Depression. They came from cities and rural towns across Australia, and from diverse backgrounds, often from large families of modest means. Most left school at the junior level to earn a living. Only a small number enrolled at university or embarked on a professional career. Very few had ever travelled interstate, let alone venturing outside Australia. During the lean years of the early 1930s, these young women observed their mothers' stoic efforts to 'make ends meet' by sewing clothes for the children, keeping house frugally, and in rural areas, working alongside the men on the farm. Influenced by their strong maternal role models, these daughters were able to draw on their own inner strength to deal with whatever future challenges life served them.

War bride Dorothy (Mary) Bourne (née Cook) was born in Meekatharra, in the Western Australian goldfields, north-east of Geralton. Her father was a gold miner and Mary remembers how difficult life was for her mother:

> *The terrible goldmines! It was terribly hard work in 110 degree weather. The family lived in tin shacks, no air-conditioning, not even any fans. They slept outside in the night. It was too hot to sleep in the houses – if you could call them houses! My mother stayed at home with the children. There were five of us, four boys and me.*[5]

Mary was thirteen months old when her father died and her mother moved to be near her sister in Albany. Mary recalls:

> *She took us all – lock, stock and barrel – and eventually settled there, although she said she was so sorry to leave all those wonderful friends in the goldfields, and she felt absolutely alone. The frogs used to croak in the cemetery nearby and she said it was absolutely awful, until she took in English migrants who had been brought out to open the roads in Western Australia. The men would be shipped or bussed or trucked or 'horsed' out to the roads, while the wives stayed in Albany and rented rooms from mother. She said that's what changed her life.*[6]

Mary's mother was resourceful, and a great role model for her daughter. As well as providing accommodation for the English wives, she had her own cow and chickens for fresh food supplies. She learned tailoring and made the four boys' clothes, and in Mary's words:

> *She was one remarkable woman. I never remember her asleep when I was little. She was always reading when I went to sleep. She was a mother in a million.*[7]

An Australian Childhood

War bride, Hazel Walker (née Castledine) grew up in suburban Brisbane in the 1920s. The middle child, with an older brother and a younger sister, she has happy holiday memories:

> *Each year we spent three weeks at the beach when my dad had his holidays. We swam, played in the sand, and went fishing with my dad. Some days I went out in the boat with him, and my brother put down nets for crabs.*[8]

Hazel (left) with sister Beryl wearing 'beach pyjamas',
Redcliffe, Moreton Bay, Queensland, 1920s

The family lived in a 'Queenslander' – a weatherboard house with large verandahs all round, built high above ground and supported on tall posts to allow cooling breezes to pass underneath. Hazel's father grew the family's vegetables in the large garden which was also home to a variety of abundant fruit trees – mango, paw-paw, lemon, mandarin, peach, plum and fig – from which Hazel could pick fruit to eat after school each day. She recalls:

> *My mum made marmalade every year and my dad often stood at our front gate and handed out oranges to the kids coming home from school. He'd also give our extra fruit to neighbours who didn't have such trees.*[9]

Hazel Walker's family home, The Brea, 1944.

Hazel and her siblings played on the swing under the camphor-laurel trees which grew down one side of the yard. When it rained, there was another swing under the house they could use. They also enjoyed sitting high up in a frangipani tree, so they could see over the fence and talk to the girl who lived next door. Hazel loved to read and recalls:

Even in my teens, I used to sit in the biggest mango tree and read my books. My dad had a great library, and after dinner in the evening, he would tell us about the book he was reading and we'd discuss it. The books were often about the power of the mind over the body, and other such things, not fiction.[10]

Hazel Mary Walker (née Castledene) (left) 2 years old in 1923. Father Charles Harold, mother Mary Donald, sister Beryl Elizabeth and brother Donald Joseph.

In summer, the large pods from the 'monkey nut palms' split open and a cascade of yellow flowers spilled out. Hazel recalls:

The pods were about a meter long. The insides were smooth yellow and the outsides were ridged. We used to sit in them and ride down the grassy slope in the field across the street from us. After each of us (my sister, brother and I) had one, the other kids we played with would ask for one, which my dad would give them. I wanted to do everything my brother did. I played with him and his friends a lot, as well as with my sister and girlfriends.[11]

The family pets included two horses, 'Sparkling Sultan' and a mare called 'Lady'; a bull-dog called 'Lion Jack', who used to bail up the milkman as he tried to leave the yard; a hen called 'Game' and many chickens. Hazel still remembers all those years ago, eating the stems of the paspalum grass flowers, chewing on what she thought were shamrock leaves, and sucking the juice out of brightly-coloured nasturtium flowers.

It was a typical idyllic Australian childhood marked by the freedom and innocence of the days prior to Australia's involvement in WWII.

The 'Yanks' Arrive in Australia

After the Japanese bombed Pearl Harbor in December 1941, great change took place in Australia. Queensland became an important base for American forces and the first American troops arrived in the city of Brisbane, which saw a massive influx of 45,000 US troops over just six days.[12]

Hazel Walker clearly remembers this time:

> *There were hundreds of Yanks wandering around the streets downtown, looking lost and lonely. Waiting at the tram or bus stops, they would stop and ask the girls if they'd like to go to the movies. Brisbane parents showered them with friendship, invitations to our homes, and fed them meals. We were grateful to have them there, because I knew the Japs were coming to land one day and most of our troops were in the European Theatre or Malaya. We were to be evacuated below the Brisbane Line[13] when the Japs landed...everyone knew about it. It was in our newspapers when it was set up and we were told how we would be notified when we were to be evacuated. I carried a ball-peen hammer in my purse to hit the Japs on their heads when they invaded. Is it any wonder everyone in Brisbane welcomed those Yanks?[14]*

In January 1942, the US headquarters moved from Brisbane to Melbourne and in March, under the command of General MacArthur, thousands of American GIs arrived in Melbourne aboard their troopships for an extended stay.[15]

US troops in Melbourne, April 1942
[Source: Australian War Memorial AMW 012016]

The visiting 'Yanks' were generally perceived by Australians to be saving the country from Japanese invasion. The threat of the 'Yellow Peril' – invasion by Asiatic hordes to the north – was symptomatic of xenophobia, alive in Australia since colonial days. With the bombing of Darwin in the north and the presence of Japanese submarines in Sydney Harbour in early 1942, and especially when HMAS *Kuttabul* was torpedoed and sunk with 21 sailors on board, invasion seemed imminent. In July, Brisbane once more became headquarters for MacArthur's South-West Pacific Campaign, with Lennon's Hotel in the city-centre being turned over to accommodate US military officers. MacArthur's War Room was set up on the third floor of the ten-storey AMP building (now named MacArthur Chambers) and US bases were established right across Australia. By June 1942, there were already 89,000 American troops based in Australia, escalating to 140,000 by August 1943.[16] Fear of Japanese invasion at that time meant that these troops were warmly welcomed in Australia and were generally hailed as 'heroes' and 'saviours'.

Patriotic Duty: Welcoming the American Troops

Australian women were encouraged to contribute to the war effort by volunteering at canteens and dances run by the Red Cross and other organisations. Volunteer hospitality bureaus were set up in major capital cities under the auspices of the Australian Comforts Fund to extend hospitality to the American troops who were far from their homes, families, and friends. Wartime stereotypes portrayed Australian girls who fraternised with American servicemen as 'good-time girls' and adolescent girls having sex with soldiers were the subject of frequent reports. However, they were expected, as part of their patriotic duty, to volunteer at clubs, dances, and canteens, as well as to wait on tables, wash dishes, and sew buttons onto uniforms.

Interior of Milk Bar, Mackay, Qld. c.1943.
[Source: Australian War Memorial AMW P00561.023]

They were also encouraged to dance with the servicemen. This was often in addition to their normal, paid day-time work as shop assistants, bank clerks, and secretaries. In fulfilling this wartime obligation, these women often became the romantic targets of attentive, lonely young American servicemen looking for companionship in a foreign city.

Dancing with an American soldier at a nightly social run by staff of Australian retail organisations. [Source: Australian War Memorial AWM 012266]

The city of Melbourne, in the southern state of Victoria, 'went all out to help the war effort' according to war bride Allie Rudy who, as a 19-year-old, found it an exciting time. She looked forward to dancing weekly at the Trocadero 'just over the Yarra River Bridge' and at the Palais de Dance on St. Kilda Road. She remembers:

These dance halls were filled to capacity seven days a week. There was music and laughter with men in uniform and lots of Australian women who loved the 'Yankees'. Their salaries went a whole lot further than the Aussies' pay and they were more than generous with it.[17]

In the city of Sydney, in New South Wales, a dance hall also named Trocadero provided a popular venue for those like Sydney war bride, Nancy Lankard, who loved to dance. She lived in the city, as her father managed a funeral parlour on Elizabeth Street opposite

Hyde Park, and the family lived above. She recalls the night clubs on Martin Place and Pitt and Castlereagh Streets, which were on the basement level and not visible from the street. She remembers the excitement and how she 'loved dancing' to the music of the 'big bands' and says: 'We had really good times!'[18]

Australian women loved to dance and this popular leisure activity provided them with the opportunity to have fun with young men while serving their community in wartime, and it gave them a new sense of social freedom. However, restrictive 'red tape' was quickly introduced to prevent girls from leaving the clubs with any servicemen.[19] In this way, even dancing became regulated in an attempt to avoid liaisons which might lead to hasty marriages between Australian girls and the American servicemen.[20] In spite of these restrictions liaisons were formed, due to the huge presence of over a million American troops passing through Australia during the war years, as well as the mingling of soldiers, sailors and marines with civilians when off duty.

Dancing at Melbourne Town Hall, 1944 [Source: Australian War Memorial AMW 083660]

It was at the 'Dugout' Club, set up by Myer's department store in Melbourne, that Jean Fargo (née Robertson) met her future husband. Born in Sea Lake, Victoria, in July 1925, Jean was the younger of two girls. Jean's father had met his Scottish-born wife when he was an Australian soldier in France during

WWI. He was wounded and sent to Scotland to recuperate. So, her mother came to Australia as a WWI war bride. During Jean's childhood, the family moved between several towns in Victoria because of her father's occupation as a banker. Although the family was Presbyterian, the last two years of Jean's education were spent at St Fintans' Ladies' College in St Kilda, which was run by nuns. Jean explains:

> *My mother thought we'd get better training and because they wore uniforms there, she thought my sister and I would become ladies and we'd be 'nicer' – and there were no boys there.*[21]

After leaving school, Jean and her sister both did clerical work at different banks during the day, and one night each week they did their bit to support the war effort by volunteering at the Dugout Club.

Artist's impression of 'The Dugout' Club, Melbourne, Victoria. Volunteer clearing tables. [Source: Australian War Memorial ART 25127]

Open seven days a week, the Dugout Club provided a place for servicemen to eat, shower, have a hair-cut, clean their clothes, and have their shoes shined. After eight-o'clock each night there was dancing. Jean and her sister used to 'clean up the tables, wash dishes, or sometimes…dance, or just sing around the piano and be friendly'. One evening someone was playing the piano and Jean felt a sudden touch on her back. She recalls:

> *There was this navy guy – not an officer, just a navy guy. He said, 'When the music starts will you dance with me?' So I said, 'Oh, sure!'* [22]

Jean danced with him quite a bit that evening, and although she declined his offer to escort her home, the American's persistence led to their meeting again. She recalls her first impressions of Albert, who was her 'first true boyfriend':

> *He had a nice soft voice and he was quite handsome. He was older than the marines and fifteen years older than me. I didn't realize that at first. He was from a large family in Philadelphia and worked in the State Department in Washington DC. He seemed kind of sophisticated.* [23]

Jean dared not tell her mother she was dating an American, as she knew 'she would not have approved'. So, each week they met at the home of an older couple in their sixties, who had two sons fighting overseas, and used to open up their house to the servicemen. Jean recalls:

> *This lady and man just loved Albert, so we went every Sunday to their place…for a whole year and a half, before we got married.* [24]

In establishing this system of 'self-chaperoning', Jean displayed her strong moral character, despite the opportunities for personal freedom offered by wartime conditions. This friendship was by no means a fast and short-lived infatuation and contradicts the stereotypical view of 'war brides'. In January 1945, Jean and Albert were married, not in haste, but 18 months after they first met.[25]

Iris Craig (née Adams) was born in Brisbane and grew up in Sydney. During the war, she worked in Sydney for the American Army as a comptometer operator in the finance department. One night Iris and her sister went to a dance in aid of the war effort where they met two American servicemen. One of them spoke to Iris first, and the other man, Jim, danced with her sister. Soon after, Jim was transferred to New Guinea and Iris recalls:

> *When he came down on leave, he called at the house and my sister happened to be on vacation, so he asked me out. He said he wanted to ask me out in the first place, he wasn't fast enough!*[26]

Iris was twenty three when she married Jim about four months later in Trinity Church, Dulwich Hill, Sydney. It was a small wedding with just the immediate family, and Iris explains how it was to marry in wartime:

> *Material was hard to come by, but I just happened to have this white dress with lace on it and it just worked out nicely. The reception was at my mother's place. We just had savouries, the usual fruit cake and a few glasses of wine. I went to work the next day.*[27]

Iris Adams' US Amy ID

Iris Adams and Jim Craig, c.1943

Across the land couples met at dances, skating rinks, clubs and cafes; on blind dates through friends and relatives; at work; on public transport, and simply in the street. Away from home and family, in a foreign land, thousands of American boys actively sought companionship and someone to talk to, often about their own families back home. They were keen to visit family homes to share a home-cooked meal, play the piano and experience a little 'normal' home-life amidst the uncertainty of wartime.

Many Australian families were hospitable and empathised with the young American men and their loneliness in a foreign land, recognising that in their fate mirrored the fate of their own menfolk who were serving overseas. Some families, however, were not happy for their daughters to go out with Americans. They were aware of growing criticism in the press and from the general community, who believed Australian girls should reserve their affections for Australian soldiers and not succumb to 'Yankee charms'.[28] Also, the rape and murder of three women in Melbourne by a US soldier in May 1942, followed by ten more American servicemen being charged with rape and attempted rape by the end of the next year, spread fears that Americans were sexually aggressive and predatory.[29]

At first, the great influx of American troops into Australian cities was seen as the 'friendly invasion', but before very long Australian attitudes changed. Thousands of US servicemen were viewed as taking girls away from young eligible Australian men who had enlisted and were away fighting the war in Europe and New Guinea. American men, drafted into the US Army in the early war years, were typically single and much better paid than their Australian counterparts. With twice the spending money, they could afford to woo young women with gifts of scarce commodities.[30]

The Americans appeared to be more exotic, bearing gifts in wartime, looking glamorous in better-fitting uniforms of better quality cloth than those issued to the Australian troops, and speaking with a 'soft American accent' only heard before in Hollywood-produced films at the local cinema.[31]

Naturally, being so far from home, the Americans were lonely and sought companionship in a society where the art of courtship was not something the average Australian man had generally cultivated.[32] Undoubtedly there was jealousy on the home front and, in time, the description of the American troops as 'heroes and saviours' changed to echo the British cry of 'over-paid, over-sexed, and over here'.[33] The perception of American servicemen (influenced by romantic Hollywood films) being a type of 'celluloid hero' quickly changed to become a real threat to the sexual status quo.[34]

A sense of social and moral panic developed during the course of the American occupation and, by early 1943, newspapers reported a high incidence of venereal disease among young Australian women. Double standards employed in vice squad raids saw young women blamed for the spread of the disease, with attacks on their morality by assorted male authorities. The young women who fraternized with Yanks during this time were vulnerable to moral attack and criticism.[35]

While not all women interviewed were aware of these critical attitudes in society, war bride Hazel Walker clearly remembers the way some people 'looked down on girls who went out with Yanks'. The memory still irritated her when she pointed out:

> There were no other boys to go out with for a start. Our parents invited them to our homes. They were like cousins and brothers to us! [36]

The women interviewed for this book certainly demonstrated a conservative approach to sex. Some told how they included dates with their boyfriends within group outings, others mentioned sexual abstinence before marriage, and some emphasized the fact that their first child was born more than nine months after they were married. These young women were not well informed about sexual relations. Sex education was almost non-existent for this generation of women and, as a result, ignorance about sex was the norm. According to surveys conducted in Australia in the early 1950s, while women were experienced in kissing and 'petting', most young unmarried women at this time had not had sexual intercourse. These surveys concluded that it was common at that time for young women under twenty-four years of age to abstain from sexual intercourse before marriage. The majority of the war brides were younger than twenty-four when they married, and knew little about sex.[37]

War bride Hazel Walker recalls when she was a young girl that 'Nothing was ever said about sex'. It was about 1930 when she first asked her mother where babies came from and she was told that 'a stork brings them'. Her mother continued to give the same answer each time Hazel asked, even when she told her mother that she knew it wasn't so. She was fifteen in 1936 when her periods started, but her mother gave her no explanation, telling her not to worry about it as it was quite normal.[38]

Like most young Australian girls in the 1940s, Hazel was ignorant about sex and the anatomy of reproduction. She remembers:

> When I got engaged, one of my close friends, Heather, did almost at the same time (1944). We began to wonder what would happen after we married, and we went together into a book shop and bought a book explaining all about sex. Our mothers wouldn't tell us anything![39]

War bride Nancy Lankard was a Sydney girl who was having a lot of fun in the 1940s, despite having a very strict father. She was one of seven girls who lived with their parents above a city funeral parlour which was managed by her father. She recalls the night clubs on Martin Place and Pitt and Castlereagh Streets, which were on the basement level and not visible from the street. She loved dancing to the music of the 'big bands' at the Trocadero and other nightclubs and says: 'We had really good times!'[40]

Nancy Lankard, about 18 years old.

Nancy danced with a lot of 'Navy men – Aussies, Brits, and French' and had dates with many of them. She remembers:

> *There were six of us who were friends and all went out with Americans who were all very well mannered – we just kissed and that was all!* [41]

She recalls her teenage years:

> *We were very moral, very Catholic, very young and innocent. At 16 you thought you could become pregnant from kissing! That's what we thought in the 40s!* [42]

Despite young Australian women's general ignorance regarding sexual activity and its consequences, powerful wartime stereotypes prevailed. False perceptions regarding women who fraternised with American servicemen were perpetuated in cartoons, comic books, and in novels, even after the war had ended. [43]

G.I. War Brides comic, June, 1954

G.I. War Brides comic, October, 1954.

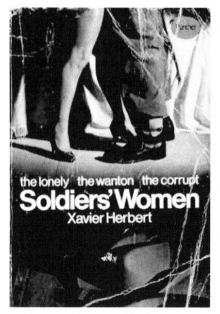

Xavier Herbert – Soldier's Women

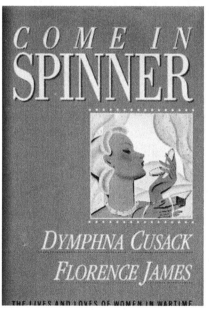

Dymphna Cusack & Florence James –
Come in Spinner

Many Australian women, keen to fulfil their patriotic duty by working for the Allied Forces, met their American husbands at work. Hazel Walker was only fifteen when she started work for paint and hardware merchants, R.S. Exton and Company Pty Ltd., where she spent a year as an 'office girl'. Her duties included small typing jobs, opening and stamping the mail which she collected from the GPO twice a day and posting the mail on the way home each day. Hazel was promoted to secretary to the Chief Accountant, and then to secretary to the Company Secretary.

Hazel in her first job, collecting mail from the GPO in Brisbane, March, 1937.

Towards the end of 1942, Hazel's boss decided to join the Navy and he suggested that she should go to work for the Americans for the duration of the war, which she did. Hazel remembers the first day in her new job as a secretary in the US Fifth Air Force Service Command Adjutant General's Office in Brisbane:

This red-headed young Yank soldier from the next office came by my desk, winked at me and said 'Hullo'. I later told one of my fellow workers, 'That red-headed fellow in the Message Center winked at me and I haven't even been introduced to him yet.' She said, 'Oh, don't take any notice of him. That's Eddie Walker. He winks at all the girls.' [44]

After talking with him and others in the snack bar at break time over several weeks, Eddie asked Hazel to go to the movies with him. She clearly remembers that night:

> *After he brought me home from the movies, he tried to kiss me 'goodnight'. I wouldn't let him. He said, 'I've met girls like you before who play hard to get'. I was irritated to think that he thought I was 'playing hard to get', instead of realizing that, in my culture, it was the way a young lady was brought up to behave. I was so annoyed with him that I didn't speak to him for weeks. I expect, by US standards, I'd have been considered 'a prig'.*[45]

Hazel dressed for church one Sunday morning, 1941. *'We wore hats and gloves in those days!'*

Eddie Walker with Koala in Brisbane, 1942.

Eventually, Hazel accepted dates from him again, and Eddie respected her feelings on how a young lady should behave. The couple dated for a little over 18 months, and then Eddie was suddenly sent to hospital with tonsillitis. Hazel remembers his 'romantic' proposal of marriage:

One day, while he was in the hospital, he called me at work. I answered the phone: 'Colonel Morgan's Office'. He said, 'Hi. I was just lying here in bed thinking. Do you want to marry me?' I said, 'What?' He repeated, 'Do you want to marry me?' I said, 'I don't know'. He said, 'Well, either you do or you don't. Make up your mind!' Just then Colonel Morgan, who apparently had picked up the phone at the same time I did, said, 'Tell him yes. Ha ha ha. Tell him yes!''. I said, 'Yes' and hung up the phone. I was dumbfounded! [46]

In a wartime atmosphere, with air-raid sirens filling the air, day and night, and with most young Australian men away overseas, Hazel remembers:

One lived day to day and didn't plan ahead very far. As far as the 'Yanks' were concerned, the general expectation was that they would eventually be transferred away and, after the war, would be going back to the US. Thinking about marrying someone, let alone one of them, never entered my head! [47]

Betty McIntire (née Waddell) also worked for the Americans and literally bumped into her future husband in a wartime 'brown-out' in Sydney. Born in Melbourne, Victoria, on 22nd December, 1922, Betty left high school at the age of fourteen and worked for four years as a secretary in a manufacturing company before working for the US Army. When the war broke out in the South Pacific region, Betty decided to 'do her thing' for the war effort and was hired by the Quartermaster Corps, USASOS, headquartered in Melbourne. As the war advanced, the USASOS moved north, and Betty moved with them. First to Sydney, then to Brisbane, and finally up to Townsville, in the latter part of 1944, where she worked as a secretary for the General Headquarters. It was while working at the Quartermaster Corps in Sydney that Betty became friends with Shirley Nicholls, a fellow-worker. Their fates took an interesting turn, as they met their future husbands while working together and went on to become lifetime friends.[48]

Shirley Norton (née Nicholls) was born on 12 June, 1929 in Melbourne. The middle girl of three daughters, Shirley left school at the age of fifteen and went to Stott's Business College to learn Pitman's shorthand and typing. She hated shorthand, possibly due to her having a broken arm at the time, which hindered her dexterity. Shirley also wanted to support the war effort and enjoyed working as a clerk with the Quartermaster Corps in Sydney, where she and Betty McIntire became friends. The two shared a flat in the eastern suburb of Rose Bay. After work one day, in early 1943, they were walking from the Grace Building (which had been allocated to the US military) towards a tram-stop, to wait for a tram to take them home. In the dim light of a wartime 'brown-out', the two young women were suddenly illuminated by light from the opening doors of the Hotel Australia as two US servicemen came out. Shirley recalls:

> *These two Yanks came along – one tall one and one short one! That's how they chose us!* [49]

The taller of the two was Bob, who was on leave after just finishing a training course in Queensland on chemical warfare. He introduced himself to Shirley, and the shorter man, Mac, greeted the diminutive Betty. The girls arranged to meet them the next day at the Grace Building.

Robert (Bob) Norton

It was love at first sight when Betty met Mac. He was very charming and, unlike most Australian men at that time, he 'liked to flatter', which was a new experience for her. She remembers that after three weeks leave in Sydney they were 'hopelessly in love', although it was to be some time before they could marry. Mac was transferred to his new duty station in Townsville, as Transportation Officer, and his letters came almost daily along with many phone calls. Betty had moved to Brisbane with the Quartermaster Corps, but she remembers how she 'longed to go north to be with my man!' An opening came up at the General Headquarters office in Townsville, so Betty quit her job in Brisbane and travelled north. She recalled that time:

> *We spent many months together, going to the Officer's Club in Townsville, taking boat trips to Magnetic Island and other places, and just plain being in love!* [50]

Shirley and Bob also fell in love and planned to marry, but first he had to go back to New Guinea to seek permission from his Commanding Officer. It was another six months before they could marry.

Some Australian women decided to enlist in the military to support the war effort. Sunny Sansing (née Potts) enlisted as a Wireless Telegraphist in the Australian Air Force from 1944 to 1945. Dorienne Minna Potts, (later nicknamed Sunny by her husband) was born in Sydney, on 9 September, 1918. Sunny's father was a returned soldier, wounded in Gallipoli, when

Shirley Nicholls and Robert (Bob) Norton

he married her mother, who she says was a 'social butterfly' at that time. Sunny's parents separated when she was five years old and she never saw her father again. When the divorce was going through, Sunny's mother took a job selling lingerie and hosiery and became 'the first travelling saleswoman by car from Sydney up the coast'. Being an only child, Sunny was put into boarding school at Mount St. Joseph's, Gladesville at the age of five and spent school holidays with her grandparents in Lane Cove. Her childhood was not a happy one; because of the divorce and being separated from both her parents. At age eleven, although from a Protestant family, she was sent to a Catholic convent in Narellan, south-west of Sydney. The convent was part orphanage and part boarding school and there she stayed until she finished school. From the age of five until sixteen, she knew nothing but the Catholic religion and says:

> *I had always wanted to belong to it – like a family – so, when I turned sixteen years of age, I became a Catholic.*[51]

Sunny's mother remarried and by this time Sunny had changed her first name to Nea and had taken her stepfather's surname, Hawkes. Now known as Nea Hawkes, she desperately wanted to go on the stage when she left school, but her mother wanted her to go to Ross Heinz' School of Dressmaking and Tailoring. At the Heinz School, she learned skills which were to prove useful in the future.

In the early 1940s, Sunny met and married a young Australian man who enlisted in the military and, by necessity, was away a lot of the time. After several miscarriages and finally going through the traumatic loss of stillborn twin babies, Sunny and her husband could no longer cope, and reluctantly, their marriage broke up.

Sunny was heart-broken and needed a new direction in her life. She decided to do her bit for the war effort and on 22 February, 1943, as Nea Minna Dorienne Woolard (her married surname), she joined the Australian Air Force as a radio operator at Garbutt Air Force Base in Townsville, in far North Queensland.

Sunny worked between the direction-finding station and the pilots in the air who had become lost and she intercepted distress calls from crippled aircraft during conflicts such as the Battle of the Coral Sea. She worked for the North Eastern Australian area where the radio code for her location was 'NEA'. As her first name was also Nea, she ran into trouble when making radio contact with US Air Force pilots. When they asked her name and she repeatedly spelled N-E-A, they were confused and thought she was simply being difficult. Sunny found the work 'very fascinating' although she admitted it was 'very, very tiring':

Aircraftwoman Nea Minna Dorienne Woolard, known as 'Sunny', in her WAAF uniform.

> We worked an eight-day week, which was very difficult, but we were young and we were 'gung-ho' and working for our country, you know. We had no intention whatsoever of coming to America! That wasn't in our minds at all.[52]

When her much-loved Grandfather died, Sunny needed transport to Sydney to attend his funeral. The Signals Officer, and her 'boss', John Goffage (later to become well-known as Chips Rafferty, the Australian film star) was somebody she was proud to call 'friend'. This man, she comments was 'not the prettiest to look at' but 'was very kind' and he was responsible for Sunny meeting the man she was to marry.

John Goffage – better known after the war as Australian actor Chips Rafferty. [Source: Australian War Memorial OG0068]

In early 1944, interstate travel by train was impossible due to wartime restrictions, and Sunny's Signals Officer sent her to the American sector of the base operations camp at Garbutt Field to find a flight back to Sydney for the funeral. This area was normally 'off limits' to Australian Air Force women, and the appearance of a petite, blue-eyed, blonde in their midst caused a commotion among the American men. Upset by all the whistling and cat-calling, Sunny was in tears by the time she reached the man behind the counter. She thought 'he was a little fresh' and called him a 'smart-Alec Yank'. To which he replied, 'No, Ma'am, I'm not a Yank, I'm a Southern gentleman!' This man was Major Richard Sansing from Tennessee and he then told Sunny that: 'Yes, I will give you a ride if you promise to go to a dinner with me when you come back!'

Sunny remembers:

> *I said 'of course!' – never meaning I would. But when I arrived back, and we landed, there was a jeep right alongside the runway and when the plane stopped and the door opened, he walked up and said, 'You! Out!' and I had my first date with him.*[53]

Sunny had never imagined that she would marry an American, but the 'very good looking Major Richard Allan Sansing, Pilot, US Navy Air Corp. with those silver wings and a twinkle in the eye', as Sunny described him, was persistent in his attentions over the next few months. She recalls:

He was very thoughtful and very kind and he treated me a little differently to what the Australian men did. We couldn't get too many things in Townsville at that time and he never failed to turn up with a bag of fruit, which was impossible for us to get. We couldn't get any ice up in the tropics and he would always take me somewhere where I could get iced water to drink. It was just a lot of little things…the Australian men sort of took us for granted and felt like they should walk one step ahead of us. The American men, if anything, put us ahead of them. They opened car doors for us, it was just that little difference, you know.[54]

Nea Woolard, AC1 WAAF and Major Richard Sansing, 5th Army Corp, Garbutt Field, Townsville, Queensland.

Richard, or 'Dick' as Sunny called him, had to get permission to go out with her, because she was enlisted and not allowed to date officers, so he had to carry a permit in his pocket. He nicknamed her 'Sunny' because of the way the sun shone on her strawberry-blonde curls, 'like the sun shining through corn silk'. She has answered to this name ever since, which also matches her 'sunny' personality. The couple spent evenings dining and dancing at the officers' club and enjoying picnics out of doors. Romance was in the air, but their opportunities for courtship were limited in the busy wartime months in 1944.

As the war escalated, Dick Sansing left Townsville and moved up into the Islands. Before he left, Sunny wept as she said to him, 'I know I'll never see you again'. Dick had been engaged back in Memphis, but told Sunny he had broken it off. He did not exactly ask Sunny to marry him, but said 'How do you feel about coming over to the States?' to which Sunny replied:

Well, when you go back to the States, you'll meet the girl that you were engaged to and you'll look around at all the American girls. Then, if you'll send me my ticket, I will come! [55]

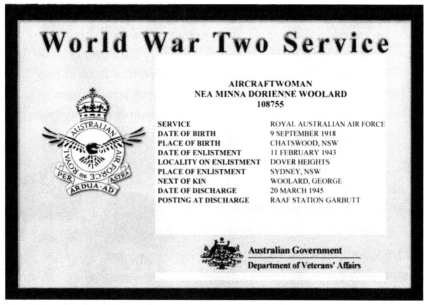

Sunny's WWII Service Record

Sunny left the Air Force in the middle of 1945. She worked as a waitress at Eaglefarm in Brisbane, serving the families who were being released from the Japanese internment camps. She did this for three months, but found it emotionally stressful and 'couldn't take it any longer', so moved back to Sydney to wait, like many other brides and fiancées, for transportation to the US to reunite with her husband-to-be.

Similarly, on the western coast of Australia, women were enlisting to support the war effort. Joan Byer (née Hughes), originally from Adelaide in South Australia, was nineteen when she joined the Women's Royal Australian Naval Service (WRANS) and trained at Fremantle Naval Base in Western Australia.[56] Her future husband, Raymond, was in the US Navy and was stationed at Fremantle on the submarine repair ship, SS *Peleus.* Joan tells how they first met:

*The band from the Peleus used to play down on the wharf
during lunch time. I was in the Women's Australian Navy
and…seven of us girls…used to come over occasionally to listen
to the music, and that's where I first met him. He asked me
for a date, and I said 'No'. I didn't mix my social life with my
working life. But then later, we met at the Embassy Ballroom
in Perth, where they had dances at least once a week, and a
lot of the servicemen used to come. I was a hostess there with a
friend of mine. And that's where we met again and he asked me
to dance, and I did, and then we starting dating.*[57]

This was the dance that changed her life, although at the time
Joan was not interested in a serious relationship. She says: 'I was
not ready for anything permanent; I was having too much fun'.[58]
Much of Raymond's appeal to Joan was his difference to most of the
Australian men she had dated before and his gentlemanly manner.
She found that the Australian guys were 'more "rough-shod"… they
weren't as attentive to women as the Americans were.'[59]

When Joan met her future husband, she was working for the
degaussing department of the Royal Australian Navy and what they
called the 'degaussing shed' was down on the beach in the Port of
Perth where all the ships came in. After regular basic training,
Joan was chosen by Lieutenant Whinney, who was in charge of
the degaussing, to be part of a team of seven women. Joan was
selected to be the liaison between the degaussing office and the
ships coming into port. Joan explains that 'degaussing' is a process
of demagnetizing the ships to protect them from being blown up by
mines. She recalls:

*Each ship had to have the degaussing equipment on board;
otherwise they had to stay in the harbor until it was taken
care of. So, I would go on the ships with the instructions from
the officers at the degaussing department and see the captain
and give them to him and then return them to the office.*[60]

Joan loved her work and found it very interesting. She said:

Everybody felt like they needed to do their part for the war effort and the navy just intrigued me as a unit to get into.[61]

Joan and Raymond Byer, Vista, CA, September, 2001.

Joan and Ray 'dated regularly, but not exclusively at first'.[62] As the couple got to know each other, Joan started introducing him to all her friends. During 1943 and 1944, Joan and Ray spent their free time together enjoying such pastimes as 'dancing, visiting friends, hiking, going to the beach or movies, attending various Navy Submarine parties, or just lazing around the house'.[63] Joan's narrative clearly indicates that not all war brides fit the stereotypes which painted a perception of them as 'one-night-stands' who simply sought sexual pleasure in their involvement with American servicemen.[64] At the time I interviewed Joan, at the couple's home in Vista, California, she and Ray had been happily married for almost sixty years.

At the outbreak of WWII, Merle Archer (née Brosius) was Head of Department at the Perpetual Trustees Office in Sydney. She wanted to be a Trust Officer but women were not allowed to apply for this position. So, after working for the Australian Red Cross Service, Merle went to work for the US Army, and she recalls:

> *I went to the Grace Building to work as Secretary to the Adjutant who said, 'You decorate the office!' I went back to work at the Red Cross again, and was then sent to New Caledonia and did administration work.*[65]

Merle tells how she enjoyed this unusual wartime experience:

> *This was Head Quarters for the South Pacific and I was there for 13 months working hard – long hours, six days a week. It was a wonderful Head Quarters near the beach and we went to the Army mess for food. I organised some functions for the Navy and had to date officers. They had the transport, so it was safer. If we were taken prisoner my status would have been that of a Captain.*[66]

Merle explains:

> *I was one of eleven Australians chosen by the US Army to go to New Caledonia in a move to 'get the girls across the Pacific'.*[67]

When the war was over, Merle was sent back to Sydney, and because of her connection with the Red Cross, she was one of two women asked to be a hostess to visiting VIPs. The Captain of SS *President Munro* was not keen to take women on board this vessel. However, persuaded by Admiral Calhoun and entertainer Bob Hope, he eventually consented. Merle was able to sail to California on this ship which carried 2,000 troops returning home.

While in Sydney, Merle had met an American serviceman and she remembers:

> *I wanted to continue with the Red Cross…I was not sure I wanted to live in the States. However, he got his orders to Japan, so we married in California – he was afraid he might lose me – and we lived in Washington DC.*[68]

Many Australian women enlisted and carried out responsible wartime duties in various capacities. Joann Patterson (née Nicholls), born in Melbourne in December 1923, the youngest of three daughters, also joined the services to help the war effort. Joann joined the Australian Women's Army Service (AWAS) in August 1943, at the age of nineteen and was discharged as Lance Corporal Joan Nicholls, LHQ Signals AWAS, in November, 1945, just before her 21st birthday. Before enlisting, Joann was working as a secretary at the University of Melbourne Veterinary Research Institute, which happened to be located at Melbourne Zoo, near where the American troops were camped.

Joann (right) and her sister Shirley in the garden of the family home

Early in 1942, Joann and a girlfriend were in a restaurant in Melbourne, having dinner before going to an evening class together. She recalls:

> *Across the room was an American sitting in a booth… he kept looking our way and our eyes met. We finished our meal and were walking up Swanson Street towards the Technical School. I glanced behind and here's this American following us at a distance. So, we didn't pay much attention and we went in and did the class.*[69]

Much to their surprise, after their class, the two girls came out to find that the American was still there. Joann was 'a little ticked off' and she asked him what he was doing. He said that he just wanted to say hello and wanted to meet some Australian girls. They chatted for a while and he offered to escort Joann and her friend home on the train. Joann explains:

> *It just happened that my girlfriend went home first, so then he escorted me home and found out where I worked. The next day, about lunch-time, he turned up and we had lunch together. That just really lasted a few days before he was moved up to Townsville, and from there, he went up to the Islands. Then we started corresponding and there were a lot of letters.*[70]

Contrary to popular wartime stereotypes which saw the war brides as 'throwing' themselves at the Yanks, the American servicemen were persistent in wooing their Australian girlfriends and often would not take 'no' for an answer, with thousands of marriages eventually taking place.

When Dorothy Thompson (née Leishmann) first met her American boyfriend, Leroy, at the Trocadero in Brisbane, she was most reluctant to go out with him and had no desire to form a permanent relationship.

Dorothy Leishman holidaying at Coolangatta, Queensland in 1943.

Although attracted by his 'good dancing and politeness', she claims that she wasn't interested in Americans. She went out with other boys while she and the 'little Corporal', as she jokingly called him, went out 'on and off'. It was much later when he told her that from the very first time they had met, he had made up his mind to marry her. But Dorothy remembers that time:

> *I didn't want to get married until I was 25…and least of all, marry an American*.[71]

Dorothy was reluctant to accept the notion of romantic love displayed by her American suitor. Claiming disinterest in his original attentions and continuing to go out with other men, she initially refused to wear his engagement ring and almost seemed to be willingly deterred by obstacles surrounding the eventual arrangements for her wedding. Dorothy appeared to resist the inevitability of fate, but Leroy's persistence finally won her affection.

Dorothy Leishman and Leroy Thompson, shopping in Sydney, 1944.

Perhaps Dorothy had already realised her ultimate reluctance to leave Australia and her seeming disinterest may have been caused by fear of the unknown. Dorothy's rebellious feelings against accepting Leroy's serious advances were possibly a natural response, and in fact, were the 'very stuff' of romance.

Similarly, Betty Paukovitz 'wasn't wild about' Ski when they met at the 'old-time dance' at North Fremantle Town Hall. Born in Dundee, Scotland, Betty had migrated to Australia with her widowed mother when she was fourteen. Three years later, she met Ski, who was eleven years her senior. She purposely didn't tell him her new address when she and her mother moved to a new house, but through sheer persistence he found out. It was three or four months after they met that they decided to marry and then it took six months for their papers to come through.[72]

Rather than 'good-time girls' who virtually threw themselves at Americans, these war brides recall initially resisting such liaisons and being actively pursued by their husbands-to-be, some of whom confidently decided on their first meeting that this was the girl they would marry.

The wartime perception of the powerful military male as hero and saviour, and the passive young female waiting to be wooed created an atmosphere of heightened romance, rather than simply one of physical pleasure. Sometimes, finding their Australian dates reluctant to go out again, the Americans were undaunted and pursued their romantic targets, wooing them with flowers and other gifts.[73] The very persistence they displayed in their romantic quests sometimes paid off when they won the hearts of their Australian girlfriends.

Rhona Jones was a Sydney girl whose father had organised for her to work for the Americans at Macarthur's USASOS Headquarters in Brisbane. In the Office of the Chief Quartermaster, Memorial Division, her grim, but important, task was to match the names of US soldiers killed in action to the correct grave numbers.

In a letter addressed to 'Mummy Darling', dated 1 December, 1943, Rhona wrote of the weather being 'very muggy...a different heat to Sydney heat', and she commented that 'these fibro buildings are not as cool as they could be'. She found it was 'almost too hot to type'. The letter gives insight into the conditions in which she worked hard as she contributed to the war effort:

> *I have worked flat out for two days, not letting up for one minute, and I mean work. Yesterday I worked from 8.30 a.m. till 11.30 p.m. and I really was tired. Then today I didn't lift my head for a minute, so much so that I got*

a cramp in the back of my neck...We really have been extremely busy, and that's putting it mildly...I have never seen such storms as we are having...and the mosquitoes are very bad, we can't sit in the office without getting riddled. So --- don't let anyone fool you into believing that your little daughter isn't helping to win the war. She is certainly doing her bit, and it isn't fun all the time.[74]

Some time, however, was set aside for fun and recreation. It was a casual encounter at an officer graduation party in Brisbane when Minnesota-born Frank Osborn laid eyes on the beautiful Australian girl, Rhona Jones. It was love at first sight.

On the night they met, Rhona danced with the handsome American and later, when she was leaving, he offered her some 'PK' chewing gum in return for her phone number, which she scribbled on the back of the gum wrapper. This was to seal their fate, although at the time, Rhona thought she would never hear from him again. However, Frank's persistence paid off when he called her and asked for a date.

Romance blossomed and just three months later the couple were engaged to be married. Frank was then assigned to SS *Contessa*, an American transport ship which sailed to and from New Guinea carrying fuel for the Australian and New Zealand Army Corps. After months at sea, the *Contessa* docked in Sydney Harbour for repairs on Christmas Eve 1944. A wedding was organised in 'double quick time' and the young couple were married at St Marks Church, Darling Point on 3 January, 1945. Major Frank Osborn was discharged from the US army in January, 1946. In Minnesota he bought a hardware business, in preparation for a new life with Rhona. However, when it was time for Rhona to sail to America, she was ill with appendicitis and 'missed the boat'. On hearing the news, Frank set sail for Australia and the couple settled in Sydney and raised a family of two daughters. Frank only returned to his home town Minnesota once in 1974.[75]

Rhona Jones and Frank Osborn, St Mark's Church, Darling Point, Sydney, 3rd January, 1945. [Source: Sydney Morning Herald, 24 April, 2009.]

In 1944, Betty Kane (née Denton) was already engaged to be married to an Australian man when she met her American husband-to-be. She recalls:

> *I was working in a bank in Perth and boarding in Subiaco with a woman called Norma. She had two children, but she was a bit of a party person and entertained a lot of Americans.*[76]

One night, the red-haired, freckle-faced young woman came home to find Norma was having a party. As she opened the door, she heard: 'Where did this little flower come from?' and she thought, 'You are a silly man!' She recalls:

> *I didn't usually go to Norma's parties, but I stayed up and this 'silly man' and I talked all night, about semi-serious stuff.*

He was a Chief Petty Officer. After that he came round every third night when he had liberty and stayed for dinner.[77]

Betty Denton, c.1943   Bob Kane, US Sailor., c.1943.

Bob Kane had intended asking Betty to go out with him, but after noticing her engagement ring and realising that she was already betrothed, he refrained. After a time, Betty and her fiancé had a falling out. She explains:

I handed back my ring after five years. I cried and cried. Bob and I dated then – he was very good looking and very good company, but I was determined not to fall in love again.[78]

Bob was offered a job which extended his stay in Australia, and Betty says: 'Our love just grew'. The couple's courtship followed the urgency of wartime romance and five months after they had met, the couple were married in Perth, in September, 1944.[79]

Many wartime romances between Australian women and American servicemen developed into permanent relationships over a period of time, often through letter-writing, which proved to be a significant part of wartime courtships as young couples had few opportunities to be together.

The experiences of women in Australia during wartime reflect many common characteristics during an extraordinary time for women throughout the world. However, the war brides' decisions to marry an American serviceman hoisted this group of women into another category of female wartime experience where special circumstances, specific legislation, and red tape, dictated their futures. The consequence of being the wife or fiancée of an American serviceman compelled these young women to discover or develop their inner resources of patience, commitment, resourcefulness and stoicism. By drawing upon these qualities, they overcame the many challenges that faced them after their decisions to marry, and to courageously embark on a journey to a new life in a land they knew little about.

CHAPTER TWO

RED TAPE

And so in the forties these two were wed,
On the edge of the war a strange life was led,
Waiting and hoping he'd be able to stay,
Soon hopes were shattered, he was on his way.
(Betty Kane, 'The War Bride', November 2001)[1]

Cynthia Peter (née Roberts) was born in Mosman in May 1925, the younger of two daughters, and grew up on Sydney's north shore. She was unhappy at school, so left at the age of fourteen to enroll at Miss Hale's Business College in the city. After her schooling, she worked at an insurance company and a lawyer's office, and then, during the war, worked for the Red Cross at their office in Sydney.

Cynthia met her husband on a blind date:

My best girlfriend in Sydney worked for the Americans in York Street. She called me up one day and said 'How about double dating with me tonight, there's supposed to be a nice young man here for you from the Navy.' I said, 'Oh, I don't know about Americans!' And she said 'Oh, give it a try! Come home with me after work and they'll come out to my house.' So that's what I did and that's when I first met Ray. As soon as we saw each other – I don't know – something clicked! It was a good feeling. I guess it was his gentle manner and he had a nice face.[2]

Ray was on a US supply ship docked in Sydney for a week, so
Cynthia was able to see him again. The ship went back and forth
to the war zone, coming back to Sydney each time to reload. The
couple dated for a year before they became engaged, but after about
ten months the war had moved further north and the action was in
the Philippines, too far north to return to Sydney. At that time, Ray
began to go through channels to arrange for Cynthia to enter the
United States as his fiancée.

They had been engaged for a year when Ray unexpectedly
returned from the Philippines and called her from Brisbane,
saying: 'I'm coming down, so we can be married!'[3] They had
three days' notice.

Cynthia was twenty when they married at St Mary's Cathedral
in Sydney on July 24, 1945, her new husband's 25th birthday.
Generous friends gave her clothing coupons and, in those three
frantic days, her mother made her wedding dress and trousseau from
satin and parachute silk that Ray had sent. Cynthia remembers the
urgency of the time:

> *Of course you didn't send out invitations in those days. You
> got on the phone and said, 'Can you come to a wedding –
> next Tuesday?'* [4]

She remembers that it was 'a lovely winter's day and the weather
was beautiful.' The couple honeymooned in Katoomba in the Blue
Mountains, and then Ray had to return to his ship in Brisbane.
Cynthia applied for special permission, which was required to travel
interstate by train due to wartime border restrictions, and joined her
husband in Brisbane.

One day in August, Cynthia asked her husband, 'What is an
atom bomb?' She had just read the press report of the first bomb
that had been dropped on Hiroshima! Shortly after that, the Japanese
surrendered and Ray's ship was sent back to San Francisco. By this
time, Cynthia was pregnant and she had to apply to the Admiral for

permission to sail to America, but he did not approve her application. She had to wait for the birth of her son Richard, by which time her husband, keen to be with her, had returned to Australia.

*   *   *

Despite soaring marriage rates for all age groups in Australia at the outbreak of WWII, getting married in wartime was not a simple matter and for a young Australian girl marrying an American, it was made even more complicated by specific wartime regulations and red tape.[5]

These women had to deal with extraordinary obstacles put in the way of their weddings. Couples who wished to marry faced opposition from both Australian and American authorities who urged caution and actively discouraged Australian-American marriages. As early as July 1942, the US Chief of Naval Operations issued orders that members of the Naval, Marine Corps or Coast Guard Forces could not marry without the approval of their Commanding Officer. In August of that year similar orders were issued by the US Army Headquarters, Southwest Pacific Area. Also, a directive was sent to all Celebrants in New South Wales requesting that they not perform marriages of a member of the United States Army Forces without written authority from his proper Commanding Officer. Marriages between American servicemen and Australian women were seen to hamper the war effort and were therefore to be avoided at all cost.

Permission to marry was entirely at the discretion of the prospective bridegroom's Commanding Officer and that permission was either granted or not. It often took months for the paperwork to be completed. In an effort to prevent hasty and ill-planned marriages, it became mandatory that after permission was granted, there had to be a 'cooling-off' period of six months before the wedding could take place. The US Secretary of War issued a directive that those personnel who married without authority would be subject to severe disciplinary action.[6]

When Joan Byer's American boyfriend, Raymond, asked her to marry him, she remembers how difficult it was to organise:

> *Ray had to get permission from his commanding officer to marry while overseas. That was not easy to do. The Navy was reluctant to grant such permission and put all sorts of obstacles in our path. We needed birth certificates from both sets of parents, letters of recommendation from our superiors, character references from long-time friends and the pastor of our church, plus a citizen's report from the police. We also had to write personal letters detailing our reasons for getting married. It was somewhat of a nightmare, and not for the faint of heart.*[7]

Ray finally obtained permission to marry Joan just a few hours before the wedding was to take place on 19 August, 1944, at St Joseph's Catholic Church in Subiaco, where Joan had been a parishioner all her life.[8]

When Dorothy Pence Berry, who grew up in Sydney, met her American boyfriend it was the beginning of a whirlwind romance! She was working at Lennon's Hotel in Brisbane which was frequented by US servicemen. She recalls:

> *He was in the US Navy and he was telling me all night long that I looked like an American. I thought that was a new line! We got together immediately and set up house, but the navy wouldn't let us get married!*[9]

After waiting six months, the Captain still refused permission, so the couple decided they would 'fool the whole world' and have a baby to expedite matters. Dorothy tells how this made no difference and she was four months pregnant when they finally married in August 1943. She remembers with indignation:

*It wasn't a very good feeling for us, because I was a very
proud Australian. I thought I would make a good wife, and
the Navy didn't think so!* [10]

The reason the authorities gave Dorothy for not allowing their
marriage was that 'they didn't want any more marriages to foreign
wives', and yet, Dorothy says, 'I didn't feel "foreign"!'[11] The couple
had a very small church wedding in Brisbane, with only her
husband's and her own best friends as attendants. Her husband was
shipped out three months later.

Dorothy and Everett Pence on their wedding
day in Brisbane, 13 August, 1943.

During the war years, wedding arrangements were often
made with as little as three or four days' notice. In the urgency of
the wartime atmosphere, despite the importance of the white
bridal gown and its symbolic qualities, wedding preparations
were sometimes forced to give way to expedience, economy, and

availability. In place of the traditional white wedding with 'all the trimmings', the bride quite often wore borrowed bridal gowns and veils, had small gatherings, and ceremonies were conducted in haste.

Dorothy (Mary) Cook with her mother, outside family home in Albany, Western Australia on her wedding day, 24 February, 1943.

Brides-to-be were challenged by wartime rationing of luxury goods such as bridal dress fabrics, as well as the shortage of alcohol and the scarcity of photographic paper. Commodities such as petrol were also in short supply and honeymoons away were rare occurrences. Some brides married one day and went back to work the next.[12] Yet, despite these difficulties, many of the Australian war brides and their families still made enormous efforts to have a traditional white church wedding.

When Mary Bourne (née Cook) married Herb in Albany, Western Australia on February 24, 1943, she wore a borrowed wedding dress and a borrowed veil. Her bridesmaid wore a dress previously worn at another wedding and the reception was held at a Greek restaurant, which her husband called 'the greasy spoon'! Wartime petrol shortages disrupted their honeymoon trip when 'the taxi driver had to stop in the middle of the road…to put charcoal in the burner.'[13]

Similarly, Rita Hopkins (née North) had a small wartime wedding on May 27, 1943 in Brisbane. She borrowed her aunt's bridal dress and her cousin had 'a piece of lace that was way, way old and had been in the family forever', which she used for a veil. Being a schoolteacher, resourceful Rita overcame the fuel shortage and took ingredients to work where she used the school's cooking facilities to make the wedding cake for her 'sit-down' wedding reception.[14]

Rita and Franklin Hopkins
married on 27 May, 1944

It seemed that having a church wedding in bridal regalia, even though problematic in wartime, was important to many war brides. Weddings in wartime were very different to peacetime weddings. The traditional white wedding gown had for decades been standard regalia, symbolising qualities of purity, virginity, innocence, and promise.[15] Participating in the pageantry of the wedding ceremony became as important as changing their individual and social status by marriage.[16]

When Dorothy Thompson finally made her wedding arrangements, the minister said 'we have one opening at four o'clock next Saturday – don't be late!' With only five days' notice, Dorothy and her bridesmaids made their own dresses and her mother's friend made the cake. Dorothy describes the confusion caused by multiple weddings at the church:

> *The Minister told us not to be late, but one bride was coming out as the other was going in...you didn't know whose family you were with...all the churches were very busy because a lot of the Yanks were getting married.*[17]

Dorothy Leishman married Leroy Ferdinand Thompson on 27 May, 1944 at Albert Street Methodist Church, Brisbane.

Due to their personal circumstances, not all war brides married in the traditional white gown or had the pageantry of the church ritual. Sometimes a simpler wedding seemed more appropriate, especially in a time of national austerity.

Joan Hamilton (née Handley) grew up in the country town of Deniliquin, New South Wales, and while her mother was getting established in Sydney as a dress designer, she went to boarding school at Sydney Church of England Girls' Grammar School (SGEGGS) at Moss Vale. In the early 1940s, Joan worked for a defence company and did voluntary work at an American Red Cross snack bar. It was while on holidays in Sydney that she met her American husband Charles. After a 'wonderful interlude', Charles went back to New Guinea, but the couple got to know each other during the ten months between meeting and marrying.[18]

Joan describes herself as 'a run-away bride'. She had known her husband for almost a year, but her mother, who was a sole parent, would not give permission for Joan to marry. She had initially been unhappy at the thought of her only child leaving Australia and going 'into the unknown'.[19] Joan recalls:

I was 21, so I packed my bags and took the train from Goondiwindi to Brisbane...I stayed with a friend, an older woman whose daughter was my attendant.[20]

At a small wedding in the Albert Street Methodist Church, Brisbane, Joan wore a pink linen suit, as she had no coupons for a bridal dress. As she had run away from home, she felt that it was inappropriate to have a big wedding. The couple spent their honeymoon in a hotel because 'Charles didn't have time to take a proper holiday'.[21]

Last minute cancellations and changes to schedules caused consternation for some women planning their weddings. Joyce Olguin (née Kelly), from Bundarra, in outback New South Wales, had known her fiancé for a year, but had only seen him three times before they married. The first time was when he had seven days leave, then again when he had ten days leave, and then suddenly, when they planned to spend some time together, all leave was cancelled. She recalls:

We were planning our marriage...I had a cake ordered, and I was taking in the sugar coupons, when they cancelled Americans! Then I cancelled everything! Then all of a sudden he shows up on an Australian holiday – and then, we found five cup-cakes![22]

Joyce wore a street dress of 'very pretty blue crepe'. Her aunt had given her coupons to buy gloves and others gave her coupons for stockings and a hat. As well as wearing 'something new' she had no choice but to wear 'something old'. She recalls, 'I had the same shoes and the same underwear, as I didn't have enough coupons for anything else!'[23]

Brides, whose husbands were shipped out soon after they were married, suffered a real sense of abandonment. Lola Atkins (née Wilkins) married Tom in the Catholic Church in the country town of Northam, Western Australia on December 16, 1943. She wore her sister's altered wedding gown and invited family and friends to a reception in a hotel there, with a wedding cake and all the trimmings. Tom's reassignment to the US came quickly, with orders to leave just thirteen days after the wedding. It was an eventful two weeks that included her father's death the day before her husband was shipped out. Lola says:

> I felt excited, scared and slightly abandoned when Tom said, 'I'll see you in Frisco!'...but it did feel like an adventure.[24]

In Melbourne, Dawne Balester was seventeen years old, and working as a temporary female assistant for the Australian Army, when she met her American boyfriend on a train crowded with hundreds of young men just back from fighting on Guadalcanal. She remembers, 'He was the handsomest boy I had ever seen in my life'.[25] He visited her family home and, with her mother's permission, took her to a movie. From that point on they saw each other constantly. Dawne writes in her journal of the powerful emotions elicited during the uncertainty of war:

> Early in our relationship I realized that I was in love. Not a quiet love. I knew what passionate love was now. It blinded me. Fred never used the word love, I never mentioned love. After all what future did we have? I was seventeen, he was nineteen, how could we ever be sure of a life together? He would have to leave Australia to fight again and would never return... So, I made the most of every moment and never worried about the outcome.[26]

In this wartime atmosphere of urgency and uncertainty, Dawne seemed to 'live for the moment' and not to consider long-term outcomes or the longevity of a relationship, as in more normal peace-time society. Dawne's mother, 'the strictest of women where her daughters were concerned', seemed to like Fred and saved the meat ration to cook dinner for him and Dawne was impressed with the way he put up with her little sister, who was a pest and a tease.[27]

Dawne Balester.

Certainly there were some 'whirlwind' romances and some babies were conceived before marriage, perhaps due to the women's ignorance of sex and its consequences. While actual wedding ceremonies were often arranged with short notice, most marriages were the result of weeks, months, and sometimes years of getting to know each other. These protracted romances were partly the consequence of their fiancés being shipped off to fight in New Guinea and the Pacific islands; combined with the delays of official regulations, which required obtaining permission followed by a six-month waiting period, before marriage. Initial friendships developed over time – often through letter-writing – into meaningful relationships which led to marriage.

Long distance love affairs

Shortly after meeting their Australian girlfriends, most Americans intending to marry an Australian girl were shipped out to New Guinea or some other secret location in the Pacific. This separation, for weeks and sometimes months, ensured more than a short interval of time between their first meeting and being wed.[28] Letters were the most expedient way for the couples to get to know one another and for their relationships to develop, given the special demands of wartime. Love-letters were sent from unknown locations due to wartime censorship, and for some couples, these formed the most important part of their courtship.

Despite requests and the intentions of several war brides to send copies of some of these letters to the author, only one was received. This might indicate a reluctance to share such a private part of their romantic past and is understandable, as many of these women are now widowed and the letters which have been kept have become virtual treasures from their past.

Communication in this written form, during long periods of physical separation, heightened the romantic nature of these liaisons. Together with mementos and photographs exchanged between couples in wartime, their letters became treasured objects and were an important component of courtships which survived wartime separations.[29]

Memento jewellery made from silver coins by Joseph
Patterson, in New Guinea, for his fiancé and his mother.

Because their men were in the US army, long periods of separation were unavoidable and the process of letter-writing was subject to a great deal of 'red tape'.[30] Bureaucratic procedures under the Defence (National Security, General) Regulations were in force in Australia as early as August 1939.[31] These regulations prohibited the obtaining, recording, communication, publishing or possession of any naval or military information which could be useful to the enemy or might influence public opinion in Australia or elsewhere, or which might be prejudicial to the defence of the Commonwealth or the efficient prosecution of the war. This censorship affected the press, radio broadcasts, cinemas, posters, booklets as well as postal mail.[32] Both civilian and military mail could be opened and read by official censors, with sections or words of a sensitive nature, which identified the locations or activities of the armed services, either thoroughly blacked out with ink or actually cut out before the mail was delivered. US regulations made US military mail subject to similar censorship and delivery of letters was unreliable and could be long delayed.

For example, US Marine, George Gierhart, wrote to his family with important news of his wedding plans to marry June Ferreira and sent a photograph of his intended Australian bride. After two months, he wrote 'I imagine that we can write it off as lost. It was a nice picture too.'[33] Later, a letter containing photographs of the wedding was held up. The long delays resulted in extended periods of silence, which George attempts to clarify by explaining the complications caused by censorship in a subsequent letter to his parents:

> *Perhaps by now the unexplainable period of silence has been broken and you have heard from me also. The censorship regulations for June are that she is not allowed to write to you through the normal channels. She can, however, write to you and enclose it in my mail, although she too must abide by the regulations under which I come. So, if you haven't heard from her, that is probably the reason. She did write, before she found out she couldn't, but those letters were most likely held up.*[34]

Despite the official intrusion of the censor, courtships were still pursued by mail and even marriage proposals were contained in such letters. In many cases, this was the only way to develop a friendship which began with a brief meeting.

Peggy Dunbar Blackman (née Duncan) had only two dates in Australia with her husband-to-be before he was shipped out and she felt that letters proved to be an excellent means of communication:

> *We both found that we were good letter-writers and so we discovered that we had many common interests and liked the same kind of books, and music and theatre, and all of those kinds of things.*[35]

Love-letters were sent back and forth between Joy Shaddle and her fiancé, Lloyd, a dentist in the US Navy. Joy lived with her family in Lane Cove and always had a love of Australian flora and fauna, at one stage keeping a pet kangaroo on the tennis court. Joy worked in the fashion department of David Jones' Department Store in Sydney and a serendipitous meeting during her lunch-hour, at a luncheon bar in Sydney, was when the young couple first set eyes on each other. The young man in uniform sat down next to her on the only stool available. Joy recalls:

> *It was Sunday; October 6, 1944...I can remember it like it was yesterday because it was the most amazing day of my life! I'd placed my order when he came in – Lloyd Shaddle – I didn't notice him at all because I was reading a newspaper. There is no way we would ever have met except for a funny quirk of fate!*[36]

The waitress accidentally swapped their orders and Joy remembers:

We looked up at each other and saw what had happened and laughed! I went on eating my lunch and I could feel his eyes watching, looking at me. I didn't look too bad in those days! [37]

The two struck up a conversation, but Joy had to get back to work. Before she left, Lloyd asked for her phone number, as he said he would like to see her again. Joy thought:

Well, if I just give him my phone number he can't murder me or anything! Just a phone number! So, I gave it to him. I kept thinking he is probably short, because I'm tall, and when we stood up to leave I couldn't believe it. He towered over me by at least seven inches. Oh, he was tall – and very handsome! He looked gorgeous in his uniform. [38]

That night, her mother told her there was a phone message from an American. A return call allowed Joy and Lloyd to arrange their first date and she remembers:

So, I got all 'glammed up' and went back into town. I met him and we had dinner at Rose's – they used to have little bands there where people could dance. There was Rose's and Romano's and we used to go to both. So that was the beginning of it, and then he was transferred. [39]

Lloyd G Shaddle,   Joy Parker, c.1945.
US Navy, 1945.

After seeing Joy during his ten days' leave, the handsome American left, but the two continued to write letters to each other over the next two and a half years. Eventually, Lloyd wrote: 'The war is over, but I can't get you out of my mind. Would you marry me and be the mother of my children?' Joy accepted the proposal and, as his fiancée, travelled to New York to marry the man she says had 'stolen her heart'. Their letters were such an important part of Joy's courtship with her fiancé that she keeps them in a box tied up with ribbon. Joy proudly relates that she still has every one of the 'love-letters' he wrote to her, and now, at ninety years of age, they bring back memories of her late husband and tears to her eyes.[41]

The love-letter represented much more than simply a means of communication, especially when the couples' separation was prolonged, and letters were often tied into neat bundles and kept in boxes or placed in scrapbooks so that they could be re-read.[42]

Letter-writing was also an important part of the courtship of Jean Wilk (née Reeves). The daughter of a Mounted Policeman, Jean and her family moved from place to place during her childhood, and she grew up in various suburbs of Perth. During the war, Jean joined the Navy as a Signaller and was stationed at Rottnest Island, off the coast of Western Australia. She met her future husband when she went home on weekend leave and he came knocking on the door. She recalls:

> He was looking for another girl he had met. I didn't know her, so he stayed! His name was Casimer Wilk. Wilk means 'wolf' in Polish![43]

As he was often on duty and his leave didn't always coincide with Jean's time off, they rarely saw each other. Jean remembers:

> I knew him for a year. We wrote letters after he went back to America.[44]

The couple's courtship blossomed through letter-writing and led to marriage, after the war had long ended, on Treasure Island, a naval base in California, in June 1947.[45]

Jean Reeves and Casimer Wilk on their wedding day in June 1947.

It was through correspondence that Dorothy Hammon (née Salinski) was also able to get to know her future husband. Dorothy was twenty-four years old when they first met and it was only one week later that her boyfriend was shipped out. Dorothy remembers announcing to her family that she was going to marry this American. Her father said, 'I'll give it three months and you'll forget all about it.' However, this was not the case, and she tells how 'we just kept writing each other letters and getting in deeper'.[46]

Similarly, Joann Patterson corresponded for two and a half years with her future husband before they married, because he had left Melbourne and gone north to Townsville. Joann recalls that he was able to get leave every once in a while:

> He would come down and look me up, sometimes with great difficulty, because by that time I had joined the service, the AWAS, and I would be moved from place to place and he would have to track me down – which he did![47]

Although he was persistent and visited when he could, Joann maintains that most of her courtship was conducted through letters, despite the heavy censorship regulations in place at that time. While the official invasion of privacy resulting from the censorship process did nothing to foster effusive expressions of love and desire, the reliance on having to 'read between the lines' in some cases intensified the romantic nature of these communications.

So, despite mandatory censorship, the flow of letters between the young women and their American boyfriends over extended periods created heightened romantic expectations as well as offering opportunities for freedom of expression. The influence of advertising, women's magazines, contemporary fiction, and Hollywood films during the war years presented women with a new language in which to write about their feelings of attraction and their relationships with men. It also provided the narrative of 'the love story' in which to frame their experiences.[48]

Such a narrative of love is written by war bride Dawne Balester who tells in her journal of the passionate romance that she and her American boyfriend conducted by mail during their wartime separation. Fred Balester left Australia to fight in the Pacific and Dawne made up her mind to forget this man with whom she was passionately in love. She writes: 'He was just gone, gone from Australia, gone from my life, gone! I had no address for him.'[49] Then a letter arrived from him and 'the letter writing years began'. Although she dated a lot, Dawne always 'compared the men to him' and subsequently left them. She tells how: 'waiting for letters became the main part of my life.' She remembers: 'Mail was slow, irregular and heavily censored' and 'one page full of his writing was a windfall'. Fred always ended his letters simply, 'Love, Fred', but after the couple became engaged, he ended his letters with the words 'I love you' which made Dawne very happy. The letters continued to flow between the two and Dawne even corresponded with Fred's mother in America and sent photos of herself and her family.[50]

Letter-writing was an important part of Dawne's romantic relationship, as she writes:

> *Fred's proposal of marriage came to me by letter. Funny, how you can really get to know someone through an exchange of letters and how a marriage proposal can be just as thrilling when the person you love and long to be with writes it to you.*[51]

Marriages of American soldiers in Australia during the progress of the war were seen by the US Military as hampering to the war effort. In July 1942 official orders were issued stating that 'no member of Naval, Marine Corps or Coast Guard Forces on duty in any foreign country or possession may marry without the approval of the Senior Commander.'[52] The Registrar General and Celebrants in New South Wales were specifically requested not to marry any personnel of the United States Army without prior written approval.[53]

Immigration policy regarding visas and restrictive quotas also put obstacles in the way of Australian brides planning to live in America. They were classed as 'aliens' by the American government and had to conform to legal requirements and apply for permission to enter the United States as immigrants regardless of their husband's status. At that time, the immigration quota allowed for only 100 Australian-born people to migrate to the United States each year.[54] Reforms to immigration policy brought changes for the better at the end of the war. However, this was still three years away and did not help the plight of war brides and fiancés who experienced frustrating delays in making their future plans.

The war brides waiting to join their American husbands had no financial support, as military allotments had not been allocated. However, Jessie Street, a campaigner for women's rights and co-founder in 1929 of the United Associations of Women, wrote as Vice President of that organisation to the wife of the American President in June 1942. She wrote to clarify the position of Australian wives of American servicemen and the lack of provision for their maintenance and that of their children. Mrs. Roosevelt replied advising that recent legislation (The Servicemen's Dependants Allowance Act of 1942), passed by the US Congress, provided dependent wives with an entitlement of $US50 per month, partially composed of an allotment made by the soldier, and partially from a contribution made by the American Government.[55] In addition $US12 a month was granted for one child and $US10 a month for each additional child. The soldier could request that the allotments be made, or lacking such a request, a petition by the wife would be given consideration.[56] Thanks to Street's intervention, the dire financial position of some of these women was improved.

Clergymen were often reluctant to perform ceremonies for brides marrying Americans, creating yet another impediment to marriage. Church authorities did their best to discourage American-Australian marriages. In Brisbane, the Catholic Archbishop James Duhig publicly urged a ban on such weddings until the Americans could prove that they were legally free to marry, claiming that he feared bigamous mergers. Meanwhile, these marriages were not allowed to take place in Brisbane Catholic churches. This created a serious impediment to Catholic couples by forcing brides to seek permission from ministers of other denominations to marry them.[57]

In Townsville, Gladys Borger had taken Catholic instruction, as her future husband was a Catholic, but when he returned from New Guinea the priest wanted to sight his baptism papers. Gladys says:

> *There was no way you could get baptism papers from the United States then, so the priest wouldn't marry us and we got a Methodist Minister to perform the ceremony instead.*[58]

Religion was important in the lives of many war brides, as attending Sunday school and church had been a significant part of their upbringing. Disillusioned brides found their expectations of a traditional church wedding upset by the opposition from the religious establishment. However, these negative attitudes to

Australian-American marriages displayed by the church, as well as the Australian and American government authorities, most certainly heightened the whole notion of 'romantic love' for these couples. Faced with the reality of the situation, their resolve to marry, albeit in a church of another denomination, was strengthened. Although marriage did not confer US citizenship nor did it guarantee the brides' subsequent admission to the US, the couples' determination to have a church wedding demonstrated a continuation of traditional values midst the upheaval of an unpredictable wartime period.[59]

Early in 1943, when American serviceman Tom Atkins filed a request to marry Lola Wilkins in Northam, Western Australia, she was interviewed by an officer of the US Navy. Lola writes in her journal: 'The interview concerned the realities and was designed to acquaint Australian young women with enough information to be able to make a reasoned choice'.[60] During the waiting period of six months before the couple could marry, Lola remembers: 'the mixture of reality and romance gave me much to ponder'.[61] This mandatory waiting period was a sobering experience for Lola, as it was for many other war brides. It allowed them time, in the pressing atmosphere of wartime, to give serious thought to the reality and importance of their decision to marry an American serviceman. It also served to heighten romance and strengthen their sense of commitment. These young women were determined to marry the men they loved, despite the discouragement of the authorities and the hindrance of obstacles they had to overcome.

Allie Rudy remembers her wedding on November 20, 1943 at Our Lady of Lourdes Catholic Church, Melbourne (where she had attended school) as 'a glorious wedding' and the reception 'was just a beautiful thing'. The memories of the happy day flood back as she recalls how she wore the beautiful wedding gown that she had seen in a store window and remembers vividly how she 'loved the white Venetian lace veil' and the 'gardenias and waterlilies' she carried in her bouquet.[62]

Alice (Allie) Drew married Lowell
Robert (Bud) Rudy in Melbourne,
Vic., on 20 November, 1943.

Colleen Halter fondly remembers her wedding in Brisbane in November 1945, at 'the pretty little Methodist church right across from the City Hall' with a carillon which rang out for the first time since the war began. She recalls:

> We had a big family wedding, bridesmaids, best man, groomsman and flower girls – the works!'[63]

Colleen doesn't remember any problem finding a bridal gown, but does remember the three-tiered wedding cake and a large reception at home with the family catering for about fifty guests.[64]

Although these weddings took place during and just after the war, these two stories are narrated without any mention of the war itself or of the problems associated with having a church wedding at that time.

The wartime environment, dominated by rules, regulations, specific legislation and red tape, had a huge impact on different aspects of the lives of these young Australian women. Their new-found freedom was hampered by the necessary adherence to the severely limiting conditions of wartime, giving them few options and causing difficulties and frustration, putting obstacles in the way of their plans for the future.

Marriage in America

Some engaged couples were unable to marry until they were reunited in America after the war was over and this presented them with more red tape. A pre-paid bond of $US500 was required from the American serviceman to ensure that his future partner would not be abandoned on arrival and that the marriage would actually take place at the first opportunity. The bond money was to cover the cost of a possible return trip by sea, if the marriage did not take place within the stipulated time. By law, Australian fiancées of American servicemen had three months after their arrival in the US in which to formalise their marriages. For these women, their patience and determination were truly tested as they waited for passage to America to reunite with their fiancés.

Valda Goldberg (née Steigrad) and Harold Hertzberg were married on 29 August, 1946, just three days after her arrival in America. She explains:

> We had to have three days to wait to see that I didn't have VD or anything – it was Pennsylvanian law – but we were being married by a rabbi and the only one my husband knew happened to be Orthodox and couldn't marry us on a Saturday. So, we had to marry a day before, and neither of us was Orthodox.[65]

Valda tells how she was married in her mother-in-law's unit in a beautiful gown that her father had had made for her in Australia. Despite her mother-in-law's advice that 'you want a simpler dress' Valda insisted on wearing it to the rather large reception that her mother-in-law had arranged.[66]

Patricia Law (née Evans) was engaged to be married when she arrived in San Francisco on SS *Marine Phoenix* in 1947. In Sydney she had met her 'lanky Yank with a slow charming smile' while volunteering for the USO where she worked in the library. He would have liked to live in Australia, but at the time there were no openings in his line of work as a newspaper printer, so they planned that Pat would go to America and they would return to Australia later on. She checked with the shipping company each week, but her booking was overlooked. Eventually she sailed on the very last 'bride ship' and was given four hours' notice to pack and get on board, being told 'this is your last chance'. A friend put her in touch with a Red Cross nurse who insisted on meeting the ship when it docked in San Francisco. This well-meaning lady took Patricia home to stay for a week, changing her plans to travel directly to join her partner, as she had always intended. She then travelled by train to Casa Grande, Arizona where a Texan lady who sat next to her said 'You poor little thing, are you getting off here?' It was a small town of 6,000 people. Her fiancé met her at the train and Patricia recalls:

> He looked so different out of uniform...he had this big cowboy hat on. He's always very quiet, and you know me, I was telling him everything! He said 'look, we've got a lifetime ahead, slow down!' [67]

Her husband-to-be worked at the local newspaper and had rented a little apartment for her in "the ladies' yard" where she stayed until they were married six weeks later. The wedding took place in a 'beautiful old Episcopalian church in Tucson, Arizona' with two neighbours as witnesses. Patricia remembers that 'it was about a hundred degrees even in October.'[68] Although Patricia had brought a bridal dress with her from Australia, she decided instead to wear 'a crepe dress with a lot of beading on it that was very fancy' and made her feel 'kind of pretty'. The newlyweds could not spend the night in Tucson as they had to drive the two witnesses back home. However, upon their return 'the neighbours had a full-sized wedding cake and all the gifts and a lovely reception' waiting for them and the new bride was made feel very welcome.[69]

Patricia Evans married
Kenneth Law in America
on 2 October, 1948.

On the east coast of America, Joy Parker's fiancé Lloyd Shaddle had travelled by train from Forrest, Illinois, to meet the merchant ship MV *Lowlander,* which had sailed through the Panama Canal and up the east coast to dock in New York in early 1947. As soon as they could get their papers ready the couple was married at 'The Little Church Around the Corner', a historic church in downtown New York, on March 14, 1947. They honeymooned in New York and visited Niagara Falls before taking the train to the small town of Forrest, where they stayed with Lloyd's parents until they were able to buy their own house.[70]

Joy Isobel Parker married Lloyd G. Shaddle
in New York, on 14 March, 1947

The Little Church Around the Corner, New York, NY, founded in 1848.

For these fiancées the absence of their own families from the important occasion of their marriage was inevitable and somewhat similar to the experience of some war brides who married in Australia during wartime without family members present. However, for the fiancées who married in America, the absence of family added an extra dimension to the emotional experience of their wedding day, with few people in attendance, in a country in which they had not had time to settle.

It was just three days after arriving in America, and after travelling for seven exhausting days by plane, that Sunny Sansing was married at the Bellevue Baptist Church in Memphis, Tennessee on September 26, 1946. Because she had been married before and had been through a divorce, Sunny says, 'they would not marry me in the church. I was married in the basement', where the Sunday School was held. She says: 'I really didn't appreciate it at all!'[71] However, these were typical of the unexpected situations which many war brides had to accept on arrival in a new country where rules and regulations varied from state to state.

When remembering such a romantic period in their early lives a necessary component of nostalgia is normal. In the majority of cases, however, there was an almost relieved outpouring from the heart, as these war brides related their stories of love and marriage which they had been waiting to tell for many years, taking their rightful place in the public wartime arena. Rather than restructuring their stories in order to present an acceptable picture, the war brides enthusiastically told how it was for them, both good and bad. They were keen to record their stories to inform the younger generation of their part in the making of women's history in a by-gone era.

CHAPTER THREE

'LADIES IN WAITING'

All the girls around Australia,
Married to Yankee Sailors:
The fare is paid across the sea,
To the home of the brave, and the land of the free.
From west to east the young girls came,
All aboard the Bridal Train.
It was a farewell crossing of the land,
She's gone to meet her sailor man.
(Lyrics from chorus of The Bridal Train,
written and sung by The Waifs, 2004)[1]

Destined for places in the US about which they knew very little, thousands of young women travelled from rural and urban locations across Australia to embark on a long shipboard voyage to join their husbands and fiancés in America. The emotions of many plunged suddenly from the 'highs' of anticipation to the 'lowest ebbs' of frustration when their expected shipboard passages were cancelled or delayed. Most faced the prospect of meeting up with their future partners they had not seen for months or sometimes years, as well as meeting their in-laws, who were not always welcoming.

The long wait

Most of the 'bride ships', specially designated to transport women from Australia to America, sailed from the eastern ports of Brisbane and Sydney. For war brides on the east coast, securing a passage on one of these ships was challenging enough, but for those young women in Western Australia, it required determination and extra stamina. They first had to undertake the arduous week-long journey by train across the arid heart of Australia to reach the eastern states, where they then faced a long wait – sometimes months – to board a ship to the US.

Barbara Gleason (née Sheridan) was born in Fremantle, Western Australia, in 1922, the youngest of seven children. Her father, a WWI veteran, was granted 100 acres of uncleared land on returning from service in France. The family lived in a makeshift shed with an attached tent while they built a house and her father set up a small dairy farm. Twice a week they sold cream to the butter factory at nearby Manjimup. This was the family's only source of income. Barbara's father became ill and her parents 'couldn't take it anymore'. She remembers:

> There was just no money on the farm, so being that he was a carpenter, we moved back to Perth, but unfortunately, he didn't live too long. He died when he was about 54.[2]

Although the family was poor, Barbara had a happy childhood on the farm:

> I loved the country, although it was a little lonesome. We really had a good life. We didn't know we were poor, because we always had everything we wanted to eat. We always had shoes and clothes. So we actually did very well. I was the youngest, and they say I was spoilt. It was harder on my brothers because 14 was the school leaving age – it was a one-room schoolhouse with all the classes in one room – and when they left, what were they going to do? Now we were deep in the Depression.[3]

Barbara's mother was a homemaker and a farmer and was a strong role model. Barbara observes:

She worked very, very hard. She worked as hard outside on the farm as she did in the house. She'd been a farmer all her life – her family were farmers. She'd milk the cows and just get out there and do men's work. Once a month a minister would come to the little schoolhouse and hold church. My mother always saw that we said our prayers.[4]

Barbara met her American husband on a blind date. She and her girlfriend used to go dancing at 'The Embassy' in Perth, where her friend met an American sailor who was keen to take her out. She insisted he bring along a friend for Barbara, so they could go out in a foursome. Barbara was working at Bond's Department Store at that time and her friend promised to bring him by the store so she could see if she liked him. Barbara remembers: 'All he had to do was smile, and I was hooked'. So the two girls and their American boyfriends went to see the Disney movie, *Fantasia*. Jim Gleason was serving on a submarine tender, USS *Pelius*, which had been bombed

at Pearl Harbour, and he was stationed in Fremantle, Western Australia, for two years. Barbara was 21 years old when she married Jim in February 1944. In March, she found that she was pregnant; in May her husband was shipped out; and in June she travelled by train to Sydney and stayed in a boarding house with a lot of other brides.

Barbara Faith Sheridan married Bernard James Gleason at Wesley Church, Perth, W.A. on 19 February, 1944.

Barbara remembers:

> *We called ourselves 'the ladies in waiting' – waiting to have babies and waiting to come to America! We were booked with Cooks…supposedly they would get us on a ship to come over here…but there weren't many ships available.*[5]

Barbara and two other girls at the boarding house went to town every day to check their progress with Cook's shipping agency. She remembers how the man behind the counter said 'You're going, you're going and' – pointing to Barbara - 'you're *not* going!' Her two companions left on a train to Brisbane to sail from there and Barbara was left on her own. Moving to new accommodation where other war brides were staying, she recalls:

> *We just waited and waited. We were all paying room and board and we weren't working'.*[6]

She stayed there until December, the month when her baby was due to be born. Finally, an American officer found Barbara a seat on the only train that went back and forth to Western Australia. She recalls how difficult it was travelling back home to have her baby:

> *You'd sit up from Sydney to Melbourne, then you'd sit up from Melbourne to Port Pirie, and then you'd have the sleeper across [the Nullarbor Plains]. I was eight months pregnant – I was crazy when I think about it!*[7]

Back home in Perth, her healthy baby daughter was born on December 28, 1944. As the mother of a small baby, Barbara was now at the top of the priority list to sail to America, but still there were no ships available. She was living at home with her family when she received a call to come to Fremantle as a ship was leaving from that port. She remembers:

> *We all went down to Fremantle, nursing our babies, and sat*
> *there for hours with all these guys typing up all these papers*
> *and when the officer finally emerged, he said 'Ha, ha, ha!*
> *Guess what? You're not going!'...so we went home again!* [8]

Barbara's report of her frustration on this occasion is typical of the disappointing treatment suffered by the brides and fiancées during the protracted wait for passage to America.

After Betty and Bob Kane were married in Perth in September, 1944, Bob returned to sea and Betty returned to the small country town of Wagin to stay with her mother until the birth of their daughter in March 1945.

Betty, now a young mother of 24, settled down to live with her mother during the war while caring for baby Susan. Bob was shipped back to the US on the 12 February, 1945. Almost 12 months later, on the 7 February, 1946, Betty received a telegram from Dalgety's in Perth stating:

Betty Denton, c.1944.

> *Mrs. Elizabeth Kane, Wagin. Please call this office Friday*

This telegram to Betty Kane, dated 7 February, 1946, is referred
to in the Waif's popular song, 'Bridal Train'.

*8th February prepared for travel to America leaving Perth
eleventh or twelfth reply. Dalgety.*[9]

After almost a year apart from Bob, Betty was reluctant to go, but
her mother insisted that she belonged with her husband. Her only
route to the city was the overnight train between Albany and Perth,
which went through Wagin at midnight. She had eight hours to
pack, organise her paperwork and say farewell to her family before
boarding 'the bridal train' to take her 'from west to east' and finally
to board SS *Monterey.*

The patience of many young Australian brides of US servicemen,
some with children, was sorely tested as they endured long and
frustrating periods anxiously waiting to be transported across the
Pacific. Newspapers claimed that the delays were not caused by red
tape or unsympathetic administration, but that it was due to 'the
necessities of wartime shipping'.[10]

Priority in obtaining a passage to America was given to the
war brides who had already married in Australia, and then it was
according to the date on which the girl's visa was issued. A US
Consular officer admitted that 'it sometimes takes a long time to

move up the list'.[11] A Joint Transportation Committee, made up of Army, Navy, War Shipping Administration and the US Consulate, were in control of shipping and 'were anxious to help get these girls to the States'.[12] However, while the war was still being fought, the war brides' transport came second to the war effort, and they had no choice but to wait.

Establishment of Clubs for Wives and Fiancées

The women anxiously waiting to sail to America had no idea how long the delay might be, and some who waited in accommodation away from home worried that their money might run out before they were allocated a berth on a ship. As early as March 1944, *Pix* (a popular Australian magazine at the time) ran a story about the hundreds of Australian girls who had 'married their new-found sweethearts' and who had 'since been left behind, temporarily, while their husbands kept their appointments with Tojo in the far-flung fronts of the Pacific'.[13] Wives and fiancées packed into the libraries of the US Information Service in Sydney and Melbourne to learn more about America.[14]

The magazine reported the formation in Melbourne of the Friendship Club for Wives of US Servicemen, the first of its kind in Australia. The Club, founded by a group of lonely war brides had a membership of more than 400, including fiancées as well as wives, and 25 babies classed as junior members. The object of the Club was social contact, and activities included culinary trials of recipes for American dishes, outdoor meetings in a city park, 'singsongs', exchanging news and comparing notes from letters, especially those from new relatives in America.

The need for such organisations existed all over Australia and similar clubs sprung up in other cities. In Sydney, the Club for Wives and Fiancées of US Servicemen met weekly. The first Australian woman Senator, Dorothy Tangney, elected in 1943 to represent Western Australia, was a strong advocate for women's rights and was Patron of this Club.[15]

Lecture Girls also learned something of the land to which they will go when transport is available. Instructor is Miss Harriet Root, who established and manages the US Information Library in Sydney. All except one of the girls in these pictures are natives of New South Wales. Some have been waiting nearly a year for passage to US.

Members of the Wives and Fiancees Association attend
lectures at the US Information Library in Sydney.

War bride Nell Rassmussen remembers visiting this Club during her wait for transport to the US:

> *I went to the Wives and Fiancées' Club which held their meetings in the Museum on the corner of William Street. We mostly wanted to hear about transportation. My father had paid 500 pounds to a man who said he could get transport - my father never saw him again! I still have a copy of a letter from the Prime Minister in answer to a request from my father for assistance in getting transportation for me to get to America.*[16]

In Brisbane the Australian Wives' and American Husbands' Club was set up during May 1944.[17] Organised by the Allied

Relations Committee, a two-day school was held at Newport on Sydney's north shore, for wives and fiancées of American Servicemen to help the girls to brush up their knowledge of Australia and to learn something of American customs and history before they left for the United States.[18] In January 1945, a lecture on America was given by feminist politician Mrs Crawford Vaughan,[19] attended by 50 members of the First NSW Wives and Fiancées of US Servicemen's Club, which was located in Castlereagh Street, Sydney. The young wives and fiancées showed keen interest in social and economic conditions in their adopted country and asked such questions as: 'Can a woman become President?'; 'Is housekeeping really so much easier than in Australia?'; and 'Will we find the weather very extreme?'[20] The young women also were anxious to know exactly what happened regarding their nationality and that of their children when they married and entered the US.

Towards the end of the war in 1945 when there were many more brides waiting to join their husbands in America, more clubs were formed in Perth, Townsville and Rockhampton, which offered companionship and other useful services. At these clubs, brides also learned more about Australia so that they could speak about their country of origin when they reached the US.[21] In this way, the clubs provided the early 'grooming' for these women who were expected to fulfil a role of 'good ambassadors' for Australia in the US. The various Clubs saw the importance of a smooth transition from Australian to American culture not only to assist these young women in adjusting to their newly married status and settling in a new land, but also to foster good relations and a lasting alliance between the people of the two countries.

Around the same time, similar clubs also began to appear in America. The Australian film actress, Shirley Ann Richards, who went to America to live in 1942, set up a club for Australian brides of US Servicemen living in the vicinity of Los Angeles. Meetings were held each month in Hollywood's luxurious Studio Club for Women.[22] *The Sydney Morning Herald* reported:

> the club will afford the brides an opportunity to form friendships with other girls from Australia, as well as to meet American women who are likely to help them.[23]

The first Australian war brides crossed the Pacific as early as 1943, but it was mainly from 1944 onwards that war brides began to sail on ships which often carried American servicemen who had been invalided home or were on furlough.[24] However, most war brides and fiancées had to wait until berths were available on ships no longer needed for carrying troops at the end of the war. It was after the Japanese surrender that there were thousands of women waiting to sail to join their husbands and fiancés. Having to compete with returning servicemen for space, these women had no option but to wait until ships under orders from the US Army Transport Service had room available to take them to America.[25]

Agitation by 'bride clubs,' and letters from US servicemen to their congressmen, highlighted the plight of these women who objected to their treatment by shipping and Government officials. In September, 1946, fiancées claimed that they were given no priority on ships to America, despite some having waited for more than four years. This was brought to the attention of Senator Dorothy Tangney, in her capacity as patron of the US Servicemen's Wives and Fiancées Association, and even US President Harry Truman was petitioned for assistance.[26] These attempts to find solutions to transportation problems demonstrated the need for urgent official intervention.

The predicament facing Australian war brides was given prominence in the American press as early as January 1945, when the *New York Times* urged that 'Washington should give official attention to the plight of the Australian war brides waiting for a passage to America'.[27] The newspaper stated:

It is certainly not a very happy introduction to their new country for the 1,200 war brides waiting in Sydney, some with babies, many with insufficient funds, and all, apparently without a definite promise from anyone as to when, where, and if they will be furnished with some method of transportation.[28]

The Sydney Morning Herald reported the next day that between 10,000 and 12,000 American-Australian marriages had been recorded since the Pacific war began, and 'probably many more of which the US Consulates and Service authorities have not been notified'. The paper stated that between 1,200 and 1,500 Australian brides and fiancées of American Servicemen had already made their way to America, and now 'nine hundred more were waiting, with visas signed, in Sydney, Melbourne, and Brisbane'.[29]

After overcoming the obstacles confronting Australian-American marriages, most of these women, once married, were quickly separated from their husbands, who were either deployed to fight in the Pacific War or shipped back to America. There were few opportunities for honeymoons, with many couples spending only a few days or weeks together before the husband was shipped out. The war brides were required to wait, some longer than others, and often under quite stressful conditions, away from their homes in the country or in another State, with little money and much uncertainty, until a berth on a ship to America became available.

Audrey Westley was eighteen when she met Private Angelo 'Bob' Capuano at a weekly dance in Strathalbyn, South Australia. They were married two years later in 1944 at St Mary's Cathedral, Sydney.

After her husband was repatriated back to America, Audrey had to wait for a berth on a bride ship. She passed the time by knitting a jumper in the design of the American flag, which she wore both departing Sydney on board SS *Monterey* in April 1946, and upon arrival in San Francisco. Audrey was featured in her 'Stars and Stripes' jumper in both the Australian and the American newspapers.[30]

Audrey Capuano's hand-knitted 'Stars and Stripes' woollen jumper.

Audrey and Angelo (Bob) at Circular Quay Sydney, August 1944.

Although frustrated by the delays in transportation, the war brides, many of whom by this time were caring for their infants, demonstrated patience and determination, traits found to be characteristic of this special generation of women.

The 'Perth Perambulator' and the Red Cross

The US Army in Australia was accompanied by social workers of the home service organisation of the American Red Cross. They recognised the threat that family separation and the slowness of transportation and mail services had to marriages and they provided a much needed service for war brides and fiancées of US servicemen. When the war came to an end, the American Red Cross, in continuing their supportive role, asked the Australian Red

Cross, the country's largest patriotic fund in WWII and probably the largest volunteer organization in Australian history, to carry on this necessary work.[31] It was 'a grass-roots, community-based organisation' with a network of branches country-wide, vigorously supported by women in rural and regional Australia.[32] When the war was almost over, the women of the Australian Red Cross Field Force accompanied the war brides across to the eastern states on a train, so that they could board a ship bound for America. An Australian Red Cross recruiting officer records her memories:

> Instead of bandages and blankets we were now collecting and packing baby food onto the train, things for the children; you never saw anything like it – napkins flapping to dry on the back of the train. What a circus they must have looked chuffing away across the sandy wastelands.[33]

The train to Melbourne took five days to cross 2,694 miles of dry, hot, dusty country stretching from west to east.[34]

Barbara Gleason was one of the passengers on that train, affectionately called the 'Perth Perambulator', because of the number of mothers and babies on board. After another period of waiting with her baby daughter, Lynette, Barbara had finally received word that a ship was leaving from Brisbane. But first, she had to get there from Perth. A special car for the war brides was put on the train from Perth, and the families of the war brides filled suitcases with food for the journey. In what seems like an understatement, Barbara recalls 'there were quite a few of us went on that train' and a Red Cross representative travelled with them.[35]

The 'Perth Perambulator' was a mammoth undertaking for the Australian Red Cross, who assigned Red Cross Hospital Visitors to accompany the war brides and their babies overland by train to the eastern ports.[36] Their work began at Perth railway station and continued day and night for almost a week until they reached Melbourne. It began by assisting in crowd management at the station as parents and friends swarmed onto the platforms to farewell the war brides. The scene was described by a Red Cross Hospital Visitor as one of 'utter chaos'.[37] Most of the passengers had packed in such a hurry that they had not been able to organise their luggage and the majority had at least two suitcases in the crowded train compartments, which 'did not add to the general comfort'.[38] The Red Cross aides spent much of their time 'soothing crying babies, cheering hysterical mothers, and re-organising luggage'.[39]

During the long train journey there was an enormous amount of community activism and support for the war brides, such as the provision of meals and refreshments at stops along the way, making up bottles of baby formula, and helping with heavy luggage at change-over points.[40] The fact that many ordinary Australians went out of their way to volunteer to help these women who were about to leave Australia, belies the often-claimed negative response to the war brides of American GIs.

The brides' train made stops at Southern Cross and Northam, in Western Australia, where hot water was put on board. At Kalgoorlie, a change to a broader rail gauge took place and a buffet car was provided with hot water continuously available.[41] When the train reached Cook, a small town in the centre of the vast Nullarbor Plain with the harshest of climates, the war brides were taken to the local bush hospital by members of the Soldiers' Welfare Community, where they were treated to an egg and bacon breakfast.[42]

On her journey, Barbara remembers the priority given to the war brides and their babies. Everyone else on the train waited while the brides were taken off. Barbara appreciated the care provided by the Red Cross and recalls:

> We sat on the verandah of this hospital and ate a really nice meal they set up for us.[43]

At Tarcoola, an old gold-mining town in South Australia, the brides were taken off the train and a special tea was provided at various nearby homes and mothers had the chance to bathe their babies while the resident took charge of the children to allow the brides to have a peaceful meal.[44] Barbara remembers the brides being taken to private houses for refreshments, and reminisces:

> *I've always been so sorry I didn't take people's names, but you were kind of numb by then. You'd get to wherever you were going and you'd kind of just fall into their arms and somebody would take your baby and lead you to where you were going.*[45]

At Port Pirie the next morning, a trained nurse gave advice on the health of some of the children and the local branch of the Red Cross served morning tea at the station.[46] On arrival at Adelaide, lunch was provided in the Railway Refreshment Rooms, and buses took the mothers and children to Red Cross headquarters where they were provided with soap, towels and make-up kits, and 'sweetly talcumed babies and rested mothers were served supper' before re-boarding the train.[47]

There were no sleeping cars on the train from Adelaide to Ballarat, where the train stopped for a brief pause. On arrival, the women felt stiff, tired and cold and were pleased to find personnel from the local branch of the Red Cross waiting on the platform with 'piping hot tea' and sandwiches, as well as fruit and daily newspapers.[48]

Barbara Gleason (right) with baby Beverley and friends June and Peg arriving at Melbourne after crossing the Nullarbor in 1945.

Once in Melbourne, a team of Red Cross personnel was waiting to take charge and accommodated the brides and their babies at the 'Lady Dugan Hostel' and at 'Edgecliffe' and 'Rockingham' Convalescent Homes.[49]

Barbara remembers being taken to an 'R & R' facility previously used for men, 'somewhere on the ocean, quite a way from town'. She recalls:

> *There were a lot of us and the babies had to sleep with you –*
> *in these high hospital beds – and we were scared the babies*
> *would fall.* [50]

They stayed there for several days and made daily trips by bus into town to take care of necessary paperwork such as procuring taxation clearances, travellers' cheques and exchange of currency. Finally, the women and their babies were once more put on a train to travel from Melbourne to Brisbane.[51]

Headlines in the daily press in early September 1945 highlighted 'pandemonium unlimited' which 'swept through Melbourne's Spencer Street station when 230 Australian brides of US servicemen, and 70 children, left on a special train for Brisbane, en route for USA'.[52] Other accounts told of 'hysterical mothers' of war brides in Sydney jumping on to the railway line at Central Station and chasing the US bride train which bore the chalked slogan 'Brides' Express'.[53] Other vivid newspaper reports confirmed this chaotic situation. In the congestion on the Melbourne platform, at the call of 'all aboard', some distraught brides tried to find their luggage and to comfort their crying babies while saying their last precious words to their relatives they were leaving behind, perhaps permanently.[54] Streamers stretched between the passengers and those on the platform and as the train slowly pulled out of the station they broke, seeming to symbolise the last bond being broken between tearful brides and their more tearful mothers and loved ones.[55]

One frantic woman on the train rushed along the corridor crying out that her baby was still with her mother on the platform. A 'big

RAAF Sergeant came speeding along the platform with the child in his arms', according to the report of a Red Cross Hospital Visitor, who writes:

> Before he reached me a toy kangaroo, a bunch of violets, and a wooden horse were thrust into my arms by various people on the platform, and then the baby was suddenly hurled at me. The force of the impact knocked me backwards on the well-nigh hysterical mother and the three of us, complete with toys, collapsed on a pile of luggage. Such was our grand exit from Melbourne! [56]

The Australian Red Cross provided 'thermos urns to heat water for babies' baths, hot-water bottles, soap, cotton wool, fruit, blankets, cushions, first-aid kits.'[57] Seven Red Cross Hospital Visitors travelled to Brisbane with the train and local Red Cross branches were on duty to assist with caring for babies when the train stopped to change engines or take on water.[58] At Albury, on the border between Victoria and New South Wales, after the change-over of trains because of the different rail gauge, a carton of cakes and sandwiches was found on every seat, thoughtfully provided by members of the Albury Branch of the Red Cross.[59] The train by-passed Sydney, but stops were made for refreshments at Gosford and Newcastle, and for a hot dinner at Taree.[60]

Travelling by train from Melbourne to Brisbane, Barbara and her girlfriend, stayed together. She recalls:

> *We had a private car where we put the babies on the seat and we slept on the floor. My hip still hurts from that! [She laughs.] At least we slept overnight!* [61]

Barbara clearly remembers the train making a stop at Newcastle for refreshments, because when her younger brother came to see her there, he was not allowed into the station and she had to go outside and talk to him. They said their goodbyes through the fence.[62]

None of the war brides was sorry when the long and tiring train trip finally came to an end. For those from Western Australia, it was a journey of nine days, with only one proper break in Melbourne. Other 'bride trains' followed much the same pattern, transporting the brides and their babies from Melbourne to Brisbane. From Sydney, one special train was used, and with extra war brides being picked up the number of passengers grew to 279 women and 85 babies.[63] For all of these journeys, the Red Cross girls provided invaluable services, their trips being 'one round after another of preparing bottles of milk and food for the babies, issuing rugs, soap, powder, napkins, barley sugar, oranges and cigarettes'.[64]

On arrival in Brisbane, buses took the mothers and babies directly to the ship. Barbara vividly remembers her first glimpse of SS *Lurline*:

> When I looked at that boat, my gosh, I'd never seen anything so huge...and it was filled with troops.[65]

It was 21 September, 1945, the war was just over, and the American authorities were keen to send the troops home. Brisbane girls were put off the ship to let the troops on, but luckily for Barbara and her travelling companions, who had come all the way from the West, they were given first priority to be on the ship. Barbara said with a sigh: 'So finally, we were on the *Lurline!*' and the first stage of her epic journey was over.[66]

Jackie Hansen tells how the war brides in Perth had been waiting for a year, sometimes more, for a ship to the US. She says:

> We kept hearing of ships such as the *Lurline* transporting brides from the east coast. I think they forgot about the brides in the West.[67]

It was a year before she could get transportation to join her husband, Lee, in the US. War brides in Perth were eventually summoned to a meeting in the Perth Town Hall, where advice was given by one of the City Councillors. Jackie recalls:

> *Councillor Caddy told us all to write to our husbands right away and have them write to their Congressmen asking for transportation for their wives. It worked!* [68]

Within a few weeks, there was an army transport ship, USAT *Fred C. Ainsworth,* sent to Fremantle, the port of Perth. Jackie remembers the protracted departure and the sadness of leaving family and friends:

> *Everyone was teary-eyed both on the dock and on the ship. The ship was delayed waiting for supplies for babies – diapers [napkins] and food. I called to my parents to go home and get some rest as they had been standing on the dock all day. The ship was not a luxury liner by any means!* [69]

War Brides and Fiancées Acts

At the end of the war, the patience of the war brides waiting to join their husbands was rewarded and their plight was relieved by the introduction of *The War Brides Act* in December 28, 1945 (59 Statutes-at-Large 659) which waived all visa requirements and provisions of immigration law for the foreign brides of American WWII servicemen.[70] Despite the passage of this legislation, however, these women still had to summon their patience and wait for available shipping before they could travel to America.

Although the passing of the US *War Brides Act* was welcomed by those who were married to Americans, it did not make any provision for the fiancées of American servicemen, and these women resented the favouritism shown towards the brides. Dorothy Hammond and her fiancé decided to marry after knowing each other for only one week before he was suddenly shipped out, and she had to wait two and a half years to join him in America. She remembers, with some bitterness:

> *The brides got to go – they were entitled and they had children – but after the war they let us [fiancées] go, and very grudgingly too!* [71]

Dorothy felt sure that the mass exodus of war brides and fiancées in such numbers was seen generally to be 'wrecking the population' in Australia.[72]

Similarly, Patricia Law recalls her wait for passage to America to be with her fiancé. She explains:

> *Because we weren't married, I was on the bottom of the list and the married ladies with children were at the top of the list!* [73]

Eventually, six months after the *War Brides Act* was passed, the *G.I. Fiancées Act* of June 29, 1946 (60 Statutes-at-Large 339) was implemented, which finally facilitated the admission to the United States of fiancées of members of the American armed forces.[74]

Mothers of war brides were concerned for their daughters' welfare as they faced the predicament of not being able to get passage on a ship to America. In Melbourne, an organisation known as the Australian Mothers of War Brides Goodwill Mission Club was formed to help publicise the plight of the war brides and to help raise funds towards costs associated with delays and the prolonged wait for passage on a ship.

The logistics of reaching the eastern ports by train, the long wait for passage on a ship, the sense of uncertainty together with the final sad goodbyes to families and friends all combined to create a stressful time for the war brides. For these women who were about to leave Australia for the first time and to sail the Pacific to join their partners, it was a defining moment in their lives requiring courage and commitment; a significant time on the brink of a new life which was imprinted in their memories.

Australian Mothers of War Brides Goodwill Mission Club.
[Source: NAA A8139, Volume 8]

CHAPTER FOUR

SAILING TO AMERICA

The U S Navy treated them grand
The Monterey' took them to their new land.
A ship full of brides and children small,
Three weeks they travelled, in no time at all
The shores of America loomed in sight,
Some scared and nervous, numb with fright.

The girl with Sue was one of this kind,
While others appeared not really to mind.
Excitement was high, excitement all round,
Soon they would have their feet on the ground.
They'd be with their men, a new life would start,
Hopefully never again to part.
(Betty Kane, 'The War Bride', November 2001)[1]

Sailing to America was a huge adventure for war bride Joy
Shaddle. In January 1947, after two and a half years waiting for
transportation, Joy sailed on the old merchant ship, SS *Lowlander,*
from Sydney to New York via the Panama Canal. She remembers this
time well:

> In those days it was like going to the moon! Nobody
> travelled. I didn't know anybody that had been outside
> Australia! Nobody! Nobody flew anywhere, only the forces
> went in planes. So it was like going to Mars, to the ends of
> the earth, after waiting so long.[2]

Sydney Harbour Bridge, Circular Quay, Sydney, c.1945. [Source: State Records NSW, 9856_A017_a017000167]

It was a sad farewell as Joy waved her parents goodbye. She was the eldest of four children, and the only girl. As the old ship sailed under Sydney Harbour Bridge in the afternoon sunset she thought she would die of grief. She thought she would probably never see her family again.

She recalls:

We only got about a hundred miles out that night, and by that time I was sick – heart-sick and really ill from the grief. I was lying in my bunk still wide awake at three o'clock the next morning, thinking 'What have I done? What have I left behind? Everything!' Suddenly, there was a dreadful explosion in the engine room and the ship shuddered.[3]

Joy went up on deck to find that the explosion had left the ship with only one engine and it could go no further. As there was no docking space available in Sydney, the ship was diverted north to Newcastle for repairs. Joys remembers:

We were back the next day! So I had all my grief for nothing! The first thing I did was get ashore and call my mother and she couldn't believe it! She was deliriously happy. She said 'I thought you'd gone for ever!'[4]

At Joy's request, her mother was able to catch a train to Newcastle right away. The Captain allowed her to stay with Joy in her cabin and they spent 'four wonderful days' together. The second departure from Australia was not nearly so sad, as Joy took her mother to catch the train home the night before the ship sailed. It took six weeks to reach New York, the old ship limping along, breaking down and being fixed several times along the way. Joy tells how one of the passengers changed his prayers to say: 'Oh Lord, give us our daily breakdown and deliver us safely to New York!'[5]

As they embarked on the long sea voyage to America, Australian war brides were excited at the prospect of travelling to a new land as most of these women had never travelled beyond Australia's shores. But, many were apprehensive about what lay ahead, wondering if they would still be in love and if they would even recognise their husbands after such a long separation.

Aust. WWII War Brides, Melbourne, leaving for the USA, 1945.
[Source: Australian War Memorial, POO561036]

At a time of global conflict and social change for women, Australian war brides and fiancées stepped out of a familiar world into one about which they knew very little. Although the journey by ship was differently experienced by each individual, it was significant in that it drew them together and brought about the development of their new identities as 'war brides'.

This was the largest contingent of Australian women ever to travel to the United States, although they were not the first to do so. Historians have documented the travels to America of high profile women such as writer and reformer Catherine Helen Spence as early as 1893; feminist suffragist Vida Goldstein in 1902; writer Miles Franklin from 1906 to 1915; and feminist Jessie Street in 1945.[6] Yet today, very little is known about the experiences of women of less conspicuous profiles, such as the war brides.[7]

In the 1920s and 30s, prior to the sophistication of modern air travel and global telecommunication, travel was traditionally seen as being the realm of men. It was understood to be the privileged experience of middle-class Australians.[8] These war bride travellers were thought to be mostly 'lower- middle- and working-class women, many still in or barely out of their teens'.[9] When Australian war brides set off for America in the mid-1940s, however, there were also some among them from upper-middle-class backgrounds where fathers' occupations included 'journalist', 'magistrate' 'banker' and 'engineer'.[10] Young women from all walks of life were setting off on a new journey together, all bound for a new life and new experiences.

Tears flowed on the ships' decks and the wharves, as many of these young women thought they might never be able to afford to return to Australia, and it seemed likely that they would never see their families again. Some were more optimistic about a return visit in the future, while others gave little thought to what lay ahead, simply wanting to be with the loves of their lives.

The passage from Australia to America, for thousands of Australian war brides and fiancées, was a life-changing journey. It offered a space outside their normal routine – a time 'in limbo' – which gave them the opportunities to make new friends, encounter new experiences, and broaden their cultural horizons. The slow, uncomfortable sea voyage was a threshold between the old and the new, where they had the opportunity to deal with the broadest emotional spectrum: grief, sadness, separation and loss at leaving their families and friends and everything familiar to them; fear of the journey itself (especially during wartime) as well as fear of the unknown circumstances which lay ahead; seasickness; concern and responsibility for their children; excitement at the prospect of seeing their husbands and fiancés again, as well as hopeful anticipation and optimism that everything would work out for the best.

The sea voyage provided a period of time in which the war brides could begin to come to terms with their own situations. Within the confines of the ship these women were, in effect, offered the opportunity for reflection and drawing on their inner strength. It was a chance to consider the reality of the consequences of the major decision they had made, to follow their hearts to America, and to begin mentally preparing for a new life in a new country.

For Jean Morse, it was a time for reflection as she sailed on SS *Mariposa* to join her husband Lyle. The couple had met at the Banyo Army Barracks in Queensland and were married the previous year.

Jean Street and Lyle Morse married on 9 June, 1945.

A time for reflection. War bride Joyce Street Morse sailing to America on SS *Mariposa*, 1946.

For these women, crossing the Pacific by sea also provided a symbolic interlude; the first part of a longer journey towards their future lives in America which would bring cultural, familial, and geographic change. The voyage from Australia to America provided an important connection to their homeland and their new country of adoption. It was the first of many links to be forged and maintained by the war brides in the years to come.

Logistics

SS *Mariposa* – refitted luxury cruise ship.

The women interviewed for this book travelled on fourteen ships, which included: SS *Arongi*, SS *David C. Shanks*, SS *Fred C. Ainsworth*, SS *General Butner*, SS *General Mann*, SS *Goonawarra*, SS *Henry T. Buckner*, SS *Lurline*, MV *Lowlander*, SS *Marine Falcon*, SS *Marine Phoenix*, SS *Mariposa*, SS *Mirrabooka*, and the SS *Monterey*. The *Mariposa* and the *Monterey* were Matson Line luxury cruise-ships refitted to accommodate war brides and their babies.

Vessels ranged from converted troop ships to ordinary passenger liners and cargo freighters to the uncomfortable 'Liberty' ships, which were mass-produced cargo ships built cheaply and quickly in the United States between 1941 and 1945.[11] By September 1946, the acute shipping problems of wartime had eased and thirty-two ships had carried Australian brides and fiancées and their children both to England and America.[12] Eighteen of these had transported up to 15,000 Australian fiancées and war brides, many with children, to the United States. Prior to April 1946, ships were not available from

Western Australia, and those women first had to make the five-day journey on a crowded steam train across the arid Nullarbor Plain to Melbourne and the eastern seaports.[13]

Betty Kane wrote to her sister Peg from SS *Monterey* as she sailed to America:

> *Well Peg you'll be wanting to hear all about my trip no doubt. It has been anything but thrilling I'm afraid and I've wished many times I was back in good old Wagin with Mum.*[14]

She described the train journey from Western Australia to the eastern states as 'most cosy' and 'it led us to believe we'd fare well all the way'. Betty continued:

> *...from Melbourne on it was extremely uncomfortable and crowded and we were thankful to reach Sydney...you know too I had a six hour wait from two o'clock till eight to have my baggage inspected and just had to wait around doing nothing. I was thankful to get aboard, but missed out on tea so, all told, had only one meal on Sunday. We sailed at six Monday morning and at six thirty I was in Hospital, having passed out with Sue in my arms. It was just exhaustion as I'd stood around holding her and waiting for a bottle too long. They let me out at mid-day as I felt O.K. but then the sea sickness hit me and kept me miserable for four days. Sue was vomiting too, so we were not too happy.*[15]

The women who travelled on these ships generally spent two to four weeks at sea, sharing crowded cabins with other war brides and babies, some in dormitory-type cabins accommodating up to 22 women. There were no facilities for washing babies' nappies and many war brides suffered seasickness. On some ships, there were outbreaks of measles which spread quickly among the children, while other ships encountered typhoons in the Pacific, which made conditions on board extremely uncomfortable. The small number of war brides and fiancées who travelled by plane did not fare much better. Sunny Sansing's flight from Rose Bay to the US, via New Zealand, took seven days because of breakdowns en route. Her arrival in Memphis, Tennessee, found her exhausted and 'deaf as a haddock' from the noisy engines.[16]

Shipping routes across the Pacific included stops at the exotic ports of Fiji, Pago Pago, Samoa and Hawaii.[17] Some vessels sailed via New Zealand, to pick up New Zealand war brides, and others via New Guinea to collect troops returning to the United States.[18]

For some of the residents in Pacific ports, the arrival of the 'bride ships' was an exciting event and the brides themselves were described as quite glamorous. In a book about growing up in Fiji, author Patricia Page writes of her impressions as a young girl and describes the 'visits of the Australian "war brides" going to join their GIs in America with a stop-over in Fiji':

> *Two magnificent liners - the* Mariposa *and the* Monterey *- carried them across the Pacific Ocean to their loves. My friends and I would rush down to the wharf to watch them arrive. The great white liner with its huge vase-shaped prow would edge into port, rows of minute far-away war brides hanging over its rails. I...was endlessly intrigued by dressed-up ladies: their little gloves, perky hats, gored skirts, padded shoulders, platform shoes...especially ones as glamorous as the war brides...They crowded into the souvenir shops to buy trinkets for their new in-laws in America and took photos of one another leaning on palm trees like Dorothy Lamour in* Road to Morocco.[19]

In reality, and unlike the glamorous screen idol, by the time the war brides reached Fiji, they were often feeling seasick and not at all glamorous.

Rosemary Smith sailed on SS Lurline in April 1946, a year after her husband had been shipped home. She remembers:

> *We were caught up in quite a typhoon...in the Tasman Sea...no one heard from us until we got to Suva. Everyone was quite worried at the time.*[20]

She remembers that 'it was a tremendous storm' and they were unable to go ashore in Honolulu because of the huge tidal wave which had preceded them.[21]

SS *Lurline,*

Iris Craig also remembers the gruesome sight, as the *Lurline* steamed into the harbour in Honolulu:

> *There were bodies in the water due to a tidal wave that had reached Hawaii.*[22]

War bride June Carver (née Arundell) sailed with her 22-month-old son on SS *Lurline* in April 1946 to join her husband in Ogden, Utah. June recalls it was a 'very rough' journey as the ship ran into a typhoon near Hawaii and 'the waves were breaking over "A" deck.'[23] She remembers:

A lot of the children were ill, and mothers as well... They set
up a hospital at the rear of the ship and the weather was so
rough that they had to tie a rope from the doors out onto the
deck to aft of the ship, and they stationed a sailor there. He'd
hold our arms and we'd hold the rope and he'd run us across
the deck to see the doctor.[24]

The Sydney Morning Herald reported that on the 2 April, 1946
a 'mighty tidal wave' had killed at least 86 people, left thousands
homeless, and caused millions of dollars' worth of damage.[25] Waves
which 'followed a world-shaking submarine earthquake near the
Aleutian Islands', reached a height of 100 feet and 'raced across the
Pacific at 300 to 400 miles an hour, piling up into terrifying walls
of water as they neared coastlines'.[26] With conditions like this it is
no wonder that, as Iris Craig recalls, the skipper declared 'it was the
roughest journey of his career'.[27]

The war brides seemed to deal with such dramatic situations with
admirable composure, possibly because there was little they could do
to change the situation, and they were eager to reach their husbands.
Every nautical mile travelled, be it smooth or turbulent, was progress
in their journey and brought them closer to their destination.

The final port for the war bride ships was usually San Francisco,
but some ships sailed through Panama Canal to New York, while
others docked at the naval base at San Pedro, California.[28] The last
vessel to cross the Pacific with a contingent of war brides was the SS
Marine Phoenix, which left Australia on 6 January 1947.[29] In this
group of women, the first bride sailed to the US in 1943 and the last
sailed on SS *Marine Phoenix* in 1947.

American/Australian wartime marriages were not encouraged,
but once married, the wives and families of the US servicemen were
entitled to travel and financial support and they were given free
passage to America by the US Government. The Australian fiancées
posed more of a problem, as they were not legally committed to
marriage and could possibly change their minds once they arrived

in America. Therefore a bond of $US500 dollars (a considerable sum at the time) was required to be paid by the American fiancé, to cover the return trip to Australia should the marriage not take place within three months of his fiancée's arrival in the US. This bond was refundable upon application after marriage.

Some war brides and fiancées – almost a hundred between December 1942 and October 1943 – managed to get passage to America before the war had ended, but most had to wait until the war was over.[30] The implementation of the *War Brides Act* of 28 December, 1945 saw the United States undertake the mass movement of war brides from all over the world. Under what was known in the American press as 'Operation Diaper Run', approximately 40,000 war brides from the UK were provided transport to the US.[31] Similarly, in Australia, 'Operation Warbride' saw a constant passage of 'bride ships' between early 1946 and 1947 back and forth across the Pacific, each carrying hundreds of war brides and their babies to America. Despite more berths on ships becoming available, a US Consular official had earlier cautioned the prospective passengers, and it was reported in the press that: 'every girl is warned that she cannot expect peace-time luxury cruises'.[32] The direct route of these vessels from the east coast of Australia to the west coast of America took approximately two weeks, with stops at islands in the Pacific. From Fremantle in Western Australia, the journey took an extra week, with a sometimes turbulent sea to navigate in the Great Australian Bight.

Up to 15,000 Australian war brides obtained transport to America under 'Operation Warbride'.[33] Most of the participants interviewed for this book were transported under this scheme.

Leaving Home

Historically, the phenomenon of travel has been primarily the domain of men, and the journey takes on different perspectives when the travellers are women. The male journey is often portrayed as a quest for glory and adventure as in tales of exploration, hunting, trading and sailing by ship to distant and exotic lands.[34] In comparison, the outcome of travel for women is more ambiguous, uncertain and multi-layered, and being a 'foreigner' in a new land is more complex for women than for men.[35]

For the Australian war brides and fiancées of American servicemen, leaving home for a new land presented all sorts of challenges, particularly for those who sailed while the world was still at war. It was a frightening journey for those on ships which had to have 'lights out' and manoeuvre in zigzag patterns through dangerous minefields in the Pacific Ocean.[36] Pregnant women, or those travelling with small children, were usually on military vessels unsuited for such a long journey.

The shipboard voyage for these women began the process of re-location from a familiar environment to one which was largely unknown, yet to be explored and evaluated. For most, it was also the beginning of their new role as wife and mother, in which they were anxious to excel, as well as to prove to their husbands and American in-laws, and their families back home, that they were equal to the task and had made the right decision in marrying an American serviceman.

The war brides' memories of this voyage to their new future confirmed a range of emotions which were full of contradictions and ambiguities. Excitement at the adventure they were undertaking was often accompanied by feelings of anxiety, fear of the unknown, as well as nostalgia and some regret at leaving their families and friends behind. Some women were optimistic about seeing their husbands and fiancés again, while others experienced palpable feelings of dread, uncertain about their reunion with a partner they had not seen for months or years. These mixed feelings are understandable given the exigencies of wartime, when these women were subject to restrictive red tape and a great deal of uncertainty. Melbourne war bride Betty McIntire, for example, had terrible feelings of foreboding before rejoining her husband, who had returned to America within a week of their marriage in Australia. After he resumed his job on the railroad in Green River, Wyoming, she recalls:

Things started to change. Sometimes I'd get a letter every two or three weeks until they got to be...every one or two months, and I got to thinking 'Do I want to go?' [37]

Betty did sail to America on board the SS *Monterey* in early April 1946, but did so with great trepidation, which proved not to be unfounded.

SS *Monterey*

Parting from family and friends was heart-wrenching for most Australian war brides and fiancées, and for some, saying goodbye to their mothers was particularly traumatic. Many women at this time still lived in the family home and were used to close proximity to their mothers in everyday life. The very strong mother-daughter bonds, which existed sixty years ago, endured for decades. This enduring bond existed despite (or perhaps because of) the cruelty of separation and the distancing of the miles, as in the case of Dorothy Pence Berry, whose bond with her mother was very strong.

On Christmas Day 1944, her last day in Australia before sailing to America, Dorothy travelled from Queensland by bus to spend Christmas Day with her family in Urbenville, a small town in New South Wales, just 25 miles south of the Queensland border. Because of wartime travel regulations, which restricted the crossing of state borders, US Navy officers took Dorothy and her baby off the bus and issued orders for her to go back to Brisbane. Dorothy recalls:

I was eight miles from my mother's, so I called her up, and I'll never forget. We both cried, and she said 'Oh, never mind. Just think about the moonlight nights on the ship'.

After returning to Brisbane, Dorothy can remember vividly:

So, here we were on Christmas Day in Australia with nothing in the refrigerator – I had taken everything out of the place because we were leaving and we were all packed and our luggage and everything had gone! Luckily I lived across the street from the Church of England and they came across and took us for Christmas dinner. I'll never forget that, at St Thomas's Church in Toowong, Brisbane.[39]

After being forced to say goodbye to her mother and family by phone, Dorothy was not to see them again for twenty-six years. She says:

It was sad, and very hard to leave Australia…I didn't know how hard until I was on board the ship and kept seeing the land getting further and further away. It was awful![40]

For Dorothy, as for many other war brides, travel by ship during wartime took great courage. She left Brisbane on board the naval troopship SS *General Mann* on Boxing Day 1944. She recalls:

There were just twenty-five women and ten babies' aboard the ship which had no special food or facilities for babies. It sailed via New Guinea, where it took on two thousand servicemen and women as well as Irving Berlin, the famous American songwriter, who was there entertaining the troops.[41]

One day, Dorothy recalls, 'the ship was rocking back and forth' and she ran to the deck to see 'all these great rusty things out in the water'. The ship was zigzagging through a minefield, and with hindsight, Dorothy realises 'how skilful that Captain was to get us through those hundreds of mines'.[42] It was a dangerous time to sail in the Pacific and a wonder that the military authorities allowed this risk to be taken by wives of US servicemen who often had young children.

Hazel Walker's son, Daniel, was only three weeks old when they sailed from Brisbane on 28 May, 1945, on board the Matson Liner, SS *Lurline,* which had been commandeered by the US Army to transport troops. Hazel had received a call from the US Military just three days after her husband Eddie had been shipped back to New Guinea, after being present for the birth of their first baby. She was informed that she would be leaving in a week or so for the US and to get her passport and fingerprint papers, and then report to their office to get the other papers she needed. Hazel replied: 'I can't go now. I just had a baby!' They said 'If you don't go now, your name will go to the bottom of the list and there's no telling when you'll go.' Her mother encouraged her to go. Hazel recalls:

My mother said she thought I was getting too settled down without Eddie around and if I didn't go now, I might never go. So I did all the paper work and was told to show up at the wharf at New Farm on 27 May, 1945.

That morning while waiting for the taxi to take me, along with my mother and father and sister, to the wharf, I walked around the house, stood on the back porch and looked at the school I'd attended, the back yard where I'd played, and thought 'I'll never see any of this again'. It was very sad.[43]

After arriving at the wharf which was crowded with war brides and their babies, Hazel remembers:

> *Eventually, after the paperwork was checked, I said 'goodbye' to my Mum and Dad and Sister, hugged them for as long as I could and then boarded the ocean liner 'Lurline'.*[44]

There were 300 war brides on board, many with babies and small children. Hazel's cabin was crowded with six bunk beds, one for each of the three women and one for each child; although the women had their children sleep with them as the bunks didn't seem safe for the youngsters, and certainly not for a three week old baby. The water from the bathroom tap was salt water, but because Hazel had a baby under one year old, she was given two buckets of fresh water every day. This allocation was shared by her two cabin mates and their two one-year-old children.[45]

Hazel remembers the hundreds of US servicemen returning home at the end of their overseas tour and how they were assigned to one side of the ships' decks, and the war brides to the other side. All day there would be announcements from the loudspeakers. Hazel remembers:

> *Every morning we'd hear 'It's 5 o'clock at sunrise. Hit the deck. Hit the deck'. In the evening...'It's 5 o'clock at sunset. It's blackout time. No smoking on the open deck. All blackout blinds will be shut'. At 10 pm there'd be an announcement...'Lights out. It's ten pm. Lights out.'*[46]

These announcements were interspersed with instructions to military personnel over the loudspeakers. Hazel recalls:

> *We had to carry life jackets every time we left the cabin. Military rules applied to everyone.*[47]

On the first day at sea one of the announcements was: 'This is an American Ship. All personnel will keep to the right using the gangways and ladders.' Hazel remembers how the Australian girls 'had been keeping to the left and the Yanks had been keeping to the right' and how they would 'often run into a jam on the "stairs" between the decks.'[48]

As the war in the Pacific was still going on, the ship zigzagged across the ocean to avoid mines in the water. Hazel remembers having numerous 'Abandon Ship' alerts, both day and night, when the war brides had to grab their life jackets and head to an assigned place to wait until there was no longer any threat. After three long weeks, the ship finally arrived in San Francisco Bay on Hazel's birthday, the 18th June, 1945.

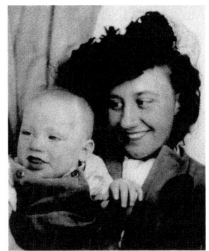

Hazel Walker with baby Danny, (6 mths) 'fresh off the ship from Australia', Chicago, June 1945.

Melbourne war bride, Allie Rudy, received permission to sail to America on the troopship SS Lurline in June, 1945. She had a six-month-old son and 'jumped' at the opportunity to join her husband. She explains that:

If you didn't come when they wanted you to come, you had to wait.[49]

She was young – about 23 – and she still remembers the anguish of the sad farewell as the train pulled out of Flinders Street Station in Melbourne. Her mother, to whom she was very close, was knocking on the train window mouthing the words, 'Don't go! Don't go!'[50] On her arrival in Brisbane, Allie, with her child in her arms, looked up in awe at the ship and thought she had never seen anything so huge! She remembers the anxious minutes when she thought 'I've got to run! I cannot do it!'[51] She recalls that there were approximately 400 wives and about 150 babies and children on board the troopship. It was still two months until the war would be over, so the ship's lights were extinguished at night, the darkness adding to her uneasy feelings as she sailed away from Australia.[52]

Similarly, Joan Moran from Western Australia recalls the fear she experienced when she left Sydney on USS *General Butner*, a converted troopship, in June 1944:

> *It was the middle of the war – and we had a submarine scare*
> *and thought we were going to be torpedoed. It was very scary!* [53]

Although it was frightening to sail in wartime, some war brides remembered the departure mostly as a time of excitement and the beginning of a real adventure. Lola Atkins and her friend Irene Perucci, both originally from the small country town of Northam in Western Australia, first took a five-day steam train journey across the arid Nullarbor Plain to Melbourne. After a long two months of waiting there, they received instructions to board a ship in Sydney. Lola's journal records that it was 'a really hectic two or three days' following the telephone call from the American Consul, and 'a flurry of activity' began for the two young women as they said final farewells, attended to last-minute business matters concerning their passports and found transportation to Sydney.[54]

On 5 April 1944, after a hurried breakfast at the YWCA in Sydney where they had stayed overnight, the two friends travelled by taxi to Wharf 12, Pyrmont, where they first saw the converted troop ship, SS *Lurline* 'in all its grandeur', the decks 'already crowded with American sailors, soldiers and nurses all homeward bound'.[55] Lola writes in her journal: 'the pier was a colourful sight with dozens of excited women, some with babies, being questioned and examined by customs officials'.[56] News passed around the ship that John Curtin, Prime Minister of Australia and General Blamey, Supreme Commander of the Australian Imperial Forces were aboard. Lola remembers how they were 'rushed to the boat deck to have pictures made by the reporters who were busily lining up women and babies and actively clicking cameras'.[57] The bustling atmosphere as the war brides went on board the huge ship is clearly portrayed in the above description. Lola remembers, with some nostalgia, the two-week sea voyage to America as 'pleasant', although she shared her cabin with five other war brides. However, she also recalls initially being 'terrified' as she remembers how she slept with her life jacket for a pillow: 'We had lifeboat drill every day. It was very scary as the war was still on'.[58] Emotions of nostalgia and fear overlapped in her narrative as she remembered the voyage.

When Gladys Borger sailed from Brisbane on SS *Lurline* in 1944, she not only left her Australian family behind, but also her American husband. He was to leave Australia after her departure, to sail north with MacArthur's troops. She remembers that day:

> My mother and cousin and sister came up, but my husband was in Sydney. He was on a special boat that was going back in with MacArthur's troops. It was called the Apache. So I was standing on the ship and I could see my mother, and I was waving to them on the shore. When I turned around my husband was at the back of me. They had let him off from duty in Sydney and he had flown up…he was on the ship and I saw him for a couple of hours before I left.[59]

For Gladys, this time was precious: she was sailing away to a new land, but at the same time she had to farewell her husband, who was still engaged in the war and likely to face further hostilities before being deployed and returning to America.

Adelaide war bride, Doris Harburt, has unhappy memories of her journey on the USS *David C. Shanks* – a Liberty ship which she describes as the first 'all-bride' ship from Fremantle and the commissioning of which was a result of the *US War Brides Act* of December 28, 1945. The brides were from all over Australia, and Doris travelled overnight from

Adelaide by train to board the ship in Melbourne. There had been some confusion as to whether the war brides were required to be inoculated for the sea voyage. Doris sought advice from the Consul who said 'it would be safer to have the inoculation', so she had it before sailing. With the huge number of war brides going to the United States, some bureaucratic disorganisation was inevitable. Doris tells of boarding the ship:

> *Up the gangplank we went and they stuck the needle in our arms without even checking whether we had already been inoculated! It wasn't very good to have a double dose, and on the 10th day when the reaction is felt, those who had a double inoculation went over like that... we were not very well for a while!* [60]

Jackie Hansen, who sailed on SS *Fred C. Ainsworth*, was another who had a bad experience as a result of an inoculation:

> *I had a smallpox vaccination on my left hip shortly before leaving Perth. I had a swelling the size of a dinner plate and it was very painful. It was difficult to sit and when turning over in bed. I went to the doctor on board and he said that it was a wonderful reaction!* [61]

There was more bungling when empty milk cans were mistakenly loaded, while the full cans were left on the wharf. As there were so many babies on board, milk was in short supply and extra supplies had to be loaded when the ship docked at Honolulu. [62]

SS *Fred C. Ainsworth*

Only having a week's notice to prepare for her journey on SS *David C Shanks,* and with little time for sleep, war bride Ruth Frost (née Dawsett) describes her departure:

> *It was hard to comprehend that I was finally on my way to the United States. It felt like a dream sequence.*[63]

It was a time of urgency when things happened quickly and events took on a surreal quality. Ruth had received a telegram from the US Army to 'report to the SS *David C. Shanks* on 28 March, 1946'. She remembers the busy time:

> *The Army, Navy, and Red Cross officers and medical staff all checking papers and passports, giving smallpox shots and getting us all on board ready to sail before nightfall.*[65]

There was 'no time to deal with the emotions of girls who had never been further than a camping trip to the beach or a visit to relatives on a farm.'[66]

Victorian war bride Shirley Norton left with her baby son, Robert, on SS *Monterey* in early April 1946.[64] Shirley's sister, Joann, also a war bride, had sailed to America just two months earlier and her parents found it very difficult to say farewell to their second war bride daughter and their first grandson. Shirley travelled from Melbourne by train to Sydney to join the ship where relatives of brides from New South Wales assembled at the end of the wharf at Darling Harbour, standing on empty oil drums as vantage points to catch a glimpse of the passengers.[67] Shirley comments:

> *I had no intention of staying away permanently – it was not to be forever.*[68]

When SS *Mariposa* sailed from Brisbane in April, 1946, Margaret Fosmo's husband was still in the US Navy and had already returned to America. She was on a waiting list and had only three days notice to prepare to board the ship. Margaret was distressed because her father, who was still in the Australian Army, was away at that time and she thought she would never see him again. Many families came to the dock to see the brides off, but as the ship was not to leave until the next morning, the crowd gradually dispersed. Margaret remembers her surprise when her father suddenly appeared in uniform on board the ship:

> *I was going to dinner and I met him in the hallway! I'd never expected it...I thought, "I'll never see my father again" – and there he came!* [69]

Margaret remembered little about the voyage, except that she 'cried all the time', and that for her it was not a happy journey. She explains:

> *My baby was ten months old and then she got sick on the ship. A lot of babies did, with the different food and the different milks...so I was stuck in the cabin most of the time.* [70]

Marge Andreatta, who sailed on the same ship, clearly recalls leaving Australia with her fifteen-month-old baby. From the porthole in her cabin she could see her mother and several other girls' mothers waving goodbye while the band played 'Now is the Hour'. Marge has not been able to listen to the haunting tune ever since, because of the association with feelings of separation. But she was also anxious to get to America to be with her husband as he had only seen the baby briefly while on leave six months previously. [71]

After a 'very, very sad' farewell to her family who were 'all there at the wharf', Australian war bride Iris Craig and her small daughter Erin sailed from Sydney on March 21, 1946 on SS *Lurline*. Iris recalls how 'it didn't help' cheer the sad occasion as the ship sailed past an island in the harbour and voices of workmen could be heard calling out: 'You'll be sorry! You'll be sorry!' This was a verbal display of the resentment directed by some Australian men towards Australian brides who married American servicemen. As Iris points out, some of the women on board did indeed appear to be sorry. After a very rough trip, the ship called into port at Fiji, where a few of the brides decided that they didn't want to continue on the long journey and 'they jumped ship'.[72]

Many war brides and fiancées found the final 'goodbye' to their family and friends required all the courage they could muster. For instance, *The Sydney Morning* Herald reported how in April 1946, less than an hour before the US Army Transport SS *David C. Shanks* sailed to America with 430 wives and children of Americans aboard, nineteen-year-old war bride Josephine Hatton from Lidcombe, New South Wales, walked off the ship. She had 'a horror of confined spaces since early childhood'.[73] Her mother, three sisters and brother had been waiting on the Pyrmont wharf in Sydney since 1.00 am to wave goodbye, and at 5.30 am

Iris Craig and her mother,
Mary Josephine Adams.

they were surprised to see her run down the gangway to the wharf gates. Her mother is reported to have said, 'She has a fine husband, but she doesn't like leaving us. She must go back on the ship.'[74]

On Board

On board ship, the war brides had to deal with feelings of grief, sadness, discomfort and apprehension combined in an uncomfortable mix with excitement, anticipation and hope. Although these young women came from diverse locations and family backgrounds, they all shared the common experiences of undertaking first-time long-distance travel to a new environment. They were all travelling to America to join their partners, who in some cases they hardly knew, and from whom they had been separated for some time. The war brides and fiancées shared the common struggle of dealing with heightened emotions caused by separation from family and loved ones; the challenges of caring for young children in uncomfortable and difficult conditions; and the anxieties about the uncertain futures they might face.

For all these young women, the voyage was a significant watershed in their lives. Although they were all sharing a similar experience tinged with feelings of adventure, separation, anticipation and some uncertainty about their future, the time on board ship produced differing memories. Some women remember little more about the sea voyage than the daily routine and survival in uncomfortable conditions, made worse for the women with babies and small children by the absence of any special facilities. Discomfort in cramped conditions was exacerbated by seasickness and outbreaks of measles, and for many there was no time for diary-keeping, which may have sharpened their later memories of the voyage.

Many women seem to remember the trip quite clearly, without the aid of daily jottings, simply because it was such a major event in their lives.

For example, Dorothy Bourne sailed from Fremantle on the *Fred C. Ainsworth,* which she vividly remembers as 'an awful...Liberty ship with no portholes'. She shared a cabin, dormitory-style, with 17 women and 22 babies. She recalls:

I was seasick the whole way. I had my little girl tied by her harness onto my wrist, sitting up on the deck for ninety percent of the way.[75]

Dorothy (Mary) Bourne (3rd from left) and her small daughter
on board SS *Fred C. Ainsworth*, 21 April, 1946

Several war brides kept shipboard diaries during the voyage. These contemporary records provide nuance and a deeper understanding of the young women's thoughts during the voyage, as well as capturing their reactions to their shipboard experiences at the time they actually occurred. Also, one war bride published her own book based on her shipboard diary.[76]

Daily handwritten entries described their thoughts and surroundings, the atmosphere and activities on board, and observations of other passengers, thus providing a degree of comfort for the young women in their new temporary environment. Confined in unfamiliar surroundings, diary notes helped them to create a comfortable space through narrating it.[77] Through writing about their experiences they began to make sense of the tangled feelings and extraordinary experiences of migration.[78] The war brides' diary entries often describe the cabin space and the arrangement of bunks, as well as frequent descriptions of shipboard food, and practical details of life on board ship.[79] The descriptions of their cabins, daily routine and activities, as well as helping the war brides to become familiar with their new surroundings, were sometimes written with their families and later readers in mind.

These personal hand-written records helped to maintain links with family and loved ones they had left behind and the process of writing helped these women to define their own lives and to shape their identities.

Lola Atkins from Western Australia remembers the two-week voyage from Sydney to San Francisco on the converted troop ship SS *Lurline,* where 'the food was good' and 'it was just like travelling on a cruise ship', except for the addition of bunks. Fritz, the cabin steward, told her that Dorothy Lamour – the famous Hollywood star and romantic 'pin-up girl' of the American troops in the Pacific – was in the same cabin on the last voyage.[80] Lola comments wryly:

> *But, she had it all to herself! Now we were six women, and we had to get up and figure out who was going to take the first quick bath.*[81]

Unlike the range of cabin-class travel earlier in the century, accommodation on board 'bride ships' was virtually one class, with berths allocated according to whether or not the brides were accompanied by children and babies. The wives travelling alone shared cabins, and mothers with children were generally placed together. As their passage was financed by the US government, class or financial distinction was usually not a factor in the allotment of cabins to the brides and fiancées.

S. S. LURLINE   *1945*

☆

SHIP'S OFFICERS

SUNDAY

☆

BREAKFAST

Stewed Fresh Frozen Apricots in Syrup   Iced Tomato Juice
Roman Meal in Milk
Assorted Dry Cereals
Scrambled Eggs with Small Breakfast Sausages
Fried, Boiled or Poached Eggs on Toast
Shirred Eggs with Canadian Bacon
Boiled Salt Mackerel, Drawn Butter, Parsley Potatoes
Broiled York Ham   Beechnut Bacon   Lamb Chop
Hash Brown Potatoes
Assorted Breakfast Cake   Dry or Buttered Toast
French Toast with Maple Syrup
Cold Sliced Sausages with Dill Pickles
Jam or Jellies
Tea   Coffee   Fresh Milk   Cocoa

LUNCHEON

Fillet of Herring in Cream   Sliced Eggs Tartare
Iced Grapefruit Juice   Dill Pickles and Olives
Chow Chow
Cream of Chicken Soup
Shirred Eggs with Asparagus Tips
Assorted Vegetable Platter with Fried Oysters
Broiled Club Steak, Maitre d'Hotel Butter
New Green Peas Francaise   Corn Saute
French Fried Potatoes
Assorted Cold Cuts with Brunswick Salad
Broccoli Salad, Thousand Island Dressing
Strawberry Ice Cream   Assorted Cookies
Cheese with Crackers
Tea   Coffee   Fresh Milk   Cocoa

DINNER

Hearts of Celery with Sliced Egg Vinaigrette   Chow Chow
Mixed Fruit Cocktail   Mixed Olives and Pickles
Cream of Chicken Soup
Apple Pancake
Italian Spaghetti with Meat Balls, Sauce Italian
Roast Young Tom Turkey, Sage Dressing, Giblet Gravy
Cranberry Sauce   Creamed Carrots and Peas
Croquette Potatoes   Fried Cauliflower
Assorted Cold Cuts with Salad
String Bean and Onion Salad
French Apple Cake   Vanilla Ice Cream
Cheese with Crackers
Tea   Coffee   Fresh Milk   Cocoa

Menu from SS *Lurline*, 1945

Food was often a recurring theme in the war brides memories of the journey. On board ship, some war brides found the American food much too rich and some longed for 'a good old fashioned baked dinner' and 'Grandma's scones and some of her tea'.[82] Others enjoyed the abundance of food provided. War bride Ruth Frost writes in her book, based on her ship-board diary, how 'the hungry girls waited in line, cafeteria-style, and ogled the sumptuous food'. After the Depression, and then wartime rationing, Ruth writes, it was a treat to view the 'different cereals that we had never seen before'.[83] It was Ruth's original diary notes on board ship which have helped her recall in detail the 'heated platters of eggs, fried or scrambled, bacon, sausages and steak plus fried potatoes, tomatoes alongside huge stacks of thick hot toast' which caused 'mouths to drool'.[84] There was 'a choice of orange, grapefruit or tomato juice plus milk and coffee – but not tea.' Ruth adds: 'The tea drinkers had plenty to say about that!'[85] The dormitory-style cabin was crowded and Ruth remembers there were 'no cupboards or wardrobes. We were to live out of our small suitcases for the duration of this voyage' and 'wet towels had to hang on the bottom of our bunks.' [86]

South Australian war bride, Kathleen Feehan Newell Bertram (known as Kay) jotted in her daily diary while sailing to America on the troopship SS *Lurline* in June 1945, before the war had ended:

> Today, Sunday, we boarded the ship, of course there was great excitement and bustle, but things have gone without a hitch, considering the great numbers of girls and babies, there are also…wounded men, American nurses, refugees, and able soldiers returning home after years abroad. The Australian Red Cross were marvellous minding the babes.[87]

Before the ship had left Brisbane, the menu on board had already provided Kay's first taste of American food. She writes: 'We had a lovely tea, turkey, sweet corn and ice cream, typically American.' [88]

Similarly, war bride Joyce Balogh first encountered American cuisine on board SS *Lurline* when she asked for jelly for her small daughter Jill and discovered that 'jelly' in America is called 'jam', and she should have been asking for 'jello'.[89] These small examples of cultural difference presented to the war brides on their journey were early hints of the adjustments they would face in America in the coming weeks and months. Kay's diary paints a picture of the ship's departure, with her small child Corinne 'sleeping through all the commotion'. The band played its last tunes, *'Now is the Time'* [sic] and *'Auld Lang Syne'*, as the boat pulled out. Kay noted:

> We have our own toilet and shower, and wash hand basin, quite cosy compared with some who have 15 and 16 to a cabin.

By the following Saturday, the diary entry was not as happy after 'a terrible night' when she was kept awake by crying babies and unbearable heat.[90]

Kay's diary compares the 16-berth cabins which are 'light and airy' with others like hers, which was 'small without portholes, 6 berths and unbearably hot'. She describes the dining room as 'nice' and 'the food plentiful', and adds 'I might say luxurious for wartime'.[91] The daily routine was fairly rigid:

> Of a morning we are called up at 6:30 am …Breakfast at 7:30 am. Lunch at 11:30 am. Tea at 5pm. We generally have fire drill, and then 10:30 pm all passage ways cleared, passengers in their cabins with lights out.[92]

Kay's diary notes: 'there are said to be 600 war brides, 190 babes on board' which she thought to be 'the most to travel so far'.[93] The long sea journey no doubt encouraged some shipboard romances, as suggested in the diary entry which mentions that there were fifteen husbands with their wives on board, but queries the fact that 'last night the sentry discovered 26 husbands ?? [sic] cuddling upon the boat deck, how come?'[94]

Leaving Brisbane on 21 September 1945, after her long and arduous trip by train from Western Australia with her small baby in arms, war bride Barbara Gleason was impressed by the size of the SS *Lurline* when she first set eyes on it. Barbara tells how 'Brisbane girls had to be put off to allow the troops on board', but because she and the other girls from Western Australia had travelled so far, they were given first priority of all the brides to board the ship. Barbara shared 'a big cabin with twelve bunks' with six women and their babies. She recalls how they had to quickly adapt to a sudden change of diet for the babies:

> *We ate down in the mess every day and they had food there for babies that we were not acquainted with – canned food and bottled food – and that was for 13 days.*[95]

Unlike most war brides, Barbara felt little emotion when she sailed away from Australia, as she had no-one to wave goodbye, and she was anxious to join her husband. She admits that if she had been leaving her home in Western Australia she probably would have felt a little different, but the ship left from Brisbane where she knew nobody. She recalls:

> *We went down the river to the ocean. The whole ship was filled with troops, so the war brides could only use the very top deck – the sundeck. We'd go to the ballroom and put the babies down on the floor which was covered with mattresses. We just sat on the floor there with the babies and spent our time that way.*[96]

Most war brides understood the difficulties of sea travel during and just after the war. When Joan Byer reached the end of her long sea voyage from Fremantle in Western Australia, she was very weary. The dormitory, with 'layered beds', was 'dank and stuffy' and Joan was sick for the whole journey. Pleased to see land when they reached San Francisco, Joan explained:

It wasn't rough, but I am susceptible to sea sickness, because as a child I used to get sea sick. It was just the fact that I was on the water for so long and I was sick for three weeks. I thought: 'I'll never go back again if I have to go by ship!' [97]

Marjory Andreatta had no problem with seasickness, but, like other mothers, she was concerned about the shipboard food for infants and remembers how she dealt with this problem:

The babies used to have all this strained food…my little girl wasn't used to that and she didn't like it. So I used to take her with me into the dining room and feed her from my plate. [98]

The health of babies was a cause for concern for many of the mothers. Apart from the sudden change of formula and the use of strained canned food, the quality of hygiene was also questionable. Shirley Norton remembers her trip on SS *Monterey* in early April, 1946:

It was sort of nightmarish at times. We were crowded …we had to line up at the dispensary to get the baby food and the diapers and all the needs and stuff for the children…we had no facilities to wash diapers. [99]

There were US Army nurses on board, but according to Shirley, the only contact the war brides had with them was when they went to get the food for their babies. Shirley's eight-month-old son contracted *streptococci* on board ship and became very ill, needing to be hospitalised on arrival in America. She was suspicious that the containers and utensils on the ship were not properly sterilised and that 'this is where my son got the infection.' [100] Conditions were difficult, especially when caring for their babies, but generally the war brides and fiancées adapted as well as they could and accepted that this was the way it would be until they reached their destination. However, they did appreciate that the navy and the staff on board made every effort to ease the difficulties and inconveniences of the voyage.

Despite the lack of facilities, there were activities on board to entertain the women and their small children. Iris Craig's small daughter, Erin, won a competition for the child with the reddest hair. The prize was a stuffed toy pig made from spotted fabric, of which she was very fond.[101]

Iris Craig (hand on head) with Erin at her feet, holding her prize on board SS *Lurline*, 1946.

Erin Craig's immigration tag dated April 7, 1946, worn on arrival in San Francisco.

According to Dorothy, the navy tried to make the journey in wartime as pleasant as possible for the mothers and their infants. For her daughter's first birthday, the Captain sent a cake covered with 'floppy pink frosting' into which the baby delighted in putting her little hand.[102] Dorothy also remembers a ceremony held in the officers' quarters when they crossed the equator. The passengers had to participate in an initiation ceremony and 'go through Davy Jones' Locker'.[103] Dorothy recalls:

> *They had us suck on a baby bottle that had alum in it so it tasted horrible and we had to wear our clothes backwards!*[104]

Dorothy still has a certificate which states 'I'm a "shellback" now because I crossed the equator'. In these small ways, she felt that the navy, despite their limited resources, did try to entertain the passengers and to make the war brides feel more comfortable, although nothing was done to ease the 'prickly heat' many suffered when crossing the equator.[105]

Shirley Tronic also remembers the ceremony held when crossing the equator, although it was two years later, when the war was over. Shirley wrote a detailed account in her diary and proudly recorded that she too had 'ascended with all the other girls, from the lowly order of a Pollywog…to an esteemed Shellback'.[106]

Shipboard life, however, had other memorable moments which were not such fun. Shirley wrote of the 'most miserable' day she spent on the ship during the whole voyage. Having congratulated herself on successfully withstanding 'seasickness, vaccination reactions, measles, diarrhoea, colds etc.' on the voyage, Shirley felt 'just about sick' to discover she had nits in her hair. The whole cabin and all the girls in it had to be disinfected. Shirley writes: 'The doctor, nurse and some assistants arrived and we all had to dip our heads in a mixture of D.D.T. and kerosene.'[107] After 15 minutes the girls washed their hair with a special shampoo, dried it and then had DDT powder sprayed into it. The bunks were stripped and everything sprayed with DDT. Shirley suffered great discomfort as she accidentally got the DDT and kerosene in both eyes and in her left ear, the latter requiring treatment with mineral oil. Shirley felt so miserable that she went to bed very early, but couldn't sleep because of ear ache. She writes:

> One of the girls got me some ear drops and that eased it a bit. Then all the girls kept coming in and we started showing photos and snaps all around and ended up by having a real jam session.[108]

Young and resilient, the war brides dealt with problems in a practical way and made the most of their time on board ship. A sense of camaraderie grew among the women as those sharing large cabins got to know each other and shared their everyday experiences, complaints, laughter and problems. As Kay Feehan Newell noted: 'Friendships between the war brides developed during the voyage'.[109] She wrote that there were 'some very nice girls on the boat', although she observes that perhaps some of the girls were not of such good character. Her diary reads:

> We have arranged to go up on the boat deck tomorrow with our children. I've been wanting to take C[orrine] up for a sunbath, but all of the officers and a lot of ? [sic] types of girls go up there, so I wouldn't go alone for fear of being thought the same.[110]

This diary entry hints that some of the women going to meet their American partners were not so blameless. But it is difficult to tell if this was the diarist's perception only, or a matter of appearance and assumption. However, Irene Franck, who travelled with eight war brides on a Swedish freighter during wartime, reported some promiscuous behaviour by one of the girls who shared her cabin:

[She] just slept with everybody – even the deckhand on the ship! They'd come in the middle of the night and slide into her bed, and you know, I'd be lying there dying [with sea-sickness] and having to listen to all of this.[111]

Later, when the ship docked in San Francisco, Irene was upset when this girl's husband was waiting for her on the dock and 'she acted as though nothing had happened' and 'was all lovey-dovey.' Irene wondered if that marriage ever lasted.[112]

On Board SS *Monterey*, Betty Kane wrote in a letter to her older sister:

You'd be surprised how many girls do gad off and leave their kids unattended…some of them don't deserve children in my opinion. There are those too who have to have a final fling with the stewards or other members of the crew before they rejoin their husbands.[113]

This sort of sexual behaviour, however, did not seem to be prevalent among the war brides. This promiscuity was not the norm and only a small number of incidents of this nature were mentioned. The war brides interviewed for this book were keen to set themselves above contemporary stereotypes surrounding girls who fraternised with American GIs. They generally disapproved of promiscuity and illicit love affairs on board ship demonstrating a higher moral code of behaviour.

'Home Duties'

Australian brides did not automatically become American citizens upon marriage and travelled on their British passports.[114] Some passenger lists for the 'bride ships' were headed 'Manifest of Alien Passengers for the United States of America', and contained columns of information about those on board.[115] Most adult passengers on the 'bride ships' were females, and their occupations were identified by the words 'home duties'.[116] Many of these women, however, had previously enlisted and served as valued members of the AWAS, the WRANS and the WAAFS, working as signallers and in other areas of responsibility during the war.[117] For example, as mentioned in an earlier chapter, Sunny Sansing, from New South Wales, was a Wireless Telegraphist in the RAAF, stationed at Garbutt Field Airforce Base in Townsville, Queensland. She proudly tells how she was designated 'Aircraftwoman First Class'.[118] Similarly, Victorian war bride Joann Patterson joined the AWAS and was assigned to the Signal branch where she worked in the basement of the University of Queensland, at St Lucia.[119] Western Australian war bride, Joan Byer, had served in the WRANS, carrying out essential work in the degaussing (or demagnetising) department. From the perspective of both Australian security and the US military, the work carried out by these women was of great importance.

Billie Ringen also joined the WAAFS, and after training at Robertson, New South Wales, was transferred to Brisbane, Queensland. Billie did general office work 'to replace a man who would go overseas' and one of her daily jobs was to take mail from her office in Brisbane to an office building 'just around the corner' where General MacArthur (Supreme Allied Commander of the South Pacific theatre of war during WWII) had his headquarters. She recalls:

> Oftentimes I'd see him drive up in his big limousine…He was a big, tall, handsome man I remember the thrill it was to see him in person. These were some of the best years of my life. Oh, yes, every minute – I loved every bit of it.[120]

Billie proudly wore her military medals (only recently received after 60 years!) as she remembered her time in service with youthful fervour; a time when she genuinely enjoyed the new opportunities and independence for women which followed the outbreak of the war.

Billie Ringen wearing WAAF badge and medals,
Garden Grove, CA, 19 September, 2001.

Jean Wilk, who arrived in San Francisco
on SS *Marine Phoenix* in June 1946,
served in the WRANS and was
stationed at Rottnest Island, just off the
coast of Fremantle, Western Australia.
She explains that during the war, the
WRANS took over the signal station
previously run by the Harbour Trust.[121]

Jean Reeves in Perth, W.A. c.1945.

Jean recalls:

> *I was a very bad traveller – I was sick every time we went over to Rottnest with the Navy in a boat that was just a little flat-bottomed thing which just rolled!* [122]

Her journey to America on board the *Marine Phoenix* was no better for Jean, who remembers:

> *There was not much time for friendship – I was sick and kept busy caring for my son.* [123]

Many other war brides had also volunteered for the war effort at clubs and canteens, in addition to their paid daytime jobs.

The contribution of these women to the war effort was important to them and to the nation, but once they boarded a ship to America, it was as if they were stripped of their work status and their valuable experience. The shipping lists reflected the gendered nature of wartime society, which saw males as heroes on the battlefield and women as supporting the war effort in domestic and voluntary capacities on the homefront, only filling vacancies in the workforce for the duration of the war. For the purpose of the ships' passenger lists, these women were seen to be wives and mothers occupied in the typical female role of 'home duties', often identified by the letters 'HD' and their immediate future seemed to promise a return to a domestic role. [124]

Passenger List SS *Monterey,* 1 April, 1946.

New Lives

The war brides' sea voyages, whether consciously acknowledged or not, represented a threshold between two worlds through which they were required to pass to continue on to their new lives. It was a liminal space 'where one is…betwixt and between'; between the comfort of lifetime familiarity on one side, and the new, unknown and unexpected on the other.[125] This was an initial and transitional stage of their ultimate journey, where the war brides occupied a space on board ship between two countries, and where they were in a state of transition between their old and their new cultures and societal roles. The voyage to America was a significant period in the lives of the war brides in which they experienced release from normal social constraints, and were introduced to a new sense of freedom.

During their voyage within the confines of the ship, in new surroundings and restricted by the rituals of shipboard routine, such as set meal times and the rite of eating and drinking together, regular safety drills, and the special ceremony to celebrate the crossing of the equator, the Australian war brides and fiancées occupied a transitional space, or threshold, between their lives in Australia and their new lives in America, where they were to step into the new roles of wife and mother. Thus following a painful separation from family and friends, and then constrained by the exigencies of the voyage, the women left behind their old lives and gradually became part of a group with a common identity of 'war brides' on board ship, thus beginning the next stage of their life.[126]

For most Australian war brides embarking on the long sea voyage to America, it was a momentous event, and they had to deal will the full gamut of emotions as they left for a new land and an unknown future. In April, 1946, *The Sydney Morning Herald* stated that one hundred brides from Victoria and several hundred from New South Wales embarked on SS *Monterey*' and described how, 'Many were tearful'.[127] The newspaper reported that the assistant State controller of the VAD,[128] Mrs.

Persia Porter, 'has a remedy for tearfulness' which was: 'Give them a dose of sal volatile, a cup of tea, and a bit of cheerful conversation.'[129] At such a time, when emotions ran high, it is doubtful that this practical solution was the panacea sought by the war brides.

Mavis Salamonski (née McSweeney) 2nd back row, 4th from right, with a group of Australian WWII war brides on SS *Mariposa*, April 1946.

CHAPTER FIVE

ARRIVAL IN AMERICA

Neath the Golden Gate to California State
We arrived on a morning fair.
Near the end of the trip, we stayed aboard ship,
We were still in the Navy's care
I was the young wife, embarked on a new life
Happiness mixed with confusion.
I'd not seen for a year the one I held dear
Would our love still bloom in profusion?
(Betty Kane, 'The War Bride', November 2001)[1]

The refurbished liner SS *Monterey* arrived in San Francisco on March 5, 1946, with 562 Australian and New Zealand war brides and their 253 children on board. A journalist from *The Sydney Morning Herald* was there to report that 'scores' of husbands were waiting on the dock, and that 'true to the reputation they established in Australia as great flower givers, nearly all the husbands clutched huge boxes of blooms' for their brides and fiancées.[2] 'Once the ship was cleared by the health authorities', it was reported, 'the husbands were allowed aboard and there were scenes in the best Hollywood manner.'[3] It was a 'journalists' day out', according to the newspaper, and 'a boatload' of press and movie photographers and special writers from all the major news services and Californian newspapers went in an army tugboat to meet the *Monterey*.[4]

Described as 'the brightest event in the lives of waterfront

writers and photographers since the war',[5] this romantic and
joyful account ostensibly described the atmosphere surrounding
the war brides' arrival in San Francisco. It was written from
the perspective of a journalist who was undoubtedly pleased
to report a happy, 'feel-good' story after the end of the war.
Its contents, however, were quite removed from the actual
experiences of these young women as they caught the first
glimpse of their new home. Although the war brides' first
impressions differed, and their reception by their husbands
and in-laws varied, for most there were periods of anxiety,
apprehension and doubt, at least until they had reached their
final destinations in their adopted country. Even then, for some,
it was not a 'Hollywood dream' come true, and there were plenty
of challenges to overcome.

As the ship, *David C. Shanks,* sat anchored in the bay of San
Francisco on April 28, 1946, Betty de St Germain wrote this
poignant entry in her diary:

> These last 19 days have not been the best, but…I would
> do it all again just to be with Ray. I didn't think I could
> love him anymore than I did in Sydney, but I find myself
> loving him more with each obstacle that comes my
> way…I know we will be happy and I have no regrets…I
> know I'm going to be so terribly lonely, but then I also
> know that Ray can give me the love to make up for those
> I've left behind. I'm starting a new life and I'm taking
> advantage of this opportunity God is giving me, but
> I'll never forget all my wonderful family and my true
> friends. I love you all and I'll never forget you, never.[6]

As well as sharing her innermost thoughts with loved ones at home
who might read her diary, her fervent words also seem to be directed
to herself, as reassurance that all would be well despite the loneliness
which she suspects looms ahead.

Betty de St Germain (née Mott) (5th from left) with other Australian
WWII war brides on board SS *David C. Shanks,* April, 1946.

Reunion

The war was still in progress when Western Australian war
bride Irene Franck arrived in San Francisco in 1944. The sea
voyage on a Swedish freighter had been anything but pleasant for
her, as she was pregnant and suffering with morning-sickness, as
well as seasickness. Upon her arrival in San Francisco, she was
feeling wretched, unable to eat or drink, and was extremely
thin. Her husband was still in service, so was not there to meet
her. She somehow summoned the stamina to travel by train to
Chicago to stay with her in-laws, who fortunately were 'the most
delightful people' and took good care of her, although she recalls:
'They looked at me as if I was a kangaroo or something!'[7]

Irene and Herb Franck with daughter
April, in Chicago, Illinois, 1944.

War bride Dorothy Pence Berry also sailed during the perils of wartime on a troopship from Brisbane, arriving at the naval base San Pedro in San Diego, California in January 1945. It was an extremely long journey of 90 days, as they had picked up 2,000 returning troops from New Guinea, as well as the great American songwriter, Irving Berlin, who was there entertaining the troops. Also, the ship was forced to make time-consuming and painstaking manoeuvres to avoid deadly mines in the water. Dorothy comments:

> *I was too young to be scared...one day the ship was going back and forth...so I ran to the deck and there were all these great rusty things out in the water. I said to one of the officers, 'What are those things?' and I'll never forget because he said: 'Those, my dear, are mines!'* [8]

Dorothy remembers that on arrival in America everything was packed up in the morning, so there were no meals on board that day; although she adds that 'the Red Cross was there to greet us with donuts!' This was her first encounter with a 'donut' as they had not yet made an appearance in Australian cuisine. There was 'nothing' for the baby. The returning US servicemen disembarked first and the war brides were the last to leave the ship. Dorothy explains:

I understand now that the servicemen were coming home
after being at sea all those months and years! [9]

At the time, though, she did not understand this order of priority
and was very anxious to disembark. On arrival at San Pedro, the war
brides were assigned to different taxi cabs and taken to a hotel where
the duties of the Red Cross came to an end. The young Australian
women then had the daunting task of finding their own way to their
final destinations. Dorothy says:

I'll never forget that experience, because my husband was
stationed at Treasure Island, San Francisco. The Red Cross
had called him and told him I had arrived – because you see
in wartime you couldn't tell people when you were arriving
– and he said 'Get the train'. [10]

So, Dorothy had to go outside the security of the hotel and find the
train station in order to buy a ticket. She asked her room-mate if she
could take care of her baby while she tried to find her way to the
train station. She recalls:

Outside the hotel, the only familiar thing to me was an
American soldier, you know. So I went up to him and asked
'Could you please tell me the way to the train station?' He
said 'Well, you know you take the N-car' and I was looking
for a car with an 'N' on it, not realising it was a tram. We
called them trams in Australia, but here it was a street-car!
So I had to quickly adapt to these different things. Anyway,
I found the station, bought my own ticket and then came
back and took a taxicab there the next day. [11]

Very few of the war brides interviewed recall their arrival in
America in glowing terms similar to the bright event described
by *The Sydney Morning Herald*. Few of the long-awaited reunions

went as was expected. Australian war brides were usually first-time travellers, already anxious as they arrived in a new country. Their anxiety grew as they searched among the crowds on the wharf for someone they recognised who might be there to meet them. Emotions ranged from jubilation and excitement to disappointment and distress, depending on whether or not there was someone there to receive them. There were inevitably feelings of disappointment and humiliation. Beset by problems such as sick babies, lost luggage, sometimes not being met or not being aware of their husbands' whereabouts, these young Australian women had to deal with many challenges on their arrival in an unfamiliar environment. Some women found it difficult to recognise their husbands and fiancés on first sighting, after the long separation. Already suffering some anxiety about arriving in America, the first glimpse of their husbands often did little to reassure them, as the men were sometimes almost impossible to recognise in civilian clothes.

Betty McIntire's husband had returned to America within a week of their marriage. Letters from him, every two or three weeks to begin with, had dwindled to one every one or two months. It was 11 months before Betty could get passage to America on SS *Monterey* in March 1946, and when she finally arrived in San Francisco, her husband was not there to meet her. The Red Cross located him in Reno, where he and some friends had stopped to gamble on their journey from Green River, Wyoming. Betty comments that 'they had such a great time they didn't make it to the ship', and she had to spend another night on board. When her husband finally 'showed up' late the next afternoon, she remembers:

> *They were the only ones on the dock and I was waiting. I thought 'Who is that?' I looked around and there was nobody else on the ship but me! I looked at these people and this guy that was out in front, he looked like the Mafia! Big broad shoulders on his Glen plaid suit, and a hat on a*

rakish angle! I was used to a uniform – he looked absolutely
wonderful in uniform. So, I finally said, 'God, that's got to
be Mac!' And it was.[12]

Arrival in the new country also brought new challenges to the
war brides as they had to deal with a new currency, a new vernacular,
new cuisines, and new customs.

Colleen Halter, pregnant and sick for most of the journey,
remembers arriving in San Francisco on June 14, 1946, to find
nobody there to meet her. When her name was called over the
loudspeaker, she remembers:

> *I walked down the gangplank and I didn't know what to do.*
> *I could just see everybody looking at me and thinking 'That*
> *poor little thing, she's pregnant and no-one to meet her!'* [13]

Colleen was ushered over to the Red Cross hut where several other
girls were also waiting. She felt sure that something had happened
to Jerry, so she used a public phone to call his Aunt Addie in San
Jose, close to San Francisco. She remembers the difficulty of doing
seemingly simple things in a new country:

> *I didn't know how to use the phone. The money looked*
> *so different and I was used to big pennies! So I asked a*
> *gentleman there to get that number for me, which he did. I*
> *talked to Aunt Addie and…she said 'You're not supposed to*
> *be here until tomorrow!'* [14]

Colleen's husband Jerry and his cousin 'Speed' eventually arrived
to collect Colleen. Self-conscious because she was pregnant and
seemingly abandoned, Colleen vividly remembers the events of that
day and how 'everyone around me had those looks of "Phew, thank
God we don't have to send her back!"'[15]

San Francisco was usually only the first stop on a long journey to a new home and many women interviewed reported that travelling alone within the United States was not easy for the war brides, and was especially difficult for those with babies and small children. They suffered discomfort due to the mode of transport, the length of the journey and, at times, the severe weather conditions, as well as the sometimes fragile health of the mother or her offspring. Hazel Walker's story provides a typical example of the stresses such a journey posed.

Hazel arrived in San Francisco on her 24th birthday. Ladies from the Red Cross came on board and took the 300 war brides in groups by car to their headquarters to arrange hotel accommodation. After a week in San Francisco, Hazel travelled by train to Chicago, and there she and other war brides experienced their first taste of resentment from American women. She recalls:

> *Every day on our way to the dining car, we had to go through a car that wasn't a Pullman, and some of the women in that car used to get down and wipe the floor after we'd walked on it and say rude things about us for having married US servicemen. We never acknowledged that we heard them, because we were brought up not to lower ourselves to the level of people like that; not that it didn't hurt our feelings. We were nervous enough as it was.*[16]

Pullman sleeping car - interior - arranged for daytime use. [Source: State Historical Society of Wisconsin visual Archives, image 34412]

There was an 'Army man' on the train who checked on the war brides every day to make sure they had no problems. When Hazel's seven-week-old baby became ill, this man stopped the train somewhere in Kansas and had a doctor come on board. The doctor said the baby was travel sick and asked Hazel how far she had come. He was shocked when she answered 'Australia' and said 'Good Lord, woman', and told her to give the baby nothing but boiled water until she got off the train. When the personnel in the kitchen would not give Hazel the water, the Army man arranged for the porter to get it for her. She says:

> *That man had been, and continued to be wonderful to us for the whole three days we were on that train. I was so grateful, that I wrote to him after I arrived in Chicago, and thanked him for his care.*[17]

Women travelling with their babies had to summon all their courage on leaving the ship, in order to make the additional journey by train to meet up with their husbands or their in-laws.

Betty Kane was exhausted after her week-long train journey from Western Australia to Sydney and was sick when she boarded SS *Monterey.* She recalls:

> *There were no stop-offs on the trip, as they had promised the US boys that they'd bring us home as quickly as they could.*[18]

On arrival in San Francisco, Betty travelled by train to Grand Junction, Colorado, where Bob was waiting, anxious to see his little daughter for the first time. Betty remembers:

> *It was 2 am when we arrived, and there he was with flowers! His family were all 'God believers' and I was not, but they were very nice. We stayed in Denver, Colorado for a couple of weeks, and then we went to New Jersey.*[19]

Rosemary Smith sailed on SS *Lurline* in April 1946 to San Francisco where her husband was unable to meet her, but with assistance from the Red Cross, she travelled to Long Beach by train. She recalls:

It all seems like a blur at times, but I remember on that train, coming down through the red desert to Long Beach, that it took almost all night...It was a regular troop train and they treated us like regular army. Every time we stopped somewhere they'd shout out, 'arm and line up', you know, just like we were part of the forces.[20]

Although no longer on board naval vessels, the quasi-military experience continued for some of these women, even after their arrival in America.

After such arduous journeys, it was sometimes weeks or even months before these war brides were reunited with their husbands. For most this was due to the exigencies of the war. Lowell Rudy was not at the dock to meet his wife Allie and their new son when they arrived on SS *Lurline* in June 1945, because he had been shipped off to Quadulan in the Marshall Islands. Never having travelled outside Australia before, Allie journeyed by train to Ohio, where she was to be met by her in-laws. Still suffering from the nausea of seasickness on the ship, Allie recalls:

My son had dysentery and in those days you couldn't buy disposable diapers...I couldn't stand to wash them, and I kept throwing them out the train window! Nobody saw what we were doing, but you dare not put them down the toilet. I kept throwing them out and I had to buy more and more. You could buy them on the train. It was just an impossible task for me to wash them, as I wasn't feeling very good at all. But we made it across country and his parents met me in Dayton, Ohio, and took me to their farm home.[21]

Seemingly abandoned by the husbands they had not seen for so long, the disappointment and despair of some war brides was tangible when they recalled that their husbands were not there to meet them.

Betty Blondon and her six-month-old baby arrived in San Francisco on board SS *Lurline* on November 14, 1946, and was then informed by the Red Cross that her husband was not there to meet her. She remembers thinking, 'What am I going to do?' His whereabouts were unknown to her and she was unable to contact him. There was a three or four hours wait for customs to clear the luggage, so she went with a few other passengers to have lunch. When she returned to check for her luggage, Betty says:

> *Someone came up behind me and grabbed me and it was my husband!' He had arrived after all...so it was a lovely surprise!* [22]

The couple drove down to Palm Springs, where they stayed with her in-laws and spent Thanksgiving with them, thus being immediately introduced to a great American cultural tradition.

Although many husbands were not able, for one reason or another, to be present to greet their wives on arrival, great efforts were made by some to meet their Australian wives. One discharged United States soldier, Amor John Mason, was so keen to be re-united with his 19-year-old Australian war bride Joyce, and his 18-months-old son Glenn, that he 'thumbed' his way across America when he learned that his family was arriving at San Francisco on March 6, 1946. It took him seven days and 22 hours to reach the West Coast from Philadelphia, Pennsylvania. He met his young wife and their son and put them on a train for Philadelphia, the family's fare being paid for by the US government. Mason did not have enough money for his own train ticket, so he hitch-hiked back again. The return trip took him eight days and 14 hours, and he arrived home with little change from the 71 dollars he had at the start of his journey. [23]

Even after arrival in America, a few women had 'cold feet' and still had to be persuaded to join their husbands and not return home to Australia. In April, 1946, headlines in the Australian press announced 'Two divorces among US Brides averted' and it was reported that Army, Navy and Red Cross officials convinced two war brides who arrived on SS *Lurline* that they 'should re-examine the situation before doing anything drastic'.[24] The paper told how 'one girl's happiness was shattered on arrival by a telegram from her husband stating the marriage was a mistake and she should return to Australia'.[25] However, the bride's mother-in-law was contacted and she invited the girl to go to her home in Missouri until the matter was resolved. Shortly after the *Lurline* docked, another war bride shocked officials by asking where she could file a suit for divorce. She was finally convinced that she should visit her husband before carrying out her plan.[26]

For other war brides, the very long and lonely wait to join their partners continued, but now in unfamiliar surroundings. For example, when May Webb sailed on SS *Monterey* in 1946, it had already been four years since she had seen her husband. She was met by her husband's sister in San Francisco, as he had been shipped to the Bikini Islands and had arranged for her to go to Wichita, Kansas, to live with her sister-in-law and her family for two years, making it virtually six years before the couple was re-united.[27]

Nancy Lankard's husband was still in the navy and his ship was also involved in the atomic testing at Bikini Atoll. On arrival in San Francisco in April 1946, she was met by the Red Cross, who 'were really wonderful' and took the war brides to Oakland to the train. Nancy recalls:

> *I was met at Denver, Colorado by my mother-in-law and her sister. They had to be identified, and then they claimed me – like a parcel! We drove down to their home in Colorado Springs.*[28]

Circumstances were different for Rita Hopkins who, unlike most war brides, was able to accompany her husband on SS *Lurline* under wartime conditions in 1944, although he was in a medical cabin, as he was being invalided home as a sick person. On arrival in San Francisco, they were met by the Red Cross and Rita's husband was transported to Latimer Army Hospital and from there to the medical facility in Santa Fe. Rita tells how she went to Monrovia, outside Los Angles, near Pasadena, to stay with her husband's aunt and uncle before going to Santa Fe, New Mexico for six weeks. The couple eventually moved to Wisconsin where Rita says she had no trouble settling in:

> *Aunt Bess and Uncle Andrew kind of took us under their wing, so we didn't have any problems. I was fine… everybody was really good.*[29]

A very positive person, despite difficulties, Rita had already demonstrated a confident resourcefulness in preparation for her wedding in Australia. When she was interviewed in September 2001 in Salem, Oregon, she was similarly positive. Her wheelchair-bound husband was very ill and attached to an oxygen tank to assist his breathing. Nevertheless, Rita was bright, spontaneous, and generous with her time, even offering me accommodation. Her hospitality during what must have been a very stressful time for her, given her husband's very poor health, is yet another example of the strength of character displayed by many of these women in the face of adversity.

First impressions

First impressions of America were different for each of the individual war brides. Knowledge of America among this group of women was fairly limited and their expectations of American lifestyles were largely coloured by what they had observed from Hollywood films screened in Australia.

Patricia Law remembers her first impressions of the United States and says:

I loved San Francisco…we went over the Golden Gate Bridge and I'd never seen that many cars!' [30]

She also remembered thinking that America did not reflect the Hollywood images portrayed in movies:

I'd seen too many movies and I didn't realise that people were just home bodies like we are and America was not all parties! [31]

Also influenced by Hollywood films, Shirley Norton was fearful after her arrival in San Francisco aboard SS *Monterey* on 22 April, 1946. She and her small son, who was ill, travelled east by train to Chicago to meet her husband. She remembers:

I thought Al Capone was still alive. I wasn't too happy going to Chicago, I can tell you that! [32]

Shirley Norton and her son Robert
in Chicago, Illinois, 1946.

The first glimpse of their new homeland was sometimes disappointing. Gladys Borger, who sailed to San Francisco on SS *Lurline* in 1944, did not expect to be met by her husband, as he was on SS *Apache* and had gone back into battle in the Philippines. She remembers her very first impression of America as a disappointment when, as the ship steamed into San Francisco, she first viewed the Golden Gate Bridge. Expecting the bridge to be 'golden', as the name implies, she was disenchanted to find that 'it was painted orange!' But she did find it impressive, and remembers that it was September and that the countryside from San Francisco to Sacramento was beautiful.[33]

The beauty of the countryside was remarked upon by several war brides. It was the landscape and environment that first caught the attention of Margaret Fosmo. She recalls that her very first impression of America was the beauty of the Oregon coast as they drove north to Seattle.[34]

Ivy Diers from Rockhampton in tropical Queensland, travelled by train to Seattle, where she was to meet her husband. She clearly remembers the wonder of seeing snow for the first time from the train in northern California.[35] Similarly, when Joan Stern settled in Amityville, New York, the knee-deep snow in winter was a new and very different experience after coming from the mild coastal climate of Sydney.

Joan Stein in the snow in
Amityville, NY, c.2001.

Valda Hertzberg's first impressions of Philadelphia were better than she had anticipated. She recalls:

> *Having been told by my husband that Philadelphia was flat, dirty and unattractive, I found…where we lived was actually outside the city limits…It was very pretty and hilly, with the river Schuylkill, and the biggest park there is!* [36]

The different climate and terrain was not always a comfort to these young women. Dorothy Thompson, for instance, came to America from the sunshine and tropical warmth of Queensland and first settled in the small town of Clark in South Dakota, in the midst of a bitter winter season. Dorothy found the move to be 'a big change' and she remembers how she was very unhappy for the first five years, and describes how much she 'hated the winters':

> *I came here in March and the snow was melting – dirty slushy snow – no leaves on the trees, and I just thought I'd come to the end of the world…* [37]

Acclimatising to new surroundings was a challenge for many war brides. Patricia Law was born at Llandudno in North Wales, but had moved with her family to Australia in 1939, as her father had contracted malaria in the Indian army and was given six months live. The temperate Sydney climate saw her father thrive and make a full recovery, so much so that with the outbreak of war, he enlisted with the Australian Army and was sent to Africa to fight against Rommel. However, this milder climate had not prepared Patricia for settling into her new surroundings in America, which she found difficult. It was very different living in the dry desert of Arizona where it was so cold that the pipes froze in winter. She describes the region as a place of 'extreme heat' and 'extreme cold', to which she had to adjust.[38]

Doris Sarff was just 21 when she arrived as a fiancée in America in June 1947. After a quiet wedding in a lovely church, with Deacons of the Church as witnesses, she and Bob drove to a house he had leased in West Seattle.

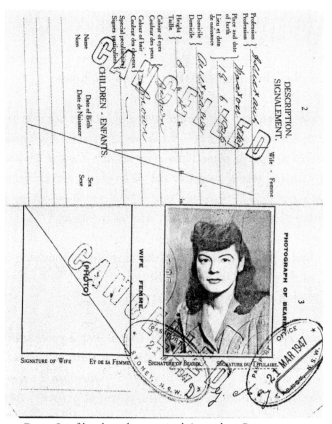

Doris Saarf has kept her original Australian Passport as a memento of her journey to America in September, 1947.

Her in-laws accepted her right away, but Doris recalls:

> *They didn't ask many questions…what Australia was like, or what my parents did, they just assumed that the rest of the world was just like this.*[39]

However, she found it very different, especially when it snowed and there were blizzards. She found it a very foreboding sort of place, and yet beautiful in some ways. She remembers:

> *I was terribly lonely when I first came. My husband would go into the city to work, so here I was high up on a bluff and I never saw any people.*[40]

Doris describes the magnificent view from the house:

> *I looked out over the Sound where the ferries were running from that part of the city – it was very lonesome. Right away I wanted to have a child. After three months I asked the doctor why I wasn't getting pregnant and he laughed…he said 'It's such a nice change. I have women here every day who are having a fit because they are pregnant!' And I wanted it so badly.*[41]

The alien landscape did not make sense to Sydney war bride, Joy Shaddle, on her arrival in Forrest, Illinois in 1947. She reflects on her first impression of the winter countryside:

> *I remember it was March and that is not a good time in Illinois, because it is neither blanketed with the beautiful snow, nor is it green. It is bare! I remember I thought 'They've had a bushfire here!' All the trees were bare. I looked around and thought 'Oh, what a pity – it's all black!'*[42]

For Betty de St Germain from Sydney, it was the night lights in New Orleans she first noticed when driving with her fiancé to meet his family:

> *It was just on dark and he had borrowed his brother's car to come in and pick me up. As we drove down Canal Street, the main street, it was like fairyland! There were so many neon lights that we didn't have [in Sydney] then.*[43]

In contrast, for Patricia Law it was the lack of night lights and entertainment which made an impression on her when she reached her destination of Casa Grande in Arizona. She explains:

> *In Sydney during wartime there was a lot of night life...*
> *clubs where you go dancing, and of course there was nothing*
> *like that in the little town where I went – just picnics and*
> *'pot lucks'.*[44]

The small town lacked the sophistication of the city of Sydney, where entertainment specifically for the troops in wartime had seen nightclubs and dance halls flourish during the 1940s.

Others were impressed by the grand scale of the roads and infrastructure, compared with Australian cities. Sydney war bride, June Carver, in her eighties when interviewed and legally blind, could still remember the strong visual impressions of her arrival in San Francisco on SS *Lurline* in 1945. Her husband had driven all the way from Utah to meet her, and the couple returned there by car. She recalls:

> *There were no freeways at that time, and I was overwhelmed*
> *at the size of the buses and trucks whizzing by. I had never*
> *seen such big trucks in my life!*[45]

After leaving San Francisco her main impression of the US was that 'it was wide', and she describes her memories of its vastness on the road trip to Utah:

> *We drove through northern California and across the whole*
> *of Nevada, and it was just a wide open desert State. Las*
> *Vegas was just a little dot on the way in those days – it*
> *wasn't what it is today.*[46]

Similarly, Joann Patterson was impressed by the vastness of the United States as she and her husband drove from San Francisco to Milford, Ohio. Coming from Melbourne which was a big city, she found 'the little towns' where they stopped along the way were quite intriguing. She found the people very friendly. She remembers visiting one small town in Kansas and declares:

> *I was a celebrity! They wanted to take me to the Chamber of Commerce the next day to make a speech about Australia!* [47]

Also impressed by the size of the country, Betty Blondon recalls:

> *It was big! And the cars scared the life out of me because they were on the wrong side of the road!* [48]

For Mary Bourne, her very first impression of the US was how the very wide roads reminded her of the 'monstrous boulevards' in Germany that were repeatedly shown at the newsreel cinemas in Australia.[49] Her husband had not been in San Francisco to meet her, she had been seasick all the way across the Pacific, and her luggage had been lost. Given these unhappy circumstances it is perhaps no wonder that such wartime images loomed large in her mind.

The number of cars on the roads signalled an apparent affluence compared to Australia, where petrol was rationed during the war and motor vehicles were often motionless, 'up on blocks' in garages.

Traffic jam, San Francisco, c.1946. [Source: San Francisco History Center, and San Francisco Public Library]

Edna Pickerel, known as Teddy, sailed on SS *Mariposa* with her small child, arriving in San Francisco on the memorable date of Anzac Day, 25 April, 1946. Her husband, whom she had not seen for six months, was waiting on the wharf with his uncle. After a few days in San Francisco with his aunt and uncle, the couple drove on to Salem, Oregon, where they spent the next six months living with Teddy's father-in-law and his wife, until finally the couple was able to buy their own home nearby. Teddy's first impressions of the US noted that 'everything was different' and 'everyone had a car'. She noticed on the drive from San Francisco that there were "all these places that said 'motel'". A motel was something she didn't know from Australia in those days and she says:

> *I didn't know whether it was a place of ill repute or what! I hoped it wasn't, because we stayed in one on our first night on the road!* [50]

Iris Craig also found the journey by car very different when she first arrived. She remarked on how strange it felt to be travelling on 'the wrong side of the road', and she noticed odd spelling on the advertising broad-boards, such as 'nite' and wondered 'is that the way they spell here' as she thought it was definitely 'not good English'. [51]

To some women, American cities seemed more affluent and advanced than those in Australia, while others thought America was lagging behind. Irene Perucci's first impression of the United States was amazement at 'all the automobiles!' She had never seen so many, and she observed that everyone seemed to go about their own business 'as if they didn't know there was a war going on'. She also noted that it seemed more affluent:

> *Things weren't rationed over here, whereas back home you had to have eight coupons for a pair of shoes. It was a very fast pace...compared to back home.* [52]

Rita Hopkins, originally from the Northern Queensland town of Rockhampton, also found the US to be quite advanced and thought that Australia was probably 'fifty years behind'.[53] By contrast, Nancy Lankard, originally from Sydney, considered herself 'a real city girl' and being used to the bustle of the city, found Colorado Springs 'a little behind the times'. She remembers that:

> *People were friendly but a little 'country-bumpkin-ish'. I was very, very lonely – coming from a big family – and it was very expensive to get through on the phone to speak to family back in Australia. Sometimes the phones were on a party-line and there would be other people on the line. It was very hard.*[54]

Similarly, Kathleen Heeren's first impression of the United States was that 'it was strange, and years and years behind' Australia. In her opinion, 'America didn't come alive until probably into the mid-50s'.[55]

The war brides' impressions as to whether America was 'behind' or 'advanced' were usually influenced by the locations in Australia from where they originally came. Compared to small towns such as Rockhampton (particularly before the influx of American troops), the US would no doubt have seemed more advanced. For those women who came from large cities such as Sydney or Melbourne, on their arrival in a small mid-west town, for example, the US would appear to be less advanced.

The different American cuisine made an impression on some war brides and fiancées. In Seattle, Margaret Fosmo's sister-in-law drove her sight-seeing to Pike Place Markets, famous for their displays of fresh fish and produce, where Margaret sampled 'a chili dog' which she thought was 'terrible'. Generally, though, her impressions were that it all seemed 'pretty much the same as at home'.[56] Norma Rehrer remembers being impressed by the home-canned fruit that some American people had stored in their basement and also by the 'chocolate covered almonds' in the shops in San Francisco.

She says: 'We hadn't had those in Australia for years!'[57] When Betty St Germain arrived at her husband Ray's brother's house in New Orleans, Louisiana, she remembers how she was accepted immediately by the family and was treated to a meal of 'red beans and rice with chili in it', which upset her digestion. Betty comments:

I don't have to tell you what happened! If you've eaten chili, you know about it! I didn't know what had happened to me![58]

New 'ethnic' cuisine was one more cultural change to which some of the Australian women had to quickly adjust.

'Foreigners' in a new land

The general attitude of Americans to the newly arrived Australian war brides, even before the war had ended, was highlighted in an article in *The Washington Post* on July 29, 1945. Under the heading, 'Thousands of American Girls Face War-Caused Spinsterhood', the article stated 'many thousands of American girls never find husbands as a direct consequence of war'.[59] The paper reported that American 'official sources hesitate about giving out estimates' but they nevertheless 'concede that more and more girls face certain spinsterhood'.[60] Among the reasons given were the surplus number of women in America when it entered the war; as well as the deaths and casualties of war, many of which were believed to be young unmarried men; and the numbers of American soldiers who 'are marrying overseas'.[61] Although the Australian Embassy was reported to have 'no figures', the Australian newspaper polls indicated in July 1945, that more than 10,000 American soldiers had married Australian girls.[62] The newspaper also reported that 'hundreds of Yank brides' are expected also to arrive from countries such as 'Iceland, Trinidad, New Zealand, Italy, Egypt, France, Newfoundland and other foreign nations'.[63] With this influx of women from other countries, married to American GIs, it is no wonder that in some instances the war brides became aware of hostility and prejudice towards them.

Australian war brides were English-speaking and had more customs in common with American traditions than most newly arrived war brides from non-English speaking countries. However, they did not escape the resentment directed at foreign brides, who were seen as having 'stolen' the young American men away from eligible American women. Overwhelmingly, the war brides interviewed expressed bemusement at being treated as 'foreigners'. As Australian wives of American servicemen, they were in fact 'foreigners' in America under US law, until they became naturalised citizens.[64] But it had never occurred to them that their husbands' relatives and friends might suspect that they would be Aboriginal, have black skin, or that they might not speak English and therefore be difficult to understand. The parochial attitude of Americans, who generally seemed to know little about countries outside their own, was surprising to the war brides. They had come from a country which was predominantly Anglo-Saxon, where Aboriginal people were not part of the mainstream population, and where the White Australia Policy excluded the immigration of Asians in an attempt to keep Australia 'white'.[65] These young Australian women, who came from a nation so closely allied to America during WWII, were shocked to find that they were treated as 'foreigners' in that country. That they should be the subject of queries about race and whiteness was something they had not expected, and subsequent feelings of alienation tested some of the war brides as they settled into their new homes.

The war brides found many instances of ignorance about Australia on the part of Americans in the immediate post-war years, which included confusing Australians with Austrians; the belief that Australians were 'black' and did not speak English; and, in one instance, believing that Australia was attached somewhere to the Southern tip of South America.

War bride Joy Shaddle, who settled in the small town of Forrest, Illinois, describes the 'open house' when her mother-in-law 'invited everyone' to meet her and 'they all came'. Joy says:

> *At that time, they didn't know what an Aussie looked like. They didn't know whether Lloyd Shaddle's wife was black or white! I think they came out of curiosity, and many of them would say to me 'You speak quite good English!' I'd laugh and say 'I can't speak anything else!'* [66]

Allie Rudy initially lived with her in-laws, and before her husband returned home from the war, all his friends from high school and various cousins, who rarely visited, came to see 'this Aussie' that Bud had married. According to Allie, the people in town knew very little about Australia, and she tells how one person in particular expected her to be a black person: 'Yes', she says, 'an Australian Aborigine!' She remembers: 'he was delighted that I was white and that I could speak English!'[67] Allie's husband was a well-known sportsperson in town - 'a wonderful pitcher in baseball' and he 'played football so very well' - and she explains how his friends were curious to see 'what kind of a woman he had married'.[68] She recalls:

> *My mother-in-law's friend had wanted to know what she thought about her son marrying a black girl! Others asked 'How will she understand what we say?' It made me feel a little uncomfortable and it was rather hurtful, but I realised it was just ignorance on their part.*[69]

As well as having to confront these unexpected issues of 'race' and 'whiteness' in a country where they expected to blend in and feel at home, there were other issues of ethnicity which tested the war brides.

Soon after arriving in the US, Shirley Norton, her husband, and their small baby moved to Milwaukee, where they rented an apartment in part of a big house. The woman who rented the house had sub-let this small apartment without telling the landlord. He found out and came banging on the door one day. Shirley remembers:

> *This was a German man that I could hardly understand! He had a very guttural voice. Milwaukee had a lot of German population. He told me I was a foreigner and should go back where I came from!* [70]

This outburst coming from a German, no doubt a resident of some years, seemed unfair to Shirley who thought, as an English-speaking wife of a US serviceman, she was less foreign than he was, particularly given the recent association of wartime alliances where Germany was the enemy and Australia an ally of the US. This experience temporarily undermined Shirley's sense of security regarding her new home.

Prejudice was often directed towards the war bride for marrying an American serviceman, rather than blame being apportioned to the American groom. Dorothy Thompson initially lived with her in-laws in a small town, where she says 'there was a lot of prejudice against us girls when we came over here'. She says: 'We married Americans and took their boys away'. She felt this local prejudice personally, as 'in a small town everyone knows you'. Dorothy says: 'nobody really bothered to come to see me', although she suspected that her mother-in-law had a lot to do with this, as she didn't want people to come to the house. Reflecting that life in America 'hasn't been a bed of roses', Dorothy adds 'but I can't really complain about it', a comment which suggests a certain amount of compromise which was necessary for some marriages to succeed. Dorothy's attitude is typical of the strength, determination and stoicism of the Australian war brides when dealing with feelings of alienation and in pursuing their goal to make a success of their marriage. [71]

Meeting the in-laws

Meeting the in-laws quite often proved to be challenging. Not all war brides were given a welcoming reception from their husband's families. Because of housing shortages just after the war, it was difficult for the newly married couples to find accommodation. In many cases, the war brides initially were expected to live with their in-laws in an unfriendly and hostile environment. There were various factors that prevented instantaneous bonding between the new bride and her in-laws.

Dorothy Pence Berry was not accepted by her husband's parents, who had earlier written to their son saying 'Why don't you marry a nice American girl instead of a foreigner?' As there was no housing available, the Red Cross provided the couple with accommodation until they could get Navy housing in Berkeley.[72] When Dorothy became pregnant, her husband suggested that she and their 18-month-old daughter should go to stay with his mother in Ohio, to be cared for during her pregnancy. It was not a happy experience for Dorothy who found that 'they didn't care' for her and they saw her as 'a foreigner' and criticised her Australian accent which she found very hurtful.[73] After returning to California, however, she realised that it was not all Americans, but just her in-laws who lived 'in their little sphere in the world'. So she adapted her attitude and relations improved. She says:

> We ended up good friends years and years later, but I was always a 'foreigner' to them.[74]

Sometimes religious differences were the root of the problem. Joann Patterson found her in-laws to be generally 'cordial', although her mother-in-law said the marriage would never last. Joann explains:

> This was mainly because they were a Catholic family and Joseph had married out of the church and married a foreigner.[75]

Her father-in-law was friendly, and Joseph had two sisters with whom she made good friends.[76]

Allie Rudy felt fortunate to be 'welcomed with opened arms' into the home of her husband's family, but she felt that her mother-in-law seemed to be bothered that Allie was Catholic and had married into their Protestant family. However, she says:

> *I won them over because I think they realised that it didn't matter, and that I was a decent person. I was a good wife, I was a good mother and I was a great help to her. So I won myself into their little hearts I think.*[77]

Allie was expected, as were most of the Australian war brides, to settle into a domestic role as housewife and mother. She did not find this difficult, as she was enthusiastic about the new experience of living on a farm. Coming from the city, she loved the idea that 'all they had for heating was a pot-bellied stove with coal'. Her mother-in-law cooked fresh eggs on a coal-oil stove. Nothing bothered her and Allie describes her as 'a real farm person' who seemed not to be aware of any hardships. She would always cook the meals, which was wonderful for Allie, as it allowed her time to take care of her son and take him for walks. Always displaying a zest for life, she enjoyed living on the farm because she knew it was 'wholesome and healthy'.[78]

Betty MacIntire's mother-in-law ran a 'ramshackle' rooming house in Green River, Wyoming, for young men working on the railroad. Betty and her husband stayed with her mother-in-law for about six months until they moved into 'a little place of our own'.[79] Betty recalls she was 'homesick right from the beginning' and 'things did not work out the way I thought they would'.[80] Despite Betty's efforts to maintain this marriage, her husband proved to be an alcoholic and the relationship ultimately failed, although not until her children were teenagers.[81] At the time of Betty's interview, she made reference to 'her story', which she was writing, and promised to give me at a later date. Keeping to her promise, she presented a manuscript to me in Denver, Colorado, in 2001. It gave a detailed and poignant account of the difficult marriage to the handsome US serviceman she had met 'in a brown-out' in Sydney and fallen in love with during the war. It contained details she had not been ready to share at our first meeting two years earlier which explained some pauses and incomplete answers to questions during the earlier taped interview (the fuller story will be mentioned in a later chapter).

Some war brides were fortunate to be genuinely welcomed by their in-laws. After 'an awful trip' on SS *David C. Shanks,* war bride Cynthia Peter found it hard to settle, but she was initially thrilled at her reception by her husband's family when she arrival in San Francisco on 23 June, 1946. She says:

> *I met his parents and his sister and his brother…I think the whole family was there! I was delighted because they were such nice people. I was so thankful for that.*[82]

Despite this warm welcome from the family, who 'were always wonderful' to her, Cynthia admits that she was 'terribly homesick for a long time'. She was not alone in suffering homesickness. This was something that affected most war brides to some extent and is referred to in more detail in the next chapter.

After two weeks in America, Kathleen Heeren's husband was ordered to Japan, and she then made the arduous journey by train to stay in Minnesota with his family, who 'were very kind' to her. But, Kathleen remembers that because of wartime restrictions, it had been previously difficult to contact the family, and 'it was like meeting strangers'. She recalls they had little in common:

> *Being a city girl I knew nothing about farming, I knew nothing about breeding animals…I didn't know anything about raising corn or soy beans. So we had nothing in common. There was really nothing to do there. I was so bored I thought 'This is not for me!'*[83]

As well as the change from city life to rural living, adjustment to life in the multicultural 'melting-pot' of America was an unexpected challenge that confronted a number of these Australian wives. Irene Perucci married into an Italian family and sailed on SS *Lurline* in 1944 on the same day that her husband was shipped out to Guam. It was a year and a half before she was to see him again. There was no one to meet her at the ship when she arrived in America. Irene and her good friend Lola, from the same small country town in Western Australia, were separated as the American Red Cross allocated them different hotels.[84] From San Francisco, Irene took the train across the country to Boston, Massachusetts, and then another train from Boston to Salem. She remembers the warm welcome she received:

> *My mother-in-law and my sister-in-law were at the depot waiting for me in Salem…I told her I would be wearing a red hat and a red coat…so…when I got off the train she just threw her arms around me and said 'Welcome to my home as my son's wife!'*[85]

Irene stayed with her husband's Italian family and initially did not feel homesick, because she and her mother-in-law had become acquainted through letter-writing. Because of their Italian background, Irene's in-laws spoke broken English and they would converse in Italian. Irene recalls:

> *Papa would come up to me and put his hand on my shoulder and say 'Mama and I no talk about you when we talking like this!'*[86]

Not wanting to appear rude, he wanted to reassure her and make her feel comfortable. Despite the warmth of her hosts, however, Irene felt isolated and recalls:

> *There's many a time I sat at the table with my mother-in-law…and she'd look up at me and say, 'Rene, ah-why are you crying?'*[87]

All the kindness in the world could not make up for the absence of her husband, as she 'missed him very much'; nor could it soothe the pain and longing she felt both for her husband and for the family she had left behind.[88]

The war brides who married second- or third-generation American immigrants often experienced different receptions by their in-laws. Some received warm welcomes and experienced the richness and diversity of the American 'melting-pot'. Others found they were not welcomed by their in-laws. These women felt excluded and as though they were 'outsiders' intruding in an ethnic enclave.

Marrying into a German family, Joan Byer sailed from Western Australia on board SS *Fred C. Ainsworth* in April 1946. She travelled by train to Omaha, Nebraska, where she was met by her husband Ray. The couple spent two days there before driving on to New Ulm. Ray's mother had died in 1925, and so it was 'a bachelor house' which they shared with his father. The couple stayed for a year and a half, but Joan was very lonely at first, as New Ulm was a German town where most people could speak English, but chose to converse with each other in German. Joan felt excluded because of the language barrier and rather isolated, as she felt that she was considered an 'outsider' who had 'married one of their own'. She recalls, 'there was a lot of that to overcome'.[89]

Similarly, it was 'a culture shock' for Joyce Balogh, who did not feel at all welcomed by her husband's parents, who spoke Hungarian in the house most of the time. She remembers, 'I felt isolated. It wasn't a good situation at all'.[90] The image of the 'Hollywood dream' was far from the reality of the Hungarian 'ghetto' in Pennsylvania where Joyce began her new life.[91]

Margaret Fosmo married into a Norwegian family. She sailed on SS *Mariposa,* from Brisbane arriving in San Francisco on Anzac Day, 25 April, 1946 to be met by her in-laws. Her husband, Olaf, was still away in the military service, so Margaret travelled north to Seattle, where she lived with his family for about two months before her husband got leave. The couple then went to San Francisco and stayed there in Navy housing. Margaret describes her in-laws as 'very nice' people, although at first her mother-in-law wasn't too pleased, as she had not chosen her to marry her son. Margaret's mother-in-law had 'a lot of Norwegian friends'. When they came to visit, they all spoke Norwegian and Margaret suspected they were talking about her. Her mother-in-law was not very nice to her 'in a lot of ways', but eventually, she felt she was accepted.[92]

Marjory (Marge) Andreatta married into an Italian family. From the ships' deck she looked for her husband as the ship docked in San Francisco and when she 'spotted him', she lifted their small daughter up for him to see her. After staying for a few days with her husband's sister in a flat above a grocery store, the couple moved in with his mother in San Mateo, about 20 miles south of San Francisco. Marge found this a difficult time. Both her husband's parents were Italian, but while her father-in-law spoke broken English; her mother-in-law couldn't speak a word of English. Despite the language barrier, Marge had no problem with the family who 'were very sweet'. Initially, she did feel some prejudice though, and thought that her husband's sisters regarded her as 'some little gold digger that wanted to come to America and snatch their brother'. But eventually, she says, they 'accepted me as a sister'.[93]

For many of the war brides, the experience of childhood in the Depression years meant that they had remained almost in a state of extended childhood in their parents' home. As well as dealing with the process of emigration and all that this entailed, these young women were also dealing with growing up and becoming responsible adults.

Rosemary Smith's husband, who was waiting for her at the train station, took her to live with his mother and his two brothers in their house in Long Beach. His father wasn't alive. It was very different for Rosemary at first. She remembers:

His mother was a little stand-offish. I think she favoured the boys so much and she was very difficult to get close to…She expected my husband to be close to her, and he being just out of the service wanted to go and do things with a friend who had been with him in the service in New Guinea and had lived in Long Beach…when you're young you don't think about things, you just think of your own enjoyment. I can understand it in a way.[94]

Rosemary was used to living at home with three brothers and a younger sister and a half sister with 'everything going on'. Now she found herself living with just adults and she comments: 'all of a sudden, you are one of the adults'. Eventually they moved out with a friend of her husband's and rented a house together and this was 'a lot of fun'.[95]

The welcome received by some war brides from their husband's family was so warm-hearted that it was almost overwhelming, and while not always preventing uneasy feelings of homesickness, this affectionate reception quickly dispelled any fears of not being accepted as part of the family.

Joan Hamilton was very happy to see her husband waiting for her at the end of her train journey, although, as Joan remembers, he looked very different in civilian clothes:

In those days the casual coats were two-toned and I'd never seen him in a hat. You know, he always had a foreage cap or a regular services cap.[96]

Joan remembers the warm welcome she received from his family that night:

We drove to his parents' house and that was the most astonishing greeting I'd ever had in my life! His whole family was there! Such a fabulous welcome, and they didn't know who I was, although his mother and I had written numerous times even before we were married. His mother came racing out and decided she was going to get Trish first. She had four boys, really desperately wanted a little girl, and of course Trish filled her dreams! So she said, 'I'm getting the baby first', and virtually snatched the baby out of my arms. Trish was wonderful, she didn't cry. She was just oblivious to all the fuss. His three brothers were there and I couldn't have asked for a better welcome. His family were so supportive.[97]

The letters that Joan and her mother-in-law had written to each before the couple were married in Australia, no doubt paved the way for good communication when they were to meet much later in person.[98]

Possessiveness and jealousy on the part of some mothers-in-law were also factors which affected the reception of new brides into the family. Valda Hertzberg acknowledges that her mother-in-law 'disliked her intensely'. She explains that her husband's father had died when he was just fifteen and he had one sister who was a year older. Letters to Valda and her small daughter Carolyn from her mother-in-law seemed very welcoming, but in retrospect, Valda said her mother-in-law did not 'want someone interfering – she wanted him – and I came first [with him], very much first.'[99] Similarly, Iris Craig received a very cool reception from her in-laws, who did not welcome her at all. She felt fortunate that she didn't have to stay with them. She explains, 'my mother-in-law had an aversion to English people and as far as she was concerned, I was English. So I cannot say I was welcomed'. Also, her mother-in-law considered that 'boys were the only children you should have', and Iris says, 'I had a girl!'[100]

Norma Rehrer had a good relationship with her in-laws. Her husband, Gene, arrived by train from Missouri to meet her, and then they travelled on a Santa Fe train to Sedaya, Missouri, where he was stationed. His parents welcomed her 'with open arms' and when Gene received orders for the Philippines, Norma lived with them in Pennsylvania for eight months. She was included in the family and spent time helping his father with his stamp collection. She remembers:

> *He had bags and bags of stamps and said he would never have gotten it done if it hadn't been for me!* [101]

Some war brides happily escaped the necessity to live in close contact with their in-laws and were able to start an independent life with their husbands all to themselves. Jean Fargo sailed on SS *David C. Shanks,* arriving in San Francisco on 28 June, 1946. She made her way by train, with carriages especially for war brides, to Washington DC where her husband came to meet her. Jean thought this city was 'just fantastic' and thought America seemed more advanced than Australia. She was well received by her mother-in-law, although she recalls:

> *She was old...in her eighties...and she seemed like a hundred to me! Then he had three older brothers living fairly close-by...all the wives were very nice, but they were all older than I was...I think that I was glad that I didn't have to live too close.* [102]

Many war brides were prepared to make the best of the circumstances in which they found themselves, some much happier than others. Their sometimes stoic acceptance of their situations and their determination to retain a positive attitude often seemed to be influenced by memories of their parents' feelings of sadness and their lingering doubts that their daughters were doing the right thing by going to America to live. The war brides' determination that all would be well, and that their lives in America would be successful, was a positive characteristic common to these women. For example, Peggy Dunbar Blackman's first impressions of the United States were 'very favourable'. She says:

*The people I met, the buildings, San Francisco Harbor – I
didn't think it was as beautiful as Sydney Harbour – but
I was not in a criticising mood and I was prepared to find
things to like. I had a positive attitude and I was bound to
make a success of this marriage. I have a lingering memory
of my mother's face as she waved me goodbye, with tears
streaming down her face. I'm sure my father felt the same.*[103]

Peggy had sailed on SS *Mirrabooka* early in August, 1945. Her
husband, Don, was not able to be in San Francisco to meet her, but
his parents came from their home in Palo Alto, California. She lived
with her in-laws for six weeks until Don came back from Manilla
and she 'got to know them very nicely'. As she recalls:

*I think they were pleased that Don had married someone
who looked like their kind of girl...I looked pretty
wholesome, I think, fifty years ago...I was their kind of
prospective family member and they were thrilled and they
welcomed me.*[104]

Before long, Peggy 'fell in love with Palo Alto'.[105] This is testimony
to her positive attitude and determination to make a success of her
new life in America. However, her recollections also reveal a recurring
theme of the strong bond between mother and daughter, and the
way that Peggy was haunted by her mother's grief at her leaving,
which fuelled her determination to succeed in her new venture. Her
positive attitude in the telling of this story perhaps masks the on-
going feelings of grief which she remembers so vividly. Like other war
brides, the strength of her positive attitude belies the deep emotions
Peggy felt when remembering her mother's tears.

Australian war brides reacted in different ways to the challenges
they faced: the sometimes alien landscape; the relationship with their
mothers-in-law from whom some learned culinary and household
skills; as well as their initial homesickness and subsequent cultural

adjustment to their surroundings. On arrival in America, they had to leave the 'security' of belonging to a group on board ship and move on to an independent life as an individual. As new wives, they were expected to fill the domestic role of housewife and mother, often living in the shadow of their mothers-in-law, while making every day adjustments to a new culture. This scenario was far from the media's picture of the promised 'Hollywood dream'.

Despite very different experiences, varying degrees of welcome and acceptance, or non-acceptance, as well as a diverse range of comfort and quality of available accommodation, many of these young Australian women felt 'torn apart' at being so far away from their parents and the support of their extended families and friends.[106] Homesickness was something which many war brides suffered in the early days and weeks, sometimes even for years, after arriving in America.[107]

CHAPTER SIX

LIVING IN AMERICA
IMMIGRANTS IN A NEW LAND

Our room up the stairs, for we were to share
That floor with a sister of his.
A wide window seat, I gazed down at the street,
My own folk I surely did miss.

So I began a new life, became a housewife,
Tried to stifle that backward look.
Learned to do things their way, as I had to stay,
And honour those vows that I took.
(Betty Kane, 'The War Bride', November 2001)[1]

For some Australian women, like Adelaide war bride Doris Harburt, the sudden change of cultural environments in America was quite alienating and it took some time to adjust to these new conditions. Doris found it very hard to settle in a strange country. She spent the first 14 months in America living with her in-laws on a ranch 70 miles northeast of Denver in Colorado, then spent the next five months in Denver, before moving to Harden in southeast Montana. She describes her impressions of Harden when she first arrived there:

> *[It was] a new town made up of all sorts of people. The Cheyenne Indians were on one side and the Crow Indians on the other. The town was originally begun by Indians. People came from all over the States and a lot were from*

American families of Dutch and European descent...After about three months the homesickness seemed to hit, so I fought the homesickness and got involved in things.[2]

Doris did not feel at home in these surroundings and in 1950, after four years in America, she returned to live in Australia where her husband had always wanted to live. Still living in Adelaide at the time of this interview, Doris and her husband had just celebrated their 60th wedding anniversary and she was looking forward to her 90th birthday celebrations in the week to come.

Migration to a different country was no easier for Barbara Edwards, originally from the sleepy fishing village of Ballina in northern New South Wales. Having migrated three times in her life, she has found each experience different to what she had expected. As a three-year-old she did not notice the first time, when her family came from England to live Australia. In 1946, when Barbara migrated to join her American husband in his home state of Maine, it was the 'happiest of migrations despite leaving my parents, my sister and my two young brothers'.[3] She stayed in America for almost 40 years, spending the last 20 years in Hawaii. Her third migration, however, was when her husband retired and they left America to return to Australia, in part to be closer to help her mother. Barbara found that coming back home is not as easy as moving to a new country. 'The whole life-style in Ballina had changed' and she no longer knew everyone she met on the street. She had to learn the new medical and hospital system and it was hard to learn the cuts of meat. While she had 'expected America to be different and it was', she had 'expected Australia to be the same and it was not'. Barbara learned that 'adaptation to a new country is easier when one is young, no matter how well you know your new home.'[4]

The passing of the US legislation in the form of the *War Brides Act* of December, 1945, followed by the *G.I. Fiancées Act* of June 29, 1946, facilitated the reunion of US servicemen with their foreign wives, fiancées and children.

Once living in America, Australian war brides had to make adjustments to cultural and familial changes. The experiences of these Australian wives, however, differed from those of war brides from other countries, as well as from other post-war migrants to America.

Despite several Japanese attacks on Australian soil, the Australian home front had not suffered the physical destruction and bombardment that Britain, Europe and Japan had experienced during the war. Australian war brides left a country which was affluent, compared to Europe at that time. Australians were well-fed, despite wartime rationing, and women were enjoying a new social freedom as they took up men's vacancies in the workforce. Even for those Australian war brides who came from large families, poor families, and from families temporarily facing lean times as a result of the Great Depression, the 'push' factor which propelled war brides from wartime conditions in Europe and Japan did not exist in the same way. The war brides' departure from Australia separated them from family and friends and a homeland where most had lived relatively happy lives, to proceed often with a sense of trepidation to an unknown future. For the Australian brides and fiancées, it was more a case of 'for love alone'.

Some young women such as Coleen Halter (nee Moore) seemed to have no fear of the future in a new country. Born in Cairns, Queensland in 1927, Colleen was only seventeen when she was introduced to her future husband by her young nephew. She fell 'head over heels' in love with Jerry and remembers her first impressions of him:

> *He was very good looking, tall, blue-eyed, blonde, great teeth, tanned skin, you know, really nice looking. He wasn't all dressed up, he was in Naval work clothes – I think it was jeans and a shirt.*[5]

Jerry Lytle, 1942.   Colleen Moore, 1944.

The couple married in Brisbane almost a year after they met in November 1945, at 'a pretty little Methodist church right across from the City Hall', and the carillon rang out to announce the happy event. Colleen sailed to America on SS *Mariposa* in June 1946, along with 500 other war brides and their children. She did not dwell on negative thoughts about what lay ahead, and had no fear of the long journey to a country about which she knew very little. She says:

> *I had no thoughts about it at all except that I was going to be with my husband. You know, I'd follow him anywhere no matter what – it didn't matter where it was, that was it! That's where I was at 18 you know, I was very young. I don't think my mother was very happy about it, but she accepted it. You know…in my family, the woman went with the man. That was it. It was the 1940s!* [6]

In some respects, the experiences of Australian war brides as immigrants to a new country were similar to those of other war brides and post-war migrants, but the Australian women were a unique group of 'aliens' in that special factors differentiated them from other female migrants. They came from a country not pillaged by war; they spoke the English language; subsequently they were not so visible as 'foreigners' as were European or Asian migrants; and cultural differences were not as major as for migrants from non-English speaking countries. Nevertheless, there was a general undercurrent of antagonism in American society towards war brides.[7]

The expectations of most Australian war brides as they journeyed to the United States were uncertain, none being quite sure exactly what lay ahead for them in the new country.

In contrast to the experience of war brides from Europe, Australian war brides were dominated by a strong 'pull' factor. This was manifested in their longing for what they hoped would be a happy reunion with their husbands, who were, in many cases, already fathers of their children. Australian war brides were also keen to make a success of their marriages which were often only half-heartedly sanctioned by their parents, who foresaw some of the difficulties they might face so far away from home, without Australian family support. Added to these factors, was also the enticement of a sense of adventure for young women who had never travelled beyond Australia's shores.

American society at the end of the War

Adjustment to life in a new country was challenging for all war brides. American society had been transformed during the decade of the 1940s, which began with one third of the nation being 'ill-housed, ill-clothed and ill-fed' with one out of four American workers unemployed.[8] By the end of the decade the American society and economy had benefited enormously from the war industry and the economy began to prosper. By 1947, with post-war recovery in full swing, the United States had become the world's leader in aviation, chemical engineering and electronics. It produced 57 per cent of the world's steel, 43 per cent of its electricity, 62 per cent of its oil and it manufactured more than 80 per cent of the world's automobiles.[9]

Despite the new prosperity which was spreading across America at this time, the Australian war brides found challenges in settling into their new lives, some finding it more difficult than others. This was dependent upon a variety of factors.

Initially, these reflected the ease with which these young women adjusted to changes in the physical landscape; the climate and the locations of their destinations; relationships with their in-laws; the severe shortage of housing; their financial situation; instances of prejudice they encountered; cultural differences and problems which presented themselves in seemingly simple matters, such as handling the new currency and shopping. Adjusting to cultural and environmental change was an additional pressure placed on these women who were also dealing with the intricacies of setting up a new life with their husbands, and in many cases learning to live with their in-laws.

At the end of the war, in America, there was concern about the noticeable increase in the number of middle-aged women seeking advice on how to prevent the break-up of their marriages of many years standing. The city of Los Angeles, it was reported in the press, had 'one of the highest divorce rates in the world, with almost one-half of all marriages ending either in divorce or separation'.[10] An organisation called the 'American Institute of Family Relations' was promoted as 'a school for brides' where 'girls learn to be good wives'.[11] This Institute also offered pre-marital courses for men on how to be 'happy though married' and also covered problems that a young wife might encounter in the early years of her marriage, even 'the perennial problem of mothers-in-law'.[12] The pre-marital course was open to both men and women. Returned soldiers, who were married and finding it difficult to readjust to domestic life, were encouraged to attend a course for counselling. The institute also offered its services as a mediator in attempting to reconcile estranged couples.[13] Such concentration on saving American marriages indicates that social readjustment was difficult in the post-war years, even for American couples. Given this state of affairs, it was not surprising that there was an undercurrent of antagonism towards the war brides from other countries, including Australian wives, who were seen to be taking men away from American women.

Cultural Change

Many of the war brides found themselves living in US locations quite different to their home towns in Australia. This was not necessarily a negative experience. Billie Ringen, for example, found the cultural differences to be of great interest to her. Her father was a forestry foreman and, until she was 13, the family lived in the New South Wales timber-town of Tenterfield, forty-one miles from the nearest town. Billie received her education via correspondence classes until she went to high school in Armidale. She recalls:

> *When I graduated from high school…I just wanted to go to the city so badly, you know, the bright lights…we had grown up in a small town and had never been exposed to all the things city people were exposed to.*[14]

In America, however, Billie settled with her husband in the small town of Billings in the wide open spaces of Montana. Despite this not providing the 'bright lights' of the city, she found it an interesting place, although quite different from her Australian home-town. Her in-laws lived in the city of Montana which she describes as:

> *An old country and western cowboy town – it was big hats, boots, the whole bit – that's exactly how they dressed and that was very interesting to me. There were rodeos, and it was real country.*[15]

Similarly, Patricia Law from suburban Sydney was also interested in the cultural differences she was presented with in Casa Grande, Arizona, a small town of 6,000 people. There were extremes of climate in the desert, from the intense heat of summer to extreme cold in winter, and she found that social life in the little town was very different to the social entertainments of Sydney. Describing the countryside as 'cowboy country' where 'the men like to dress western', Patricia recalls: 'we went to rodeos and the American football games.' Although she had been used to frequenting beaches, theatre and musicals in Australia, and missed these forms of entertainment, in America her husband used to take her driving to some historical or scenic area every weekend.[16] She remembers:

> *I was interested in the Indians. I had never seen or heard anything about them in my own life, and we were near a big Indian reservation. People in town thought I was kind of silly, but when they [the Indians] had their get-togethers, I said 'I want to go and watch'.*[17]

Patricia and her husband 'watched them do that little shuffle dance and have their own food and they didn't mind us watching'. She says: 'I didn't photograph or anything, I just watched with interest.'[18]

Some war brides had to adjust to extreme cultural conditions in very unusual locations. For example, Iris Craig found herself living on Alcatraz Island, which was home to some of the worst criminals in America. About a year after Iris' arrival in America, her husband Jim applied for a job as a correctional officer at the prison. Although there were apartments on the island, none were available at the time. Iris had to wait with Erin and her new baby son, Terrence, until one became vacant so she could join her husband.

Access to the island was on a small boat that took people back and forth, and any visitors had to be identified before they could land on the island. Iris comments: 'I didn't have very much social life there'. But she found living on the island quite interesting:

> *Once a week, one of the inmates would come with a guard to collect your laundry. Of course, you wouldn't see it for another*

week, so you had to be careful what you sent away. If there was
any work that had to be done in your apartment, one of the
convicts would come and do it, also with a guard.[19]

On one occasion, when such an inmate left her apartment, Iris
commented to her husband that 'he seemed quite pleasant'. Her
husband responded: 'He's in here for life, he's a murderer!' Iris
remembers:

> *You couldn't put any razorblades or anything sharp in the*
> *garbage because it was collected by the prisoners.*[20]

There was a playground for the children, with a small sand box,
otherwise it was all concrete. At certain times of the day when the
prisoners were let out in their yard, Iris and the children could not
appear, and they were not allowed to wear shorts at any time on the
island. After seventeen months on Alcatraz, Jim applied for a job
with the Border Control and the family moved to Imperial Valley,
where Jim worked on the Calexico-Mexicali border.

Iris Craig and daughter Erin adjusting
to life on Alcatraz Island, CA, c.1947.

Learning new ways

The majority of Australian marriages to American servicemen were happy and successful, but every Australian WWII war bride who relocated her life across the Pacific had to adjust to differences, both large and small. Among the challenges they faced were some seemingly routine matters: shopping; food preparation and cooking; using the US currency, and understanding the idiosyncrasies of language as spoken in America, as well as its ambiguities.

Shopping posed some challenges for these newcomers to the post-war American cities and suburbs, which saw the emergence of large urban and suburban shopping centres and malls with large car parks and an abundance of goods. Following the shortages during WWII, Americans were enthusiastic shoppers, and modern supermarkets sprang up across the United States to accommodate increased consumerism, their numbers doubling between 1948 and 1958. New multi-lane highways carried huge numbers of vehicles to the car parks at these retail centres, and from 1945 to 1955 the number of cars on the road also doubled.[21]

Immediately post-war, however, not all people were fortunate enough to own cars. Australian war bride, Barbara Gleason, settled with her husband and small daughter in Monterey, California, at the end of 1945. She had no car to take her shopping and she found travel by public transport, as well as the shopping itself, presented difficulties. At first, Barbara was unfamiliar with the American coinage and had trouble paying for her ticket on the bus. She recalls: 'I had nickels in my hand, and I said "How much?"'. Seeing her confusion, the bus driver pointed and said 'One of those!' Barbara was embarrassed because she 'didn't know a dime from a nickel or a quarter', so her husband sat with her that night and helped her to understand the currency. At the shop Barbara had difficulties being understood. She remembers wanting to buy some face-cloths:

> I went all over that town, and with my accent I was calling them "fayce" cloths, and they didn't know what I was talking about. So I just gave up!'[22]

Barbara also had trouble with American terminology for common grocery items. She tells how she 'never had cornflour in the house', because no-one knew what she was talking about. Then, she met an Australian woman, who told her 'If you want to buy cornflour, you will have to ask for corn starch!' Barbara found American food was very rich and difficult to get used to. Even on board the ship she had found the bread to be very rich, and there were too many 'sweets with the salads'. Despite being 'bothered' by the richness of the American food, she did learn to cook 'American' style. While she refrains from joining him, her husband still enjoys eating eggs and bacon with maple syrup.[24]

When shopping, war bride Jean Vallero (née Anderson), who grew up in Banyo, a small suburb of Brisbane, remembers having to pay additional tax on purchases. She recalls:

> *I got tripped up with that several times, because the price on the thing is not what you pay. You know, you pay it plus tax! That really threw me for a loop and we had so little money.*[25]

Similarly, Irene Perucci remembers some of the adjustments she had to make when she first arrived in America. She went shopping to buy a swede, and the shop assistant had never heard of such a thing and asked 'what does it look like?' Irene tells how she walked all the way down the vegetable aisle and said 'Oh, here it is, right here!' Irene found that the humble 'swede' was called a 'Rudibaker' in America.[26]

Such difficulties encountered by war brides, though seemingly trivial, had an impact on these new arrivals, all of whom were keen to prove themselves competent in their new roles as wives and mothers. Their inability to handle these 'everyday' tasks with ease undermined their self-confidence and added to any sense of insecurity they had in starting a new way of life in a new country.

Betty Blondon initially lived with her husband in a cottage adjoining her in-laws house in Palm Springs, California. She too had difficulties when shopping, and recalls a trip to the butcher's section of the supermarket. She asked for 'a pound of mince' and was directed to a counter where there was sweet 'mince-meat' in a jar. She discovered that in Australia meat is 'minced', whereas in the United States it is 'ground'. To confuse matters more, Betty says, in the US, 'ground beef' is referred to as 'hamburger'. She comments: 'there were lots of little things like that', such as her 'favourite rock melon' being called 'cantaloupe', to which she had to adjust. She remembers a trip to 'the Five and Dime' to buy some cotton to mend something. She discovered that 'cotton' is called 'thread' in American, whereas 'cotton-wool' is referred to as 'cotton'. Betty found these small differences very frustrating at a time when she was feeling a little isolated, and was endeavouring to settle into her new married life.[27] Betty recalls:

> *[I was] trying to live with my husband again – we didn't get along off and on you know – I was ready to go home about three times. It wasn't easy at first. It took me a while to get to understand his ways. He was quiet and always kept everything inside, and I was an outward person and had so many relatives and friends, that being by myself and not knowing anybody was hard.*[28]

Ambiguities in the language were also a source of frustration. Often an Australian expression had a very different meaning when used in America. Betty remembers:

> *I'm afraid I would hear something and my Aussie blood would boil – then I'd think, 'No that's not how they're thinking!' Sometimes I would say something and the Americans would look at me with great big startled eyes as much as to say 'What is this?'*[29]

For example, Betty tells how a lot of people used to compliment her small daughter, who was 'very beautiful when she was little with her big blue eyes and golden curls'. She recalls:

> *They would come up – especially the men – and they would*
> *pat her on the head and say 'What a cute little "booger"!'*
> *Well, that was too close to…an awful cuss word to me, and*
> *I'd shy back.*[30]

It was 'just little things like that' which were difficult at first, but Betty gradually became accustomed to the differences.

As well as the ambiguities of language, the variation in accents also caused problems with communication. Irene Franck remembers how people were not used to the Australian accent (which she had acquired after coming to Perth from Shanghai as a young girl) and they would look at her strangely. She explains: 'I had just started to acquire an Australian accent' and she found many words were pronounced differently in America, such as aluminium pronounced 'al-OOM-inum' instead of 'al-yoo-MINium'; 'zee' instead of 'zed'; and 'tom-ATE-oes instead of 'tom-ART-oes'. Irene was pregnant at the time and living with her in-laws, so she didn't have much social contact with people to practice these differences in language. She was not feeling very happy as her husband was still away on service and, as she explains, she was 'getting bigger by the minute'. When her husband finally arrived back home, his initial reaction to her did not help to make her feel more secure. She recalls:

> *My husband got off the plane – he said he almost got back*
> *on again. He couldn't believe I could have swelled up that*
> *much in nine months!* [31]

American accents were also a challenge. Valda Hertzberg settled in Philadelphia, Pennsylvania in 1946, at a time when many black Americans were migrating north from the southern states. Valda employed a woman as housemaid and subsequently had terrible difficulty in understanding the woman's southern accent. On the other hand, the housemaid could not make sense of Valda's Australian accent and communication between the two was fraught with difficulty.[32]

Some war brides had problems with other aspects of life in America. Marge Andreatta, for instance, had no trouble dealing with the new currency which she 'learned very quickly'. Neither did she have any difficulty with language and communication. The only problem she encountered was walking on the other side of the street, which really troubled her. She says she still has problems with this even now, and she comments:

> I can be walking down Market Street in San Francisco…
> on the left side, and people are bumping into me and I'm
> thinking 'What's the matter with these stupid people?' Then
> I realise that it's me and not them.[33]

Similarly she used to climb the stairs at work on the left hand side and 'invariably would bump into somebody'. As Marge observes, it was fortunate that she did not drive in those days. Betty Blondon also initially had problems with the traffic driving 'on the wrong side of the road' which she found frightening.[34] These numerous, and seemingly small, differences in their new way of life in a new country initially added to a sense of dislocation for many of the war brides as they settled into their new environment.

Stepping into a domestic role

The role into which the war brides were expected to fit on their arrival in America was also something to which women in Australia had to adjust in the immediate post war years, when there was an exaggerated emphasis on family life, a legacy of the wartime experience.[35] This gave the impression of peace and conformity, and the media image of American women in the 1950s saw them in the home and raising a family, impressions which were reinforced by popular TV sitcoms and hit records of the day. In reality, however, the fifties in America foreshadowed great social and cultural changes, with increasing numbers of women joining the workforce.[36] The participation rate for married women in America jumped from 16.7 per cent in 1940 to 24.8 per cent in 1950 and 31.7 per cent in 1960.[37]

Australian war brides, however, on arrival in America were initially expected by their husbands and in-laws to step into a domestic role of wife and mother, and as new brides of American servicemen, these young women had little choice. Their official status was that of *alien* residents until they became naturalised US citizens, this not being possible for a minimum of twelve months after arrival. This factor, along with the responsibilities of motherhood, necessitated a domestic role with traditional female duties at home, caring for small children.

In the early years for most of these women, joining the workforce was not an option, although some had already been part of the workforce in both voluntary and paid capacities in Australia. Many of these young women had not long finished school, and often had very little experience of household tasks in the kitchen and laundry. Consequently, they often accepted the help of their mothers-in-law to teach them how to keep house and cook for their new husbands.

War bride Norma Rehrer first settled with her husband in the small town of Sedaya, Missouri. She admits that she 'couldn't cook' and was 'in trouble' with her lack of culinary skills soon after she arrived in America. She used to go to a small grocery store in town where they would help plan her meals. She laughs as she recalls, in her small rural home-town of Winton in Queensland, how she had been used to her mother or father killing a hen or a rooster. She remembers how 'they'd pluck it and clean it and take the insides out'. In her new home in America she recalls:

> *I had company one night and I started to cook, and Gene,*
> *my husband, said 'where's the gizzard and the heart?'*

> *Fortunately, he came to the rescue and removed the innards*
> *from the chicken before it went into the oven.*[38]

Dorothy Thompson's husband was from a Norwegian immigrant family and her mother-in-law, who was possessive and did not allow her much freedom, was keen for Dorothy to cook in the same way that she cooked for the family. Dorothy was shown how to make Scandinavian breads and all sorts of dishes which were quite new to her. Fifty years later, she still enjoys making these recipes, using the culinary skills learnt from her mother-in-law.

Education

Education burgeoned in the United States in the immediate post-war years. Under the *Servicemen's Readjustment Act,* known as the 'GI Bill', veterans returning to civilian life could attend college, with the cost of tuition covered by the government. They were also entitled to supplements if they were married and had families, and subsequently this saw a decrease in women's college attendance. At the same time, public school enrolments grew, increasing from about 29 million in 1950 to over 40 million at the end of the decade.[39]

Keen to obtain a good education for their children, many Australian war brides took an active part in their school communities, which helped them to make friends and fit more easily into their new home towns. Betty Blondon and her husband had four children and she comments that she became a volunteer at the school her children attended, where she enjoyed the interaction with other parents and found it 'very nice making friends'.[40]

When her children were in high school, Peggy Dunbar Blackman was involved in a program at the school which helped students to apply to study abroad, and she instructed the students who came from abroad. She was then 'lucky enough to land a job' at California University in Sacramento in the International Centre where Peggy worked for fifteen years. She says:

I was paid to do what I had been doing as a volunteer. It was the perfect 'job-fit' in that I was right for it and it was right for me. I consider myself a very fortunate woman.[41]

Once their children were grown up and at school, many war brides stepped out of the home and went to work or looked to further their own education. Betty Blondon took the opportunity to go to college

Peggy Dunbar Blackman, Sacramento, CA, 29 September, 2001.

herself for two years, to study early childhood education and library science with the aim of working in a library. However, due to the introduction of a tax initiative in California, known as 'Proposition 13',[42] she says:

Instead of hiring they were firing, so I never got on. So I stayed with the school as an instructional aid doing the lower fifty per cent – the lower achievers – helping the teacher out after she had already given the main class-work. I was there for eighteen years and I enjoyed it.[43]

Ambassadors for Australia

In their enthusiasm to share their knowledge of their homeland with Americans, who knew little about Australia, many war brides were happy to give talks at schools and group meetings. Before leaving for America to marry her American fiancé, Joy Parker was a popular member of staff at David Jones' department store in Sydney for over six years. She worked in the Active Sportswear Department and was promoted to head of the Cole of California swimsuit section in 1946,[44] when California Productions Pty Ltd. promoted 'American

"Chic" for Australia'.[45] Joy's work, selling Australian women the stylish beach clothes and playsuits 'worn by their Californian sisters',

saw the early beginnings of her future relationship with America.[46] The store newsletter was proud to announce in July 1947 that Joy, who had married Dr Lloyd Shaddle three months earlier, 'is the only Australian girl to make her home in Forrest', Illinois.[47]

The paper reported that Mrs Shaddle 'has become quite a personality in Forrest', already having contributed an article to *The Forrest News* about her

Lloyd and Joy Shaddle settled in Forrest, Illinois.

sea voyage from Australia, and had photographs of her New York wedding published in *The Fairbury Blade*.[48] Already involved as an enthusiastic ambassador for Australia, Joy was reported to have 'addressed the Forrest Chapter of the Future Homemakers of America'.[49] She was asked to give talks on Australia at various clubs and also in local schools. She says that 'within two years I'd given a hundred talks on Australia'. Surprised that Americans seemed to know little about Australia, Joy states that after her efforts she feels that 'they know about Australia now!' And almost 60 years later, the schools still invite her to talk about

Joy Shaddle with her children in Forrest, Illinois, c.1953.

Australia. Always enthusiastic to showcase the country of her birth, Joy still loves to tell the younger children about the pet kangaroo she used to have in Sydney, and of the meaning of words like 'koala'.[50]

War bride Valda Hertzberg was one of two daughters of Jewish parents, her mother having been born in England and her father in Palestine. Valda's mother had been an opera singer and pianist in Melbourne and her father was in the wool business. After finishing high school, Valda was among the few war brides in this book who went to university in Australia. Although she did not complete the course, after her marriage to Harold – a radiologist – and coming to America, Valda says:

> *I did very many more courses in the United States – from anthropology to nineteenth century music.*[51]

Valda settled in Philadelphia, Pennsylvania, and from the early days she contributed her knowledge and skills in a voluntary capacity, speaking in different forums and fostering good relations between Australians and Americans.

Clubs, church and community activities

Valda was involved with was the founding of an Australian Women's Club in Philadelphia. She saw the need for such an organisation and recalls:

> *The purpose really, for people like myself, was to show that war brides weren't just 'silly little bits'.*[52]

She was very impressed by some of the young Australian women who were gathered into this club and she took delight in observing them.

> *The development of some of these kids from quarter-horse towns up in Queensland... was superb.*[53]

She also became part of an international organisation, the American Jewish Congress, as well as the League of Women Voters in Philadelphia, and is proud to have been part of a Reform group of Jewish people. Valda was very active in these organisations and says, 'right away I started doing things', always supported by her husband who she says 'encouraged me to be the person I am'.[54]

Valda was very much welcomed as an Australian in the community and 'given special treatment'. She was invited to speak to different groups informing them about Australia, which in those days 'was quite novel'. One of these groups was the Knights of Columbus, a very big Catholic organisation, and she also spoke to university women's groups and school groups, her audiences initially knowing very little about Australia.[55]

Valda Hertsberg, Darling Point,
Sydney, May 2007 (Aged 90).

In such diverse ways, formally and informally, many Australian WWII war brides were great ambassadors for Australia. By informing Americans about the country of their birth, they encouraged interest in and understanding of Australia and its people, its flora and fauna. Such activities helped to foster goodwill between the people of the two countries.

Edna Pickerel, known as Teddy, says:

All my life has been spent here [in America] – it's just that the foundation was laid there [in Australia]'. [56]

Teddy settled in Salem, Oregon, which like her original home town, also happened to be a timber town. Early after her arrival, she saw the need for an organisation to cater for war brides like herself from Australia, New Zealand, and other countries who had moved to the area, to prevent them feeling isolated and to help them adjust to life in America. Teddy was one of the founders of the Accent Club which welcomed war brides 'from all over', including members who came from England and Scotland. Teddy recalls, 'as time went on, while I still liked the girls, I felt I had outgrown it' and although she didn't remain an active member of the Club, she still meets with 'the old-timers' about once a year.[57] Teddy points out:

The Club still exists, but in more recent years it has been taken over by younger foreign women who married Americans abroad and they are now mostly Europeans. [58]

Teddy took advantage of living near Chemeketa Community College in Salem, Oregon, and enrolled in computer courses, as well as typewriting and history classes. She was also involved in a number of academic and political communities. However, more recently her involvement with the local Anglican Church has taken up most of her time. She relates:

Edna (Teddy) Pickerel (née Love)
Salem, OR, September, 2001.

The biggest part of my life is involved with my church…my daughter is now fifty-five and she was twelve when she was confirmed, so it's been close to forty-five years at this one church, St Timothy's. My close-knit group of friends are people I have known

for twenty, thirty or forty years at the church and especially now,
as all of us are single, either divorced or widows, we have been
family to each other…just like an extension of the family, and it
has been a very, very important part of my life.[59]

Like many Australian war brides, Teddy was a regular Sunday
school pupil during her childhood, religion was important in her
upbringing, and she is an active member of the church community
in Salem, Oregon. Teddy has been involved with the Episcopal
Church Women (ECW) and has run bazaars, worked on the Altar
Guild, and was also an active lector, an acolyte and chalice bearer as
well as an usher. She says:

I even high-flipped pancakes on Pancake Tuesday and I
turned chicken at the barbecue…the kind of things you do
when you belong to a church.[60]

Teddy admits she likes to keep busy, but she also values her private
time and is very happy to be by herself some of the time.[61]

Still active at over 80 years of age, Norma Rehrer also volunteers
with the Episcopal Church Women's group at the local church in
Sacramento, California. At the time of this interview she was looking
forward to the rummage sale the next week. She says:

We work every day and then on Friday we set up, and on
Saturday we sell. We have a rummage sale every six months.[62]

Norma also enjoys working in a voluntary capacity as 'server' (a 'more
polite word for "waitress"' she explains) at a local community restaurant
where she has been working for the last 27 years. She says modestly:

I work at the Casa Garden Restaurant and all our money
goes to the Sacramento Children's Home…officially I work

twice a month – but I fill in and then I work special events.
We have weddings and anniversaries and retirement parties
and I work when I'm needed.[63]

The restaurant, which is open to the public five days a week, is staffed by volunteer gardeners, cooks, servers, kitchen help and cashiers. It serves 'a lot of different chicken dishes and pork and kebabs…and scrumptious desserts'. Wearing a smart green dress and a plaid apron for work in the restaurant, Norma says that more recently, since her knee operation, she works in the pantry, which she also enjoys.[64]

Involvement in community work, through church and educational activities, was and still is a common activity of many war brides. Clearly, they have embraced their new land of adoption and consider themselves an integral part of their local communities where, after 60 years, they continue to participate in activities with energy and enthusiasm. In this way, the war brides are able to 'give back' some of the goodwill and kindness they themselves acknowledge they have received from their local communities over the years.

Norma Rehrer, Sacramento, CA, September, 2001.

Not all Australian war brides chose to join the workforce after they settled in America. Some remained at home, reflecting the trend in both Australia and America for women to return to the home after the war, where they were fully occupied looking after the home and raising children. Joann Patterson, for instance, says that she and her husband did not feel the need for her to go out to work. She says:

We weren't too much into the second car, boat, or big house. We mainly liked to travel which we did with all five of the children.[65]

In America, Cynthia Peter, while being competent at office work, chose not to go out to work. She had left school in Australia at fourteen years of age, completed a business college course, and had her first job at sixteen. She worked in an insurance company and a lawyer's office, and then worked for the Red Cross in the Sydney office. However, after settling in America, Cynthia had four children and although she chose not do paid work outside the house, she says:

I worked hard at home...I sewed for the children, I made shirts for the boys, gave them haircuts, and made little dresses for my daughter.[66]

Joining the paid workforce

While the general expectation seemed to be for the young Australian wives to fulfil a domestic role, almost half those interviewed did take up paid work after their children were a little older. Those who joined the workforce were represented in many fields of business over the years.

When Hazel Walker arrived in the US she lived with Eddie's oldest brother and his wife and family in Chicago until Eddie came home on leave. Eddie was appointed to the Recruiting Office in Danville, Illinois, about 150 miles south of Chicago, and after living for six weeks in a room, the couple found a three-room house just off the edge of town where they lived for three years. Hazel remembers:

We had a pot-bellied coal-fired furnace sitting in the middle of the kitchen to keep us warm, and a well in the back yard with a pump on the draining board of the sink to get water into the house. We had a regular 'dunny' – an outdoor toilet – in the back yard. There was no hot water and we took baths in a big tin 'tub'. At least we had electricity.[67]

Hazel says that they were lucky to be able to find that house to buy, because 'there were just no houses to rent or for sale' when the Army moved them there. She comments:

> *It certainly was a change after having left Brisbane where we lived in a Queenslander house with three bedrooms, a front and side verandah, hot and cold running water, a full bathroom and a flushing toilet connected to the city sewer.*[68]

Hazel soon found employment at an automobile dealership where she worked in the Accounts Department. A very active person, she also found time to take part in social activities and joined the Fine Arts Society and sang in the choir of the local Musical Society. Eddie called Square Dances for the City and also for a Square Dance Club at which Hazel loved to dance.

Hazel and Eddie Walker enjoyed square dancing in Danville, Illinois, 1940s.

It was in 1951, when Eddie was transferred to Luke Air Force Base in Phoenix, Arizona that Hazel felt more settled. She remembers:

> *From then on, I was part of the Air Force family and I began to feel that I belonged.*[69]

Eddie was transferred after two years to Perrin Air Force Base in Texas where the couple lived for seven years, followed by another move to Okinawa, Japan, at Kadena Air Base. After another two years there, they moved to Shaw Air Force Base in Sumter, South Carolina, from where Eddie retired and the couple went back to Australia to live.

During the 1940s in Australia, Shirley Norton had worked for the US Army at General MacArthur's headquarters. Tragically, her husband was killed in the Korean War in 1951, when she had only been in America for five years. So, as a

mother of four young children – the oldest under six years of age – she worked part-time to support the family. When her mother-in-law came to live with them in 1956, Shirley was then able to work full time. Her first job was with the government at the Naval Air Station in Maine in 1957, where she had a responsible position in control of the budget for the whole station where young men were recruited to enlist in the Air Force.[70]

Shirley Norton's children in 1954.

Sunny Sansing, who had been a Signaller in the Australian Air Force, was also widowed. As a ranking officer's wife she had travelled all over the world and says: 'I was very fortunate in that my husband was an officer, so I had privileges that I would normally not have had…I've lived a good life'. She tells how 'the only bad thing that has happened to me is that my husband died in 1970 and unfortunately, he died on my birthday'. Sunny's husband had been flying in and out of Vietnam on a C-47, in an unarmed aircraft, when he was totally disabled. It was two years after he came back from South East Asia that he died. Sunny says:

> *I've never married again, I've just gone on. I'm a firm believer in 'life is what you make of it', and I think that most Australians are that way. We make what we can of it – the very best of it. I think we are a very independent type.*[71]

Because of a severe back problem, Sunny was advised to take up 'belly dancing' for remedial purposes, and soon began creating costumes for her and for other dancers to wear. She proved to be an impressive and creative seamstress and designer, and before long was fashioning her own line of lingerie which was modelled at some of the best hotels. In this way, Sunny was able to make an income for herself while she reared her small son, showing both independence and initiative.[72]

Some war brides found suitable work in the growing retail sector in post-war America. Betty Paukovitz of San Diego joined the workforce and her main occupation in America was as retail manager for a large chain of department stores, now taken over by Macy's.[73]

Soon after her arrival in America, Rosemary Smith worked at a department store selling toys and found 'it was fun'. She says: 'I saved my money and then I went home for Christmas of 1948… to make sure I was doing the right thing' by moving to America. Since her return she says: 'I've had fantastic jobs'. Rosemary then became a buyer of lingerie for a department store, and later went into telephone communications, which she loved. After she was widowed prematurely, she recalls:

> I went to school and became an engineer. It takes a lot of work, but you know when something happens like that, it's funny how you dig in because you need something.[74]

Jean Wilk, now a proud mother of seven, a grandmother of twenty-one and great-grandmother of sixteen, originally grew up in Western Australia. After leaving school at about 15 years of age she worked as a waitress and then in a Kodak camera store, before joining the Women's Australian Auxiliary Navy as a signaller on Rottnest Island. Now a resident of Mt Pleasant, near Chicago, Jean is still in the workforce at 83 years of age. A merchandiser at a discount store, Jean works 10 hours a week, putting out stock and doing display work. She says with pride:

> *I've worked part-time for the last 25 years. I had so many grand-children that I worked so that I could buy presents – and I still do! I was going to quit at 75, then 80, and this Christmas for sure. But then I thought, if I quit work I will miss it, and they are such a nice bunch of people, mostly women.*[75]

Jean Wilk visiting the signal station at Rottnest Island in 2006.

Other war brides studied to improve their work opportunities. Once in America, Joyce Olguin, who left school at an early age in

Australia, went to night school twice a week to get a high school diploma before going to real estate school. She worked in real estate for many years, before becoming a notary in public works, work which she still does.[76]

Joyce Olguin, Garden Grove, September, 2001.

Billie Ringen trained as a Secretary in Brisbane and joined the Australian Air Force where her job was general office work which she really enjoyed. In America, this training stood her in good stead for obtaining work in a variety of offices doing secretarial work.[77]

Despite most war brides now being in their eighties and early nineties, their enthusiastic and conscientious attitude to work, both paid and voluntary, continues to survive. It points to the fact that these women, of a particular generation who grew up in Australia during the difficult years of the Depression and WWII, see the importance of contributing positively to their communities in various ways, and many did join the workforce after some years, thus fully embracing the new country in which they have chosen to live.

Unhappy marriages

Living in America, adjustment to marriage was difficult for some Australian war brides who found themselves in quite alien circumstances, sometimes living in conditions inferior to standards they were used to in Australia. Also, in some cases the man they had fallen in love with and married in wartime turned out to be quite different when back in his home-town. Among 60 war brides interviewed, there were six divorces (10%), but usually the couples stayed together until the children were older. Although the majority of those interviewed professed to have had happy marriages, it is difficult to know how many made compromises over the years.

When Betty McIntire arrived in America in 1946, she already had misgivings about her uncertain future, as her husband's letters to her had become infrequent. Lester was known as 'Mac' in Australia, and 'Bud' by his friends back in his home town of Green River, Wyoming, which proved to be indicative of his seemingly dual personality. Betty loved her husband, but struggled for many years with his addiction to alcohol, which dramatically affected their marriage and made it very difficult to maintain. Finally, after her husband threatened her with a gun following a drinking binge, she made the decision to divorce him and moved in 1966, with her teenage children, to Anchorage, Alaska. Here Betty showed great resilience in the face of adversity. She successfully sought employment and worked with the same company for many years. She

enjoyed social activities, especially 'clog-dancing', and in 1997 when she
was in her late 70s, she proudly won the title of 'Miss Senior Alaska'.[78]

Betty McIntire, Denver,
CO, September, 2001

One of the most destructive forces
in the GI marriages was alcohol,
and American servicemen, who
became addicted during the war,
often continued the habit when
they returned to civilian life.[79] In a
study of trauma and grief in post-
war Australia, the author observes:

*In dealing with painful memories of anguish, 'the war'
served to legitimise some men's erratic and unstable
behaviour and provide a coherent narrative through which
to explain why women remained in marriages that were
themselves traumatic.*[80]

This explanation can partially provide an answer in the case of Australian
war brides in America who stayed in unhappy marriages for some
time. However, the absence of extended family support restricted their
options in this regard, especially in times of marriage breakdown. Lack
of any welfare provision for abandoned wives and children also made it
impossible for unhappy war brides to leave their husbands.

Archival records show that there were some cases of rapid marriage
break-down when young brides arrived in America to find that they
were no longer wanted by their husbands who had already formed new
relationships. The Australian Department of Immigration received
frequent applications from unhappy wives of both British and Allied ex-
Servicemen, and sometimes from their mothers, for government assistance
for repatriation to Australia. In America, finding themselves friendless

and without financial support, these women sought help because of 'ill-treatment, habitual drunkenness, infidelity, or failure to support'.[81]

The large majority of the war brides interviewed, however, had lasting and successful marriages, this being influenced by a number of different factors. The war brides were stateless and treated as aliens in America, until they became naturalised US citizens, at which time they had to automatically forfeit their Australian citizenship. This legislation made it difficult for any Australian wife, when feelings of homesickness were most acute in the initial years of residence, to suddenly leave her marriage and go back home. The additional complication of raising small children in the first years of marriage, combined with the cost of travel back to Australia, also made this option impossible for many couples. Not all women had the blessing of their parents when they married and sailed for America; others were cautioned by their parents that life may not be easy for them, creating an expectation of possible marriage failure. The war brides' strong desire, in the face of any opposition, to make a success of their marriage gave them strength in the early years to fight homesickness and feelings of alienation, and to show that they had made the right choice of a marriage partner. Because of difficulties in settling due to homesickness, acculturation, and financial worries, the war brides no doubt had to make some compromises along the way.

A small proportion of war brides, however, did return to Australia after a short time in America. The press reported as early as 1945 that more than 50 Australian brides of American servicemen had returned to Brisbane on SS *Matsonia,* including divorcees, widows, and those who were 'fed up', who claimed that American women resented them for taking their men, that the pace of life was too fast and the cost of living too high.[82] In 1948, it was reported that 100 Australian war brides had returned to Australia, mostly with husbands and children, on SS *Marine Phoenix.*[83] They claimed that the cost of living in America made it impossible for families on a small wage, and that 'it was just one long scramble to make ends meet'.[84]

Betty Kane was one of these war brides returning to Australia on SS *Marine Phoenix* with her husband and two children in 1948.

After three years in America, Betty was inconsolably homesick and the family returned to settle in Albany, Western Australia, where they lived for 18 years before returning to the US in 1967, as Bob wanted his teenage children to see life in America. Nine years later, the family once more returned to resettle permanently in Albany.[85]

In the case of Betty de St Germain, who happily settled with her husband Ray in New Orleans, Louisiana, it was an unexpected rattlesnake bite that sent her home to her family. Pregnant with her first child, Betty was walking in the woods in Ponchatoula to pick some muskadines (a species of wild grapes) when she accidently stepped on the 'rattler', which bit her on the ankle. The nearby hospital carried anti-venom and Betty was lucky to survive. In excruciating pain and with 'a leg the size of an elephant', she could do very little for herself. Her husband had to give up work to care for her as she was sick all through her pregnancy, but her tiny baby girl was born healthy. The couple decided to return to Australia where Betty's mother could help with the baby, who was five months old by the time they sailed on SS *Marine Phoenix*. Betty's father arranged a job for Ray and although Betty had 'fully intended to stay in America', the couple settled permanently in Australia.

During the difficult early years in America, the war brides made efforts to meet the various challenges which confronted them and many became involved in their children's schools and various community activities. Most did not have the opportunity to return to Australia for many more years and had to make the best of the situations in which they found themselves.

Homesickness

Far away from Australian family and friends, homesickness was a major factor which impacted the lives of many, if not all, war brides to some extent. On holidays and other special occasions, homesickness was most acute. Betty Stites tells of one Christmas when her husband had been on duty for three or four days and she and her two sons were at home alone:

It was Christmas and the boys were looking out the window and everyone else's grandpas were coming to visit them for Christmas...the three of us were sitting, crying, [and] homesick. I'll always remember that Christmas. Lee was on duty until late at night.[86]

The loneliness and absence of family members was made worse for Betty who had been the target of nasty comments from the lady who lived downstairs who reproached her for 'coming over from Australia and taking our beautiful young men, when we've got lovely girls here!' Betty felt alone in her new surroundings and recalls:

She was always saying things like that to me, and not having a soul to talk to – an older person you know – it was very difficult.[87]

For many war brides, the separation from their Australian families was very distressing. In the early years, it was only the fact that the war brides now had children from their marriage to an American husband that kept some women from attempting to return permanently to their homeland.

Originally a Melbourne girl, Allie Rudy, suffered terrible homesickness. She reveals that: 'If I hadn't had children, I would have packed up and gone home. That's where my family is, you know, my roots are there.'[88] After living in America for more than 60 years, she can still experience real pangs of homesickness. Allie tells how she attended a reunion of WWII war brides in Denver, Colorado in 2001, and on meeting another Australian woman from Melbourne she says:

We started to talk and she began to cry - it's a feeling of belonging – she felt very homesick – and of course I started to get the feeling too.[89]

Allie was amazed that she could still feel that way so many years after her initial sad farewell to her mother. She tells how the memories of her mother and the family atmosphere still tug at her heart, causing her to revisit feelings of homesickness even after all these years. The strong bond between mother and daughter is again highlighted here, and for many of these women this was a significant factor affecting the intensity of the homesickness they suffered.

The stories of the Australian WWII war brides reveal that homesickness was a most powerful emotion. The stress of trying to overcome this condition, and their stoic efforts to hide it, sometimes manifested in physical symptoms causing them great distress. Homesickness, not always visible to the naked eye, affected most war brides to some degree. Manifesting itself in various forms of physical illness, such as panic attacks, sleeplessness and bouts of depression accompanied by many tears, it was very isolating for the sufferers in a new country where everything was unfamiliar, and in some cases, unfriendly and unwelcoming.

Even for women who had happy marriages, it was difficult for husbands and in-laws to fully understand the deep sense of grief and longing for family and old friends, which dogged some women for years, with one war bride relating that she was chronically homesick for 20 years.[90] The inability of their husbands to understand the intensity of their homesickness put a strain on some marriages and often the wife was the one to make a compromise, despite being well justified in her suffering. After all, it was the women who gave up family and long-time friends to join their partners – it was not the husbands.[91]

Despite sometimes chronic homesickness, however, due to reasons discussed above, very few of these women attempted to return to Australia to live permanently and in retrospect, most claim to have had a 'happy' or at least a 'successful' married life in America.

CHAPTER SEVEN

LINKS WITH AUSTRALIA

The intangible pull of our own homeland
Is something we scarcely understand
But invisible threads can bind.
We're stirred in a deep and restless way
To know that we must return some day
Those intangibles to find.
(Betty Kane, 'The War Bride', November 2001)[1]

Soon after arrival in America, the war brides purposely set about maintaining their links with Australia. They realised the importance and necessity of keeping in contact with family and friends they had left behind in Australia, and they purposefully set about doing so. As well as maintaining these links with the country of their birth, they were enthusiastic to share their 'Australian-ness' with others in America who showed an interest in learning more about their homeland.

One of the hardest things the war brides had to overcome in their new lives in America was homesickness. Even after years of living in America, a chance news item about Australia, a photograph, a phone call, or something less tangible, could bring about a nostalgic memory and a flood of emotions connected with family, friends and what they had left behind. Anxious to keep up to date with news from their homeland, the war brides made early efforts to satisfy their sometimes intangible longings for what they had given up to join their husbands across the Pacific.

Communications with family and friends

Separation from family and the vast distance from their
homeland fuelled the war brides' desire to maintain links with
Australia and strong ties have remained intact through various forms
of communication over the last six decades. In the early days, after
settling in their adopted country, the war brides communicated with
family and friends in Australia by letter and telephone, and were kept
well informed (although, in the case of communication by mail, with
a time delay) about personal and family matters. In return, their letters
informed their Australian families and friends about life in America.

Nancy Lankard and her husband first settled in Colorado Springs,
and being from the busy city of Sydney, she found this small town
'a little behind the times'. She found the people 'friendly but a little
country-bumpkinish'. Nancy missed her big family and remembers
that she was 'very, very lonely'. She made an effort to keep in contact
with family by telephone, but these calls were less than satisfactory, due
to the expense and lack of privacy on shared party-lines.[2]

War bride Iris Craig remembers that soon after her arrival in
America, calls to Australia had to be routed through Canada. She says:

> My mother and I mostly cried on the phone for about 15
> minutes, and that cost $100.[3]

Letter-writing was the main form of communication for Dorothy
Bourne, originally from Western Australia. She recalls:

> My brother and I wrote to each other every week for at least
> twenty years. We never missed a week.[4]

Similarly, Joan Hamilton, an only child, kept in touch with her
mother to whom she was very close, by letter writing. She says:

> I'd write to her every week and let her know what was going on.[5]

Her mother has kept all Joan's letters and has offered to give them back to Joan, who thinks they 'would be a lovely history' for her five daughters to read. Joan's words highlight the usefulness of recording important events in letters, diaries and journals when she says:

> *I would love…to go back and read of the girls' developments and funny things they said, because you forget!* [6]

Some war brides eagerly looked forward to regularly receiving copies of popular Australian magazines in the post, such as *The Australian Women's Weekly* and *Woman's Day*, which helped to maintain links with Australia. These magazines kept them up to date on fashion trends, social events, cosmetics and the latest recipes which were popular with Australian women back home. Newspaper articles about topics thought to be of interest were often clipped and posted by family members and friends.

Australian Women's Weekly, March, 1947,
showing family after visiting the Royal
Easter Show in Sydney.

The war brides were always interested in following Australian books, films and sports, despite the fact that sometimes this information was difficult to access in America. These links with their home country helped to ease the pain of separation from their families, but they could not completely compensate for the sense of loss these women experienced, which in many cases still manifested in involuntary and unexpected feelings of homesickness and longing for those they had left behind.

Clubs in America for Australian war brides

In the late 1940s, all over the United States, groups of women who were new to the American lifestyle began to come together regularly at social gatherings. Many of these women were WWII war brides from Britain, Europe, Australia and New Zealand, who had married American servicemen during and just after the war years. Some groups were exclusively Australian.

Australian war bride Jean Fargo, who settled in Virginia, belonged to the Southern Cross Club, (originally called the Billy Tea Club) in Washington DC.[7] This Club was founded in 1946 by Mrs Jane Johnson, who had spent four years in Canberra when her husband headed the United States Diplomatic Mission to Australia. On her return to Washington DC, she wished to provide a venue for Australian and New Zealand women, as well as American women with ties to either country, to meet.

Prior to the founding of the Billy Tea Club, Mrs Norman Makin, wife of the then Australian Ambassador to the United States, held monthly teas at the Washington Embassy residence for the many recently arrived war brides from 'Down Under.' It was at one of these teas that Mrs Johnson conceived the idea of forming a club for these young women. Although the newly formed Billy Tea Club was a social organisation, it was the responsibility of all members to promote goodwill and understanding with Americans.[8] The original name 'Billy Tea Club' was chosen as appropriate because:

This nostalgic title conjured up memories of picnics with the aroma of gum trees and burning wood permeating the air while participants sipped tea around an open fire over which the Billy boiled.[9]

Jean Fargo remembers how the Australian Ambassador in Washington DC, as Patron of the Club, used to invite members to come to the Embassy to celebrate Australia Day each January, and also to attend various cocktail parties hosted by the Ambassador.[10] These occasions served as a link with Australia on a formal level and helped to ease the feelings of displacement and homesickness which haunted some war brides, especially in the early years of living in America. The Southern Cross Club still exists today as a social meeting place for expatriate Australians and New Zealanders as well as Americans with an interest in Australia and New Zealand.

In its early years, when it was still known as the Billy Tea Club, it generated a lot of interest among members of the growing Australian/New Zealand community in the Washington DC area. It was also publicised in the American press which saw a growing number of Americans making up a membership of two hundred. In 1950, men were invited to become members of the club. Members were now drawn from a wider background, including Australian and New Zealand Embassies, the World Bank and the International Monetary Fund. In the early to mid-fifties members were instrumental in raising funds for deserving causes, among which were the Australian Flood Relief Fund and the Welfare Fund of HMAS *Sydney*, when the ship visited Washington DC. It also donated sets of books highlighting key historical events and persons in the United States to universities in Australia and New Zealand, and to some high schools in both countries. These activities of the Club were supported by members who were Australian war brides, thus not only helping to strengthen bonds between America and Australia, but also helping the war brides to take part in actively maintaining links with their homeland.[11]

The Club changed its name to The Southern Cross Club of Washington, DC in 1952, naming it after the constellation featured on both the Australian and New Zealand flags. The connection with Australian war brides is still strong, and the President of the Club and editor of the Club's newsletter in 2008 was Colleen Greer, the daughter of Australian WWII war bride, Betty Greer.[12] This Club has the distinction of being one of the oldest, Australian/New Zealand social organisations in the United States. In 1954, the Southern Cross Club's first newsletter was issued, and the publication was hailed as an indispensable bridge in communication between the resident and transient membership of the day.[13]

A number of Australian war brides joined their State's chapter of the 'Daughters of the British Empire in the USA', a non-profit, non-political American organisation originally founded in 1909. Membership is extended by invitation to women residing in the USA who are of British or British Commonwealth heritage either by birth, naturalisation or proven ancestry. This organisation, known as the 'DBE', has been a common bond for women of British heritage living in America who contribute to the good of their local communities and in particular raise funds for the support of the 'British Homes', which are retirement homes established by the DBE for men and women. Meetings are held monthly, usually followed by an informal get-together over a cup of tea or coffee, and 'in this way friendships are formed and the mutual heritage becomes a comforting and familiar bond'.[14] Australian war bride, Hazel Walker, has belonged to the Arizona Chapter of the DBE on and off for more than 50 years. Hazel says:

> *The chapter to which I belong was originally the Overseas Chapter and was comprised almost entirely of Australian war brides. Many have died or moved on elsewhere, and now there are only two Australians, one South African and the rest are English. The name of the Chapter was changed three years ago to the Union Jack Chapter, because everyone*

in that chapter had died and as it was the first one to be
formed in Arizona, the National office didn't want to name
to disappear.[15]

The changes of name from 'The Billy Tea Club' to 'The Southern Cross Club' and from the 'Overseas Chapter' to the 'Union Jack Chapter' highlight the changing demographics which have occurred over the years. The changes also demonstrate the way in which such an organisation can adapt to maintain its vital role in an evolving community.

In Seattle, Washington, a group of Australian war brides, Joy Gustaffson, Ivy Diers and Margaret Fosmo, who had all arrived from Australia on SS *Mariposa* in 1946, joined the Daughters of the British Empire, Gibraltar Chapter, in Seattle, and they also founded the Aussie War Brides' Club which had its first meeting in 1947. Joy is still in possession of a scrapbook filled with minutes of meetings, names of members and notes and illustrations relating to the club's history and its activities.[16]

Joy Gustaffson, Ivy Diers, Margaret Fosmo and Sonti the Australian Cockatoo, Seattle, 2001.

Kathleen Heeren remembers when she first settled in San Diego in Southern California in 1946, about 50 women from Australia and New Zealand got together and formed The Anzac Club. However, as the young women started having children, they were not always able to attend, and people drifted away, especially those with husbands still in service who were often transferred to other locations, and the Club eventually disbanded.[17]

John Heeren   Kathleen Heeren, c.1946.

Similarly Bernice Geist, who settled in Sacramento, California, belonged to a 'bride's club' which was not only for Australian war brides, but for 'girls from everywhere'. They met regularly at the YWCA for several years. Bernice recalls:

> *The girls' families grew, and they began to get more and more children and [had] less time to be able to do these things and the club gradually dispersed.*[18]

However, these organisations served their purpose well in the early days when it was important to the war brides to have support and contact with others from their homeland. Another lively organisation with its headquarters in Philadelphia was the Australasian Women's Club, its members being the wives of former GIs who had served in Australia. The Philadelphia chapter met regularly in the early years after the war and was particularly active, with its 40-odd members maintaining close ties with Australia and things Australian.[19] War bride Valda Hertzberg from Sydney, one of the foundation members, is still proud of the Club, and has observed the way in which the activities of the Club and the friendships formed there enabled these young women to settle into their new lives.[20]

Brisbane war bride, Muriel Locklear (née Ricketts), and her baby son, Ron, sailed on SS *Monterey* in July, 1946. Muriel reunited with her husband, Ernie, and they settled in the small tourist town of Sarasota, Florida, on the west side of the Gulf of Mexico.

Muriel Locklear in Brisbane - 18 yrs old.   Muriel and Ernie Locklear, c.1945.

Eight months pregnant when she arrived in America, Muriel's baby girl, Carolyn was born a month later. Ernie found work as a plumber at the local ice plant and later became foreman of the crew that developed the South Gate shopping complex in 1957. In that year, the couple's second son, Steve, was born and Muriel was kept busy with three young children to care for. Later, when they were all at school, she felt the need for more social interaction and, in the 1960s and 1970s Muriel belonged to an Australian Women's Club called the 'Kangaroo Club'. The members came from cities and towns all over Australia. These Australian war brides had mostly settled in Sarasota and surrounding locations of Bradenton, St. Petersburg and Tampa. The club met once a month in the homes of the members who enjoyed 'getting together and sharing things about Australia'. In time, a lot of the members moved away, and some went back to live in Australia, so the club was discontinued.[21]

Smaller, less formal groups of war brides were important in facilitating a suitable way for war brides to meet and maintain links with other Australians. Dorothy Thompson of Golden Grove, California, and a number of other Australian war brides who lived in the area, set up a regular, but informal group.

Australian WWII war brides at the home of Dorothy Thompson
(front row, left). Billie Ringen (front row, right).

One of the regular participants, Billie Ringen, gives a summary of the club's changing membership.

Most of us have been here thirty-five or forty years, and started this little club in about 1961. And so we've had new

members, and old members have passed on and so forth,
but we keep about 12 to 15 members most of the time. It's
very enjoyable. We have a good time. So many of us are now
widowed, so life has changed somewhat for many of us. I
think most of the ladies that I know have had rather happy
marriages, most of them have had children, they've travelled
and they've done a lot of nice things with their families. Their
homes are pleasant and we have more than we need to have.[22]

This group still meets regularly, although their numbers are now
dwindling due to the aging of members of the group, and sadly also
due to some deaths in recent years. Dorothy recalls:

We generally meet once a month on a birthday – whoever's
birthday it is – and we have a 'pot-luck' lunch…with a
birthday cake, and we sing 'I Like Aeroplane Jelly'.[23]

The popular term 'pot-luck' (commonly used in America to describe
a picnic or luncheon where all guests take a plate of food) is very much
part of American culture. In the same sentence, Dorothy speaks of singing
'I Like Aeroplane Jelly' (a popular advertising jingle in Australia in the
forties and fifties which promoted fruit-flavoured dessert jellies), a product
which became an icon representing part of Australian popular culture.
This juxtaposition of aspects of both cultures highlights the acceptance of
American culture, as well as demonstrating the importance to the war brides
of maintaining links to Australian culture and cuisine over the years.

Dorothy tells how the war brides take it in turn to host the meetings
in their own homes. On these occasions the table is decked with
traditional Australian fare from the forties and fifties, prepared and
brought along by the war brides. At such a gathering in September 2001,
these women sought to replicate Australian cuisine as it was at the time
they left Australia. Platters contained items such as Devon sausage slices
rolled around a filling of potato mashed with diced onion and secured
with a toothpick; vegemite on crust-free buttered white bread; devilled

eggs; fairy bread decorated with 'hundreds-and-thousands'; a trifle of jelly, custard, sliced peaches and slices of sherry-soaked jam roll; and a birthday cake with an Australian theme, decorated with green icing and two ornamental frilled lizards. This display of typical Australian fare demonstrates how the war brides have continued to present food as they remember it during their young lives 'at home' and as part of their childhood. This ossification of aspects of Australian culture and cuisine clearly stems from the migration experience of these women who still have a yearning, indeed a 'hunger' for home.

Australian WWII war brides, Helen Leira (left) and Joan Hammon (middle) at Dorothy Thompson's luncheon, Garden Grove, California, 2001.

Topping the war brides' lists of what they missed most after coming to America, was always 'family and friends', coming a close second was always food remembered from Australia. Homesickness among the war brides in this book often translated as a yearning for the food cooked by their mothers and eaten in the family home. 'Food' seemed to be a metaphor for 'home' and 'family'.

Dorothy Thompson's hand-stitched 'Australia' banner hung outside her home on 'reunion' days.

In March, 1970, the Brisbane *Advertiser* featured a story of war bride Dorothy Pence, who had returned to Australia for the first time after an absence of 27 years. A photograph showed Dorothy enjoying a cool drink with her brother and sister-in-law, obviously happy to be reunited with her family. The article noted her yearning for a 'fair dinkum Australian pie' and it quoted Dorothy as saying: 'America is a great place, wonderful people, and magnificent homes and touring attractions ... but no meat pies!'

'They Can't Beat Our Dinkum Pie', The Advertiser, March 19, 1970.

War bride Allie Rudy remembers the culinary delights of
Australia when she was growing up and how she savoured them on
her return visits, the last one being in 2006:

> *I miss meat pies and I haven't had a really decent piece*
> *of corned beef. My mother used to fix silver-side, and*
> *whenever I go home that's what they fix me. I can*
> *remember last time when I went home, my sister-in-*
> *law who's going to be 91...asked what I would like and I*
> *said I would even fix it, or I'll buy it, whatever. I'd like to*
> *have a nice big piece of silver-side, and for sandwiches and*
> *everything else, and put all those vegies around it.*[24]

Allie's focus here on home-
cooked meals in Australia indicates
a definite connection between the
nostalgic memories of home and
the food her mother used to cook.
Allie swears that she 'now loves
America'; at the same time she
comments 'but it's not home'.[25]
It is clear from this narrative that
it is not the food, but rather the
memories of her mother and the
family atmosphere that still tug
at her heart, causing her to revisit
feelings of homesickness even after
all these years.

Allie Rudy in Washington
DC, 2004.

Similarly war bride Jess Berghofer from a dairy farm in
Toowoomba, Queensland, remained close to her mother who
inspired her, despite the thousands of miles that separated them. Jess,
who settled in Texas, recalls how they corresponded: 'She and I wrote
and communicated: she could write me her problems and I mine'.[26]

The strong bond between mother and daughter is highlighted in the telling of these stories and indicates this is a significant factor in the homesickness suffered by many of these women.

Val Smith also tells of her links with Australia. After family and friends, next on her list of things most missed was food and drink. Unlike many war brides, she travelled often to visit Australia, sometimes two or three times a year, due to the discounts her husband Ben received as a senior member of staff at Pan-Am. Val thinks back with nostalgia to when she lived in Australia and how different it is in America:

> *I remember how we used to make ginger beer at Christmas time and we'd have that with fruit cake when friends came over. Well, that is foreign to people here – serving fruit cake with ginger beer...nobody likes fruit cake in the US. It is funny, but they have a real standing joke...companies will give people a fruit cake and it might circulate around that 'You might end up with a fruit cake again if you don't watch out!' They are not fruit cake people!* [27]

Val Smith in her garden, Palo Alto, California, 2001.

When visiting Val at her Palo Alto home in California to conduct an interview with her, she related to me as a fellow Australian, and proudly produced hot cups of 'proper' tea made in a teapot, rather than the teabags usually offered in America to dip in a cup of hot water. This was accompanied by a passionfruit-iced sponge which she had specially made for the occasion, a favourite of hers and a legacy of her mother's treasured recipe book – a fitting culinary treat for an Australian visitor.

Lola Atkins arranged to host a luncheon with several Australian war brides as guests at her home in San Diego, to facilitate interviews with them for my research. The cold sliced meat and salad was followed by an authentic 'Australian trifle' that Lola had painstakingly made the night before. It was the first time she had entertained this group of Australian women, and the first time she had made a trifle in many years. She was upset because she could not buy the necessary ingredient of the Australian brand of 'Foster Clark's Custard Powder', but made do with a 'Vanilla Pudding Mix' as a substitute. It was a great success and delighted the guests who exclaimed that they hadn't had trifle since leaving Australia. It proved to be an appropriate and bonding repast for these women, mostly in their eighties, who were there to share their memories of their early lives.

Lola and Tom Atkins outside their home in San Diego, CA, 2001.

Similarly, war bride Norma Rehrer invited me to her home in Sacramento in 2001 where she hosted a luncheon for other Australian war brides from surrounding areas. At this gathering, the women enjoyed meeting each other, and were keen to have their stories recorded for the first time.

Norma Rehrer, (right) hosting luncheon for Australian WWII
war brides in Sacramento, CA, September, 2001.

The camaraderie shared by a group of sixteen Australian war
brides, at the home of Dorothy Thompson in California, almost
sixty years after coming to America, was clearly displayed as they
consumed favourite foods familiar to them from their homeland.
They enjoyed singing songs which they had once sung to the
accompaniment of pianos and pianolas in their family living rooms,
when community singing around the piano was a popular form of
entertainment in the 1940s. Songs such as 'Daisy Bell' and 'The
Bells are Ringing For Me and My Girl', for example, were enjoyed
in 1940s Australia. Such romantic songs were also sung at later
gatherings and reunions in America, nostalgic reminders of the war
brides' courtships and weddings in wartime conditions in Australia.
The lyrics from the well-known refrain of 'Daisy Bell' are:

*Daisy, Daisy, give me your answer do! I'm half crazy all for
the love of you! It won't be a stylish marriage, I can't afford*

a carriage. But you'll look sweet upon the seat of a bicycle built for two! [28]

These tangible and nostalgic links to Australia, both culinary and musical, are still important to these women who continue to celebrate their Australian heritage, while at the same time they fully embrace their lives in America. Australian sport, along with cuisine and music, helped to strengthen and maintain important links to the country of their birth. For example, in 1950 when world-champion sculler, Mervyn Wood of Sydney, raced in the Schuylkill River in Philadelphia, a large delegation of Australasian Women's Club members barracked him to victory. In the same year many of the Philadelphia club members journeyed to Forrest Hills, New York, to watch the Australian Davis Cup team triumph over America in the Challenge round.[29]

War bride, Sunny Sansing, tells of her display of loyalty to both Australia and America during the sailing challenge in the 1990s:

When they had the America's Cup in San Diego I wore a T-shirt that had 'San Diego' on the front and 'Australia' on the back! And whoever was winning, I turned it around! [30]

The Australian-American Journal

The strong need for the war brides' continuing connection with Australia, and the pro-active way in which it was maintained, can also be seen in the appearance of a magazine which was set up for this purpose. The first issue of *The Australian-American Journal*, published in January 1948, was promoted as: 'a monthly magazine devoted primarily to your personal interests in Australia and America'.[31] The launch of this magazine saw the dream of Australian war bride, Pat McLean, become a reality. Pat tells of two 'soldier buddies' who were among the 'Yanks' who were guests at her family's home in Brisbane and who were taken 'completely into our home and hearts'. Pat fell in love with one of these American servicemen and relates: 'the day came when I promised to "settle for life" with him in his home in far-off America!'[32] When the war ended, Pat made her new home in Kentucky where, despite her happiness, in the beginning she 'found life in America strange and sometimes difficult'.[33] One day she was reading a letter from home when an idea struck her:

> *What a wonderful thing it would be if we Australian brides could have a publication of our own through which we could keep in touch with one another and with goings-on in our homeland!*' [34]

As Executive Secretary of the *Journal,* and with definite signs of good ambassadorial skills, Pat wrote in the first issue to the readers: 'May it prove to be a real bond of friendship between Australia and America – and may it bring about even a better understanding and a closer kinship between our two countries.'[35] So, *The Australian-American Journal* was born, displaying a boomerang and a kangaroo incorporated into the masthead design, and the cover of the first issue shows a young woman admiring a koala at Koala Park in Sydney. This tangible link with their home country became available to Australian war brides all over America for a subscription rate of $US 3.00 in the USA and $US 3.25 outside the USA.

Endorsed by the Honorable J.B. Chifley, Prime Minister of Australia in September, 1947, his words were published in the first issue of the magazine:

> The Australian Ambassador to the United States (Mr. Norman Makin) has spoken of the value of a publication such as "The Australian-American Journal" and I wish it every success in the commendable endeavour it will make to bring the people of our two countries closer together.[36]

A message from the Honourable Norman Makin, Australian Ambassador to the United States of America at that time, was also published in the first issue where he spoke of the important mission of *The Australian-American Journal*. He saw the advent of such a magazine as 'an interesting experiment', one 'born of war and the aftermath of war' and one 'destined to achieve success, devoted as it will be to the furtherance of Australian-American ties'.[37] He spoke of the 'bonds between Australia and America which were born on the battlefield' and which have been 'progressively strengthened since the cessation of hostilities' a contributing factor being 'the marriages of so many thousands of American servicemen and Australian girls'.[38] As well as facilitating a way for Australian war brides in America to keep in touch with each other, the Ambassador commented:

> It will take news of their activities to their friends and loved ones at home in Australia, who in this way will be able to follow the fortunes of their daughters in this great democracy of America.[39]

He also hoped and believed that the magazine would be "a useful contribution to Americans' knowledge of Australia".[40]

In this first issue of *The Australian-American Journal* the first page is devoted to 'Letters From Our Readers' which contain enthusiastic congratulations, comments and suggestions from the first readers, all Australian war brides. The magazine presents core information about Australia, ranging from geographical, historical, agricultural, industrial, educational and sporting perspectives. The 'News From Australia' page contains a variety of information, including: the tabling in Parliament of the 'Geneva Trade Agreement', the price of a top thoroughbred racehorse, the expansion of the Kingsford-Smith airport, and the Miss Australia Contest.[41] The 'More News From "Down Under"' page includes news as varied as the 'Nightingale Medal for Australian Nurses', the pearling industry, the continued rationing of clothing and food, and a comical story about Herbert, a port-drinking pet rabbit at the Crown Hotel in Parramatta.[42] On other pages, a headline announces a "Marine Stowaway Weds Melbourne Girl' and there are stories about the Flying Doctor Service of Australia. Pages follow filled with news of 'Aussie Activities' in America, notices of babies' births, war brides' reunions, club activities and holidays; and more pages display recipes, dress patterns and needlecraft ideas.[43] The back cover of this magazine is a beautiful scenic photograph of two young women sitting among long grasses at the edge of a lake in Yosemite National Park, California, with a huge mountain and gushing water falls providing a magnificent backdrop. This purposefully designed Journal, between its 'Australian' and 'American' covers, encompasses information covering news, food and fashion to which Australian war brides in America longed to have regular access. Its format provided these women with a place to communicate, to share their experiences, and especially for those in far-flung corners of America, to feel that they were not alone. The contents of the Journal helped to heal feelings of homesickness and isolation for Australian war brides. As well, it provided a wealth of information about Australia and its culture for Americans to read.

Subsequent issues of *The Australian-American Journal* continued to brighten the lives of the war brides. In the March, 1948 issue, with two Australian Kookaburras on the cover, a letter from Mrs Dulcie J. Mason from Stevenson, in the State of Washington, tells how much she enjoyed receiving her first copy of the magazine:

> I must congratulate you and your co-workers on such a splendid edition. I have read it from cover to cover, and shall look forward to my copy each month. I sincerely hope that lots of the girls will write in as I really enjoy reading their letters and suggestions.[44]

The cover of the April, 1948, issue of the magazine displayed a photograph of Captain Cook's Cottage in Melbourne; and in May, 1948 the cover is a photograph of a large Alsatian dog with a baby Koala riding on its back.[45]

Australian-American Journal, April, 1948.

These covers were obviously designed to appeal strongly to the Australian war brides, many of whom were homesick and seeking news from home and contact with other Australians in America. Following the design policy of this publication which also highlighted the beauty of the American landscape, the back cover of the May issue is an American scenic view of a family standing beside their car, gazing at the magnificent view of the majestic snow-capped Mount Hood in the State of Oregon.[46]

Letters to the magazine were from Australian war brides in Hollywood and Los Angeles in California, from Superior in

Nebraska, Stafford Springs in Connecticut, Columbus in Indiana, Clairton in Pennsylvania, Hardin in Montana, Libertyville in Illinois, Okeechobee in Florida, and many other locations across the United States. This diversity demonstrates the spread of locations in which the war brides settled, as well as the magazine's long reach across the vast country, and while it is not known how long this publication remained in production, it clearly served a very good purpose during the period of its publication by reaching many women for whom it was a necessary link both to their homeland and to other women in the same situation as themselves.

Holidays and travel to Australia

Holidays to Australia became popular with the war brides in America, but usually not within the first ten years after settling in America. During these years, while often homesick and longing to visit their Australian families, many were busy bringing up small children, and finances did not allow for travel. Mothers of Australian war brides also wanted to see their daughters and concerted efforts were made to fund visits to America.

Victorian war bride, Joann Patterson, tells how her mother belonged to the Victorian division of a club formed for the Australian mothers of US war brides. Her mother was 'basically a home body, not involved in going outside the home'.[47] However, after the war and after she was widowed, and having two of her three daughters married to US servicemen, Joann's mother became very involved in this organisation and held office as Secretary. The Club held bag sales and raffles, raising money towards the cost of passage to the US for two mothers to visit her their bride daughters each year. Joann recalls:

> That was how my mother came to visit me the first time. It wasn't a big organisation - maybe eight to ten people. The Club members were issued with a badge with a kookaburra on a boomerang encircled with the words 'U.S. Wives Mothers' Social Club'.[48]

This effort made by the war brides' mothers highlights the strong bond that existed between mothers and daughters and demonstrates how this assistance helped the war brides to maintain their links with Australia in the early years of separation from their home country.

Badge of the US Wives Mothers' Social Club, Victoria. This club had branches in all the state capitals. [Courtesy Australian War Memorial, AWM REL34259]

Originally from Sydney, Joane Dambly was a war bride and an officer of the Australasian Women's Club in America. She realised that there were 'just as many if not more mothers anxious to visit daughters here [in America] as there are Australian girls wanting to return home again'.[49] International air regulations allowed bona fide clubs to charter planes for travel between countries and Joane had the ingenious idea of organising travel which was a two-way exchange of Australian war brides with a group of mothers of other Australian brides who were unable to make the flight. A Pan-American World Airways Constellation was chartered in the name of the Australasian Women's Club for this two-way exchange, which cut the fares from $1,200 by half to $600 making it financially possible for twenty-five women to take a trip home to Australia. After only five years of living in America these fortunate members of the Club flew to Sydney where, together with their children, they were transported to their destinations in Sydney, Melbourne, Perth, Brisbane and elsewhere. The plane made an immediate turnabout flight with a group of mothers, all members of the "Mothers' Goodwill Club of Australia", to San Francisco where they travelled on to visit their daughters in various parts of America. The stay in both Australia and America was for four months, in which time Mrs Dambly hoped that she could have her little boy 'talking like a native-born Aussie.'[50]

Despite the war brides' strong desire to make a return visit to Australia, for many the journey had to wait until their children were older and until they could afford the expense of travel. When the opportunity did arrive, the war brides were able to strengthen their bonds with Australia by visiting their families. Barbara Gleason, for instance, regularly communicated over the years with her large family of four brothers and two sisters. Although now there is only one remaining sister, Barbara is still in contact with her extended family. She says:

> *There are oodles of cousins our age and older and we have all those nieces and nephews and grand-nieces and grand-nephews. There are literally hundreds.*[51]

Despite the long 31-hour flight from California to Perth, Barbara and her husband considered it important to return to Australia to celebrate her 50th, 60th and 70th birthdays with family and friends.[52]

Barbara and Jim Gleason, celebrating his 83rd birthday, Annaheim, CA, 2001.

Great efforts were made by the war brides to visit Australia in an effort to maintain links with their home country. Val Smith's daughter was born twelve months after she arrived in America. She says: 'I wanted to take my first-born back to show everyone'.[53]

Ben Smith, San Antonio, Texas, 1941.   Val Smith (nee Ballard) aged 18.

Val's husband had flown B-47 bombers during the war and post-war he was a pilot with Pan-Am, which entitled him to a 50% discount on fares. However, Val remembers that the air fare to Australia and back was about a thousand US dollars, which 'was hard to come by'.[54] She loved to sew, and decided to 'do a little bit of extra sewing' to help with saving, and her husband promised to sell what she made. Together they worked to make extra money, and Val tells how she put together 'little zoot-suits', made from an Australian pattern for small children's 'pilchers'[55] which were not available in America:

> *I made these little suits up and I'd embroider a little flamingo on the pocket because we were in Florida and that's their national bird symbol. Ben [her husband] used to cut them out – he was marvellous – and he would sew the buttons on.*[56]

The couple sold the 'zoot-suits' to 'a fancy store' and from this venture, Val proudly states:

> *We made enough money to put a rug on the floor and to send me to Australia…so that's how I got there the first time.*[57]

Retaining an Australian accent

In the early 1950s, about five years after their arrival in America, a spokesperson for a group of Australian war brides who were members of the Australasian Women's Club in Philadelphia declared: 'Most of us are happy about living in America, but we are all dinky-di Aussies at heart'.[58] In an article in *The Australian Women's Weekly* it was reported that although the girls 'looked completely American in their new frocks, nylons and ankle-strap shoes', when they spoke 'it was with the accents of Australia.'[59] A founding member of the Club declared: 'Most of us are proud of our Australian speech and are trying to cling to it'. She comments:

> *It is a bit of a shock at first, though, to hear your kiddies talking with an American accent. The children pick up the speech around them and there is not much you can do about that.*[60]

Many of the Australian war brides proudly declare that they have not lost their Australian accent despite having lived in America for six decades. Certainly, there are some who still sound quite Australian with hardly a trace of an American accent. However, while it is sometimes possible to detect a hint of their Australian accent, those who profess to 'still sound like an Aussie' often have a recognisable American 'twang' to the Australian ear. While proud of their Australian accents, the war brides find it is rarely recognised as such by others in America. For example, Betty McIntire says that a lot of people when they hear her speak ask: 'Are you from Boston?'[61]

Sydney war bride, Iris Craig, made an effort to change her Australian accent especially to please her husband, but without success. She recalls:

> One day my husband said to me 'Why don't you try and speak more like an American?' And so I thought, well if that pleases him, I'll try. But when I discovered myself putting R's where they weren't supposed to be, I decided enough's enough, just take me as I am, I'm not going to change![62]

War bride Joy Shaddle has a slight American accent, but her Australian accent is still most discernible. She comments nostalgically:

> I have tried very hard to maintain my accent...because that's all I've got left of Australia! I've left everything else behind.[63]

Proud of their Australian accents, this distinction from other women in America still serves, after many years, as a link to the country of their birth.

Memorabilia collections

Betty Bridges and her 'Australiana Corner', Seattle, 2001

During visits to the homes of Australian WWII war brides to conduct interviews, items of Australiana were visible in all sorts of different forms. For example, at Betty Bridges' home in Seattle, Washington, she had a special 'Australiana corner' where items such as Aboriginal masks, paintings of Australian landscapes, drawings of koalas and other artefacts were proudly displayed.

Australian memorabilia also abounded at the home of Dorothy Thompson in Golden Grove, California, when she hosted a luncheon for a gathering of war brides. The teapot was kept warm in a hand-knitted woollen 'koala' tea-cosy. She also had various Aboriginal artefacts on her living room wall, as well as growing passionfruit and frangipannis in her garden. Barbara Gleason in Anaheim, California, delights in displaying a framed picture on her living room wall of a special 'black-butt' tree from Western Australia. On a visit to Australia her husband had spied this tree and said 'I think that looks like an elephant!' Since that time the tree has become a tourist attraction, and Barbara's grandson gave her the picture of the 'elephant tree' for remembrance sake.[64]

Similarly, Dorothy Hammon is proud of her items of Australiana:

In my house I have a hallway – I must have about 15 or 20 items. There are Aboriginal bark pictures, a picture of Captain Cook, a poem about the Flag, a beautiful tapestry done by an Australian friend, and a beautiful flower arrangement set in a frame that my sister gave me many, many years ago and it has kept beautifully. Oh, and a picture of Sydney Harbour.[65]

As well as these above-mentioned artefacts, some war brides kept other types of mementos from Australia. Joy Gustaffson, for instance, kept a lively sulphur-crested white cockatoo – a bird native to Australia – which spent some months in quarantine after it had been brought from Australia by her daughter. This large bird named 'Sonti' takes 'centre stage' in her home, and at 30 years of age has 'ruled the roost' for many years, being a living link with Australia and providing Joy and her visitors with much entertainment.[66]

Joy Gutaffson and Sonti, her Australian Cockatoo, Seattle, September, 2001.

Interviewed during a visit to Australia, war bride Joy Shaddle was staying with one of her three brothers in Sydney in 2002. Of all the things Joy misses most, apart from family, is the 'flora and fauna' as 'it never changes, and it seems to me when you leave your country, you don't want things to change.' Nevertheless, Joy notices that changes have taken place, and comments:

> *I come back and I feel I don't belong here. It's different - the people are not the same...This is a real melting-pot now and it's bubbling very furiously, more so than America. So, actually the people where I live there in little old Forrest [in Illinois] are like what I left behind!* [67]

What Joy loves about Australia is 'the timeless stuff', and she comments:

> *I saw two Kookaburras yesterday and I was thrilled, and some magpies, and then the flowers — the bottlebrush, the wattle. I'm so glad that the wattle is blooming.* [68]

Joy also speaks fondly of a pot containing a Lantana plant which she bought from a nursery because it reminds her of Australia. It is not her original Lantana plant, as being used to a much warmer temperature it doesn't always survive the Illinois winter, and she regularly replaces it with a new hardy plant. But she loves the smell of the Lantana leaves which reminds her so much of 'home'. It seemed appropriate that the table, where we sat to talk that day, had a centrepiece of a large jar of Vegemite!

Australian literature, magazines and popular culture

Books by Australian authors, for some war brides, have provided another tangible link to their homeland over the years. Betty McIntire, a keen reader, had enjoyed Colleen McCullough's book,

The Thorn Birds, which she thought was a wonderful story.[69] Peggy Dunbar Blackman, herself a published author in America, is always interested in Australian authors, particularly Jill Kerr Conway, whose books she has read and has purchased copies to give to friends.[70] Similarly, Betty Paukovitz has Australian books in her collection. She says: 'I have all the books about Weary Dunlop', (an Australian military hero) and 'Sarah Henderson' (an Australian pastoralist and author), and 'a history of Sydney Harbour'.[71]

Interested in Australian movies, Betty McIntire enjoyed *Crocodile Dundee,* starring actor Paul Hogan, and as for Australian actor Mel Gibson, she says 'I love him!'[72] Of course not all war brides shared the same taste in films. Peggy Blackman was not impressed by Australian film star Paul Hogan. She disliked his 'swagger' and found the 'excesses of the Australian accent offensive to the ear'. Peggy, a well-read and elegant woman, was forthright about not wanting to be represented as an Australian by 'that kind of man'. She declared:

> *If you get to be too much of a dilettante, then you're never going to cut the mustard in forging ahead in a foreign country.*[73]

Jean Vallero was keen to receive the first issue of an Australian magazine to which she had recently subscribed. She also had a subscription to *The Australian Catalogue* from which it was possible to buy Australian food products, books, videos, T-shirts. She also was interested in Australian film actors such as Mel Gibson, Bryan Brown and Rachel Ward.[74] Collecting Australiana of all descriptions was almost an obsession for Patricia Law, who says:

> *My daughter and I buy Australian books everywhere we go. I've got a whole collection of Australian videos. Every time there's one I buy it, and I've got every Australian stuffed animal. I've got a whole collection of koalas, all sizes, every time they bring one out I have to get one.*[75]

Children's and Grandchildren's interest in Australia

As mothers and grandmothers, the Australian WWII war brides living in America consider it important that their children and grandchildren are given every opportunity to learn about their Australian heritage. This shared Australian-American bond, a legacy of the war bride's wartime romance and marriage to an American, is a significant link to their homeland. The maintenance of this link through an interest in Australia by future generations is seen by the war brides as an important investment in Australian-American relations for years to come.

Dorothy Thompson, always reluctant to leave Australia, took her children back to visit Australia in 1950 when her eldest daughter was five. She says:

> I really intended living there. I was going home and I was going to stay there. But it didn't work out that way.[76]

Dorothy had left everything in America packed up and had intended giving her husband the following choice:

> 'Send my stuff over or come over to me', which I knew he would have. I was so sure that he would, because he did love me and he loved his family. He was a good family man.[77]

However, Dorothy says, the outbreak of the Korean War changed her plans. Because she was not a US citizen at the time, she was afraid that if the war escalated, her children who were US citizens might be taken back to America. Dorothy admits:

> I didn't mind getting stranded in Australia – that would have been wonderful – but, like mother said, 'Think about it, you don't want your children to be without a father'.[78]

So, her husband arranged for Dorothy and their children to fly Pan-Am back to the US. She remembers that it was very difficult flying with small children on a trip which took 36 hours at that time. When Dorothy's mother died in 1962 she travelled to Australia again, taking her second daughter who was three years old. On this second visit, Dorothy still would have liked to stay in Australia, but they couldn't really afford the move and her husband was not keen to emigrate. Many years later, in 1995, Dorothy made another trip to Australia with her eldest daughter. She remembers taking her to the Sydney suburbs where she used to live:

> It was really nice to show her all around Harbord and Manly. When we went to Brisbane I would take her to the mall…and I said, 'This is where your Dad used to buy me chocolates' and I'd start to cry.[79]

In Australia during the war, when Dorothy was a sales assistant in Woolworths, her husband-to-be had sent her a dozen long-stemmed red roses each week. Dorothy recalls:

> The florist used to come with this big bunch…I was the envy of the whole store.[80]

Dorothy pointed out to her daughter the shop where her Dad had bought the flowers, and they ate in a restaurant in Albert Street where the courting couple had once frequented. Mother and daughter also visited the Beach House at Coolangatta where Dorothy used to 'hang out' when she was younger. Dorothy was delighted to have been able to acquaint her daughter with the places which meant so much to her. She comments:

> So, she got to see all the things that I'd talked about, and it meant a lot to her because she'd heard about it before, and being the eldest and being born there, it really meant a lot to Beverley.[81]

Some Australian war brides had opportunities for their children to have an Australian education. When war bride Hazel Walker's husband retired from the military in 1962, the family sojourned in Australia and her son Rusty spent the next four years studying art at university in Queensland. He painted watercolours and oil landscapes of the indigenous ghost gums on location in Australia. He happily reports:

> *I sketched the laughing kookaburras outside my window. I painted in the Botanical Gardens across from the college and endured the alarming charge of black swans and swooping magpies, with their sour dispositions, one encounters along the Brisbane River.*[82]

During his four year undergraduate work in Australia, he also played in music bands on the Gold Coast with his guitar and blues harmonica.

Hazel Walker with son Rusty on her 90th birthday, Phoenix, Arizona.

He subsequently graduated from Queensland Institute of Technology (now Queensland University of Technology) in Brisbane, Australia, and later completed graduate studies in the United States. From his time in Australia his combined passion for the visual arts and music has continued and he is now a well-known and successful artist.[83] Rusty's mother, war bride Hazel Walker, is justifiably proud of her son, not least of all because of his involvement with life in Australia, and so continuing the links established between the two countries.

The war brides also wanted their grandchildren to maintain links with Australia. War bride Coral Ayraud, for example, was keen to introduce her grandson to Australia. She tells how:

> As recently as six years ago, I travelled to Australia with my grandson, who is blind. He enrolled at Newcastle University and now has a Masters in Chemical Engineering. He has a problem with breaking limbs because of his condition, although that has improved. He now has a job with the government and is engaged to be married. I am very proud of him.[84]

The WWI War Brides Association

It was not until 1996 that the WWII War Brides Association was officially registered in America. This organisation was the inspiration of two daughters of WWII war brides, Barbara Scibetta, the daughter of a German war bride and Elfrieda Shukert, the daughter of an Austrian war bride. Together they wrote *War Brides of World War II* which was published by Presidio Press in 1988. During five years of research for the book they made many contacts with war brides from many countries who had settled in America. In 1985, the authors organised a reunion of WWII war brides on board the Queen Mary, a ship which had transported many British war brides to America, and which was docked in the harbour of Long Beach, California. The reunion was attended by 500 war brides and their husbands and the gathering attracted a lot of media publicity all over the US. Ten years later, another national reunion was organised on 8 May, 1995, in San Diego - exactly 50 years after the end of World War II in Europe – and was attended by 200 war brides and husbands in San Diego. British War Bride, Eileen Orton, volunteered to write a monthly bulletin for all war brides, which was later called 'The Courier'. Eileen herself organised the next year's reunion in Laughlin, Nevada, at which time a Board of Directors was voted in. Eileen established bylaws and registered the organisation with the IRS (Internal Revenue Service) as a non-profit organisation.[85]

The Association's bulletin, now titled 'War Brides Courier' is the Official newsletter of the WWII War Brides Association. According to German war bride Connie McGrath, one of the Association's founding members, since its early days this newsletter has 'helped to bind us together, to attract new members, and to plan a national reunion in different parts of the US every year'.[86]

At a time when the war brides are reaching their mid- to late-eighties and some are 90 and over, many can no longer travel to attend the reunions. However, there are a number of staunch regulars who still make the journey, and the Association is still receiving applications for membership from Australian war brides who have only recently learned of its existence and are keen to join. The Association met in Orlando, Florida in October 2008, in San Francisco, California in October 2009, (the port where most Australian WWII war brides arrived in America in the mid- to late-1940s), in St Louis, Missouri in October 2010, in San Diego, California in 2011, and the latest reunion in Boston, Massachusetts in August 2012, which I was privileged to attend.

In Boston, I was seated at dinner next to an Australian war bride, Mary Maciel McCormack (née Swift) who was attending her first reunion of WWII war brides, since arriving in America in 1946. Her son Michael, had heard about the event, and at short notice was able to accompany his mother. I recognised her name and asked her if she had ever had a 'pillow fight' with other young war brides. I was delighted to discover that she was indeed the subject of a photograph I had in my collection, copied from a 1945 issue of Pix magazine. Mary had been one of a number of young women attending a two-day course for wives and fiancées of US servicemen held at Newport on Sydney's north shore all those years ago, while waiting for transportation to America on SS *Lurline*.

Rumpus After lights out the girls staged a pillow fight before turning in. Mrs. McCormack is being attacked from three sides by Miss Joan Maurer, Mrs. Stella Frey and Mrs. Gloria Sutcliffe. Mrs. McCormack said later that the course was thoroughly enjoyed by all the girls. "They didn't think they could have so much enjoyment being educated," she said

Mary McCormack (née Swift) 'Pillow Attack'
[Source: Pix, 5 May, 1945, p.15]

Mary Maciel and son Michael McCormack, at the 2012 Reunion
of the WWII War Brides' Association, in Boston.

The membership of the WWII War Brides Association is made up of war brides from Australia as well as those who came from many countries including Britain, Germany, Austria, Italy, France, the Philippines and New Zealand. The existence of such organisations today demonstrates their important role in maintaining links with the war brides' countries of origin and strong bonds with their homelands, which have remained intact. Australian war bride Sunny Sansing says:

> *This [America] is where my son is and my two grandchildren and my great-grandchildren are, so this is where I'll be. America has been good to me I don't think you can take the 'Australia' out of Australians!* [87]

Sunny still misses her homeland and says: 'I still call Australia "home."' However, she quickly adds 'I also call San Diego "home"', and describes this city as 'about the closest thing to Sydney' where she is happy to live. Sunny tells an amusing story which demonstrates her feelings of loyalty to both countries:

> *I'm a 'dinky-di' Aussie. I go back to 1814 to a convict great, great, great grandfather of whom I'm very, very proud. His name was Robert Woodley from Devon, England. He was 39 years of age and was a government servant..* [88]

Sunny Sansing at the official dedication of the WWII War Memorial in Washington DC, 004.

Strong attachment to one's homeland is an inevitable part of the process of immigration and applies to others as well as Australians. War bride Hazel Walker tells how she once took a class called 'Chicano History and Culture' at a local Community College. Near the end of the course, the professor went around the class and asked, 'How long do you think a person lives in the US before he feels American?' Most of the young people in the class said varying years from 18 months up. When it came to Hazel's turn she said: 'Never! I'll always feel Australian'. Hazel tells how Doris, another woman in the class, agreed with her and said: 'My husband is American, my kids are American, but I'm Mexican, and I'll always feel Mexican'.[89]

It is clear to see the importance to these women of maintaining links to their homeland. The bonds originally forged during their lives as young Australian women during wartime, when there was a heightened sense of national pride, have been nurtured and maintained. The preservation of these links has been vital to the welfare of these women as they settled in to their new homes in America, often originally isolated from other Australian women; where they had to adjust to geographical and cultural change and deal with the challenges of homesickness and longing for a lost time and place.

In establishing various means of communication and meeting places, the war brides clearly recognised the need for such action in the early years of their lives in America. It is a sign of the strong spirit of the Australian war brides that they sought practical solutions to their particular problems and dilemmas, and made positive decisions to improve their experiences as newcomers to America by taking action.

The establishment of these strong links with Australia has provided the war brides with a solid foundation on which to build their new lives in America. These bonds have been vital to their psychological wellbeing, especially in the early post war years when they were officially viewed as 'aliens' in a new land, at least until they became US citizens, a topic to be discussed in the next chapter.

More recently, with the development of modern technology, various websites provide communications which now help expatriates keep in touch with their homeland, but such aids were not available to the war brides in years gone by.

Links to Australia have also been vital to the development of good relations between the two nations, fostering goodwill and furthering knowledge of the people of each country. Over the years, the Australian WWII war brides have proved themselves, sometimes consciously and sometimes unwittingly, to be good ambassadors for both Australia and America.

CHAPTER EIGHT

US CITIZENSHIP FOR AUSTRALIAN
WWII WAR BRIDES

'It was a sad day... like saying goodbye to
everything I'd ever known.'
[Joy Shaddle, reflecting on the forfeiture
of her Australian citizenship in 1953][1]

'I never thought it would take so long –
I have come full circle!'
[Joy Shaddle, on reclaiming her Australian
citizenship in 2007][2]

In 1944, Lola Atkins, from the small country town of Northam in Western Australia, left her home and went to the United States as the wartime bride of an American GI. Eleven years later, she became a US citizen. She remembers, 'it was a sad day for me'.[3] Her husband Tom told her she needed to do so, and because her children were American citizens, she too felt that it was necessary to take up US citizenship. Lola tells how she went through the process of being tested and interviewed twice:

> *The Immigration Officer, a veteran of forty-plus years in the INS [Immigration and Naturalization Service], had been arrested for accepting bribes. This necessitated recall with many other innocent persons to repeat the process with another staff member. Perhaps this contributed minimally to my haunting ambivalence.*[4]

Lola felt truly 'divided' about taking up US citizenship and having to relinquish the citizenship of her homeland. She recalls how terribly difficult it was and how she cried. A good friend gave Lola a surprise celebration with candles and American flags on the cake, but she just couldn't enjoy it and 'tears bubbled over during the celebration'. She

answered her friend's question with one of her own: 'How would you like to renounce your native land?' On her first return trip to Australia, thirty-seven years after she had originally left, Lola was a naturalised American citizen. 'Ah!' she says, 'but I was still very attached to the land of my birth. I felt that I had one foot in and on each beloved continent.'[5]

Lola Atkins, San Diego, CA, 2001.

Australian WWII war brides such as Lola, who migrated to America and took up US citizenship, automatically forfeited their rights as Australian citizens under section 17 of the *Australian Citizenship Act 1948,* which provided that adult Australian citizens lost their Australian citizenship when they acquired the citizenship of another country. Nothing could be done about this situation, which was entrenched in law.

The experiences of WWII war brides highlight the moral, emotional, and legal difficulties inherent within citizenship. Torn between allegiance to their old country and their new country of adoption, these women reveal the factors which motivated them to become US citizens, despite the consequential loss of Australian citizenship, and the severance of this symbolic tie to their country of birth.

In the late 1940s and early 1950s, Australian WWII war brides living in America turned their thoughts to whether or not they wanted to become US citizens. Their 'voices' illuminate the dilemmas they faced when deciding whether or not to become US citizens, especially at a time when they also felt strongly about maintaining their

Australian citizenship. Despite this predicament, only three of the 60 war brides interviewed have remained Australian citizens.

Preparation to become a US citizen varied across the United States, although it usually involved applying for naturalisation and taking classes to learn about American history and government. The applicants then were required to pass a test before taking part in a formal ceremony, where they received a certificate authenticating their US citizenship. It was a difficult and emotional decision for Australian WWII war brides to become US citizens as they felt loyalty to both countries: a special tie to the country of their birth and a need to embrace their new country of residence.

Legislation regarding citizenship thus had a significant impact on the lives of these women. In most cases their children who were born outside Australia had no access to Australian citizenship through their Australian mothers. It has been documented that 'various unfortunate historical quirks' in Australian citizenship law, meant that it had 'a complex and confusing history'.[6] The concepts of Australian citizenship and nationality conveyed by political theorists and other practitioners have been communicated with 'a range of varied and sometimes contradictory meanings' making it difficult to arrive at an acceptable single definition.[7] The history of citizenship and nationality in Australia has been complicated by Australia remaining part of the British Empire, and therefore the focus was on imperial categories of civic belonging, rather than national ones.[8] The rights and obligations attached to Australian citizenship have been defined in an ad hoc manner adding to its complexity. There was no coherent concept of Australian citizenship, to capture the whole relationship between citizen and state.[9]

At the time of Federation in 1901 a legal category of Australian citizenship did not exist, the Australian Constitution provided no definition of citizenship, nor did it claim any power over it. The term 'British subject' was the only formal civic status in Australia, until Australia Day 1949 when the *Nationality and Citizenship Act 1948* was proclaimed. This Act created a legal status of Australian citizenship, but because it lacked any new substance, most legislation continued to use the category 'British subject' rather than 'Australian citizen' until the 1970s. It was not until 1984 that Australian citizens actually ceased to be British subjects.[10]

Becoming a US citizen

Australians, including WWII war brides, who became naturalised US citizens on or after 26 January, 1949, and before 4 April, 2002, automatically forfeited their Australian citizenship under the provisions of Section 17 of the *Australian Citizenship Act 1948*.[11] The prospect of simultaneously giving up the citizenship of the country of their birth was difficult and sometimes traumatic for the war brides, especially at a time when many were homesick and still grieving for the families they had left behind.

The oath of allegiance to the US,[12] sworn as part of the US naturalisation process, may have sounded to Australian war brides taking up US citizenship as if it was some sort of 'renunciation' of their Australian citizenship. However, as the oath was made under US law, it had no legal effect on their citizenship under Australian law. Under established principles of national sovereignty, a country can only make laws about its own citizenship, not that of another sovereign nation. However, Section 17 of the *Australian Citizenship Act 1948* functioned by operation of law (regardless of whether the Australian authorities knew about the US naturalisation) to automatically take away their Australian citizenship under Australian law, its purpose being to prevent dual citizenship.[13]

Changes to Australian citizenship policy and law

Although there were minor amendments to the *Australian Citizenship Act 1948* over the ensuing years, Section 17 was part of the legislation from 26 January 1949, and its wording read from 22 November 1984 to the date of repeal on 4 April 2002 as follows:

Section 17

(1) A person, being an Australian citizen who has attained the age
    of 18 years, who does any act or thing:
    (a) the sole or dominant purpose of which; and
    (b) the effect of which, is to acquire the nationality or
         citizenship of a foreign country, shall, upon
         that acquisition, cease to be an Australian citizen.

(2) Subsection (1) does not apply in relation to an act of
    marriage.[14]

However, it should be noted that the period in which this
wording applied was long after most Australian WWII war brides
had become US citizens, and they had already forfeited their
Australian citizenship.

Becoming US Citizens

Up to fifteen thousand Australian WWII war brides went to
live in the United States and all, at some time, were faced with the
decision of whether or not to become US citizens. The motivation
and reasons behind their decisions were varied.

Betty Blondon, a war bride from Newcastle, New South
Wales, felt guilty taking the oath of allegiance to become a US
citizen. She explains:

> *During the war there's such a strong feeling for your country,*
> *and then to come to another country and forget your first*
> *country – no, you can't!* [15]

Australia has always been home to Betty. She comments:

> *Even though I was only there twenty-one years and I'm 75*
> *years old now, but you know, it's still home.*[16]

Despite this predicament, which was experienced by most Australian war brides, Betty did become a US citizen. Only three of the 60 war brides interviewed have remained Australian citizens.

The war brides' stories provide an important new lens through which to view the way in which these Australian women responded to their right to vote and to citizenship. Having grown up in a country where women had been able to vote in national elections since 1902,[17] and where compulsory voting at federal elections was introduced in 1924 for citizens over 21 years of age, these women found it very different as residents of America where voting was not compulsory. Australian war brides generally embraced their new country of residence, and it was some time after they had settled in to American life that many decided to take up US citizenship.[18]

Citizenship for women

Early in the period between the wars, Australian women, particularly married women, were unrelenting in their battle for economic independence. The issue of citizenship had become increasingly important in this period, with feminists asserting that 'rights of full "self-expression" and of "earning a living" were "rights essential to every citizen"'.[19] Though the Australian war brides were not necessarily feminists, they were nevertheless concerned over their own loss of nationality and citizenship upon marriage.[20]

Citizenship has been defined in various ways and can mean a number of things, political, economic, social and emotional',[21] but there is an elusive quality at the symbolic heart of citizenship which is difficult to define.[22] Writing, songs and paintings that depict the land, are all important in identifying the shared values that define a country's cultural heritage.[23]

Historical studies of migration have shown that when arriving in a new country and stepping from the ship onto land, immigrants look around for signs of continuity with the land they left behind.[24] This is true of the war brides' experience as Australian migrants to

America in the mid-twentieth century. They first glimpsed their new country and looked for familiar examples of flora and other signs in the seasonal landscape which reminded them of Australia.[25] For many of the Australian war brides it took years before they overcame chronic feelings of homesickness and were settled enough to consider taking out US citizenship and swearing allegiance to their adopted country.

Citizenship legislation and Australian WWII war brides

In the 1940s, there was a great deal of confusion regarding the citizenship status of Australian war brides, and it was also a time when there was little universal support for the rights of married women and their children.[26] After processing the necessary paperwork in the form of permissions, references, declarations, official personal certification, health and police clearances, the United States accepted entry of Australian brides of US servicemen as residents, but only within the legislative framework at that time which categorised them as 'aliens'.

Under American law, after the passing of the Cable Act of 22 September 1922, an alien woman married to an American did not automatically acquire her husband's domicile or nationality.[27]

In March 1943, the Australian Minister for the Army clarified that an Australian bride of an American serviceman did not lose her Australian citizenship until she acquired American citizenship, which did not automatically occur upon marriage. Information of an ambiguous nature was circulated in July of the same year by the Director General of the authoritative Manpower organisation, regarding the legal position of Australian girls (who then were known as 'British subjects') on their marriage to American servicemen. It stated that 'an Australian girl marrying an American will lose her British nationality and become an American national' (which implied, incorrectly, that this would happen automatically) with the proviso 'unless, under American law, she is prevented from acquiring the nationality of her husband'.[28]

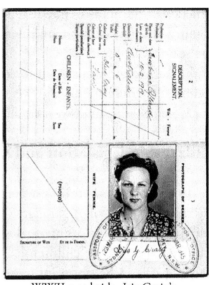

Iris Craig's British Passport cover.   WWII war bride, Iris Craig's
                                                      passport photo

Bottom, Iris's passport stamped 'British Subject

A year later, on 29 August 1944, the Director General of
Manpower clarified the true position under Section 18 (2) of the
Commonwealth Nationality Act 1920-1936. Under this Act a female
subject did not lose her rights to Australian citizenship unless she

acquired the nationality of her husband.[29] Under Australian law, a woman who was a British subject immediately before her marriage did not cease to be a British subject upon her marriage to an American soldier. If she was to acquire US citizenship in due course, she then ceased to be a British subject.[30]

However, for the Australian wife of an American soldier, it was not a quick process to acquire US citizenship and it seemed that it could be a long wait for some of these women to gain a true sense of security.[31] Their anxiety was made worse by lack of access to maintenance, as no arrangements had been put in place by the US forces for the distribution of allotments to foreign wives.[32]

Initially, the Australian wife had to obtain a visa and comply with immigration formalities for entry into the United States. Then, they had to reside in the United States for one year before making application for and obtaining naturalisation papers. In addition, the Australian wife was required to pass a test before the citizenship ceremony took place.[33] Many attended night classes in America to study for this test. Dorothy Berry recalls 'it was a six-week course and…it was two nights a week'. She remembers learning the Constitution and considering herself a good student. She took her citizenship test in front of a 'regular US Judge' who asked why it had taken her thirteen years to become a citizen. Dorothy recalls:

> *I said 'Well your honour, I have been a little busy' and he asked 'Doing what?' I said 'Well in the past eleven years I've had six children!' He said 'Oh!' and that came out in the newspaper.*[35]

Speaking up in this situation gave Dorothy confidence and she went on to be PTA President at her children's school and she became quite a community leader. This involvement in her neighbourhood helped her finally to feel accepted in her country of adoption.[36]

While many Australian war brides were keen to become naturalised and take up US citizenship, they nevertheless found it very difficult and sometimes traumatic to give up the citizenship of the country of their birth. Ivy Diers, who grew up in Rockhampton, Queensland, remembers:

> *I decided if I'm going to live here I should become a citizen. I feel pretty strongly about that really. it wasn't difficult to say 'I want to be a US citizen...but the hardest thing I ever did was to put my hand up and say – and we had to say – that I was going to give up my Australian citizenship'.*[37]

Ivy Diers, visiting Sydney, 13 November, 2006.

Certainly, anyone wanting to become a naturalised US citizen had to swear as part of the oath of allegiance to the US that:

> *I absolutely and entirely renounce and abjure all allegiance and fidelity to any foreign prince, potentate, state or sovereignty; of whom or which I have heretofore been a subject or citizen.*[38]

Similarly, Mary Bourne took up American citizenship and clearly recalls the day she gave up her Australian citizenship:

It was one of the hardest things I've ever done in my life. As welcome as I was here, I was still an Aussie.[39]

Dorothy (Mary) Bourne,
Sacramento, 2001.

The wartime experience of these women undoubtedly sharpened their sense of national identity when they were faced with the prospect of having to forfeit their Australian citizenship and sever this connection to the country of their birth. Although, as mentioned earlier, while it was timely that various issues affecting the status of women be considered at a national level, some years were to pass before new Australian nationality and citizenship legislation affecting the war brides was to be implemented.[40]

The immigration quota for entry of Australian immigrants to the US at this time was only one hundred per year.[41] In cases where the Australian immigration quota to the US was not full, the Australian woman married to a United States soldier had to obtain a visa from the American Consulate, which required in particular, evidence of good health, as well as evidence of the means of the applicant, so that she would not become a public charge (this being strictly enforced), and then she had to comply with immigration formalities.[42]

On the other hand, if the immigration quota was full, then a petition could be made through the American Consulate to Washington on the grounds that the applicant is married to an American citizen. If granted, this could overcome the quota difficulties but it did not waive the other immigration requirements, particularly good health at the time of actual entry and that the person entering would not become a public charge. Such a petition took five to six months to be sent to Washington and returned.[43]

This draconian situation was relieved soon after the end of the war when, under American law, *The War Brides Act* of December 28, 1945 (59 Statutes-at-Large 659) waived all visa requirements and provisions of immigration law for members of the American armed forces who, during World War II, had married nationals of foreign countries.[44] Six months later, the *G.I. Fiancées Act* of June 29, 1946 (60 Statutes-at-Large 339) was implemented, finally admitting the fiancées of American servicemen to the United States.[45] Once settled in America, war brides turned their thoughts to whether or not they wished to become citizens of their new country.

Not all war brides became US citizens, and some chose to keep their Australian citizenship. Barbara Gleason, for example, readily admits that 'it is amazing' that after 60 years of living in America that she is still an Australian citizen. She says:

> *I did consider it at one time, but I just couldn't do it. Once an Aussie, always an Aussie!'* [46]

Similarly, Margaret Fosmo says, 'I'm Australian' and she has never wanted to become an American citizen, although people have been critical in the past. She recalls:

> *People said 'your children will want you to be an American', but my children have always kind of liked it that I'm Australian...I'm what they call a 'resident alien'.*[47]

As such, Margaret has a card which is pink in colour, although it is still referred to as a 'green card', which has to be regularly checked although she has been an upstanding citizen for more than 60 years. [48]

Reasons for becoming US citizens

Most war brides, however, did become US citizens and were variously motivated to take this action. The strong bonds of motherhood, apparent from the experiences of some of these war brides, were significant factors behind their motivation to become naturalised US citizens. The maternal bonds strengthened the women's decisions to take the serious step of becoming US citizens, despite having to relinquish their cherished Australian citizenship.

For Joyce Balogh, the security of her children was the prime motivation to take up US citizenship. At her home in Tigard, Oregon, she looked fondly at her framed certificate of citizenship and tells how her husband, Alexander, had said to her: 'If I'm sent overseas anytime and you and the girls are with me, you will be sent to the British section and the girls and I will go to the American section.' Joyce recollected:

> *I had no other reason, I was happy being an Australian. I didn't mind leaving Alexander, but I couldn't dare leave my daughters.*[49]

It was after her children started school that Joann Patterson wanted to become a naturalised US citizen. She was interested in her children's education and was keen to 'have a say in what was going on in the school'. She also wanted to be able to vote as she had been able to in Australia.[50]

Joann Patterson, Portland, Oregon, September, 2001.

This continuous theme among the war brides' stories highlights the relationship between motherhood and citizenship, where their main motivation to become a US citizen was in the interests of their children. In their role of 'mother' these women had a natural concern for the security of their offspring. In the period from the late 1940s to the early 1950s, the outbreak of the Korean War was juxtaposed with fresh memories of the war just over. Matters of security were heightened at this time, and it seemed prudent for the children and both parents to be US citizens in case of military conflict which might threaten the family unit. The war brides also demonstrated normal maternal concern for good education for their children, and having US citizenship enabled them to express their opinions via the right to vote.

Some war brides took up US citizenship to facilitate easier passage through immigration checks when travelling, so they would not be separated from their children. It was for the sake of her children that Joan Moran took up US citizenship after being in America only a short time. Her husband Tom warned her that in the event of another war she could be separated from her children 'because they were US citizens'.[51] It was their strong maternal ties to their children that strengthened the women's decisions to take the serious step of becoming US citizens, despite having to automatically forfeit their Australian citizenship.

Joan Moran, Garden Grove, CA.

Similarly, Betty Stites took up US citizenship for the sake of her two young sons. Betty had made two visits home to Australia since arriving in America, and remembers on returning to the United States always having to leave her two little children 'over on the side' while she went through customs as a 'non-American' to collect her baggage. She recalls: 'With those little kids waiting in there, it scared me to death'.[53] Separation from her children because of her 'alien' status was a great worry to Betty and it was the main reason that she decided to become an American citizen, although dual citizenship would have been her preference, had it been an option at the time. The process of becoming a citizen of the United States proved to be fairly easy for Betty, apart from the strong emotion she felt at giving up her Australian citizenship. She tells how she went to night school and 'studied everything under the sun – every book I could find about America'.[54] Betty's husband drove her to take the examination, and even then she was not sure that she wanted 'to give away' citizenship of her 'own country', and she almost changed her mind. Betty clearly remembers this occasion and the person who conducted the interview:

> He was very high up…and he invited me into his office and asked me all these questions. I kept looking at him and thinking 'Why does he want to know all about my family and my family in Australia and all that sort of stuff?' He didn't ask me a thing about the Constitution! [55]

Betty enquired if he planned to ask her more relevant questions. She said 'I want you to know that I've really studied and I've taken classes and I can answer any question that you want to ask me!' The examiner's response was 'I know that! I knew that the minute I saw you' and he said 'I know you're going to make a wonderful citizen!'[56] When Betty received the notice for the citizenship ceremony she recalls:

I almost ran…you know how you sometimes get panicky?
I thought to myself 'What are you doing?'…all these other
nationalities were all over the place…hardly anybody like
me there …anyway I raised the flag and…he gave a lovely
speech about how we don't want you to forget your own
country…it will always be your homeland, but you will be
a citizen of the United States as long as you live here.[57]

Joy Shaddle settled in the small town of Forrest, Illinois, and still lives in the same house almost 60 years later. She was very sad to have to give up her Australian citizenship to become a US citizen, but like many others, she did it for the sake of her three children. She felt that 'it was the wise thing to do' as her children were American citizens and she thought, 'if anything happens; I'd better be one too'.[58] Joy was in Peoria, Illinois, seven months pregnant with her third child, Jimmy, and nearby a group of Mexicans were celebrating becoming American citizens, but Joy was not so happy. She remembers 'I stood there with tears flowing'.[59] It was difficult to explain to her four-year-old daughter why she was crying. But she felt she had to become a US citizen and relinquish her Australian citizenship, for the security of her children. If anything happened to her husband, she didn't know what would become of her and her children. Over fifty years later, she reflects on that day in 1953 when she became an American citizen and automatically forfeited her Australian citizenship:

It was a sad day…like saying goodbye to everything I'd
ever known.[60]

Some war brides took up US citizenship in order to obtain employment. Jean Fargo's motivation to become a US citizen in 1950 was to get a job with the US government, which required her to hold US citizenship. Jean said:

Other Australian girls and I thought it was the thing to do
– I have a son who lives here – it was just the thing to do'.[61]

Similarly, June Carver who lives in Ogden, Utah, became a US citizen so that she was eligible to work for the Federal Government. Starting out as a key-punch operator, June worked for the Treasury Department in the Internal Revenue Service for twenty-six years and was in the position of supervisor in the audit section when she retired.[62]

Other war brides found it necessary to become US citizens in order to facilitate their husbands' employment. Renouncing her Australian citizenship was not easy, but Iris Craig decided to take out US citizenship in 1949 to ensure that her husband's job application was successful. She studied hard for her US citizenship test by correspondence through the University of California, although the test turned out to be easy for her. Because her husband was employed in the Border Patrol, Iris had met quite a few people in the Immigration Department. During a general conversation when she happened to be visiting the office at that time, one of the immigration officials asked if she had been studying. As there were a few things that puzzled her a little, they discussed them. He then asked her a few more questions, which she was able to answer. Iris tells how easy it was:

The next thing, he says 'You passed!' I said 'Passed what?' He said
'I just gave you a test!' I didn't realise I was being tested!'[63]

Iris was working at the time and was allowed time off to go to the court for the citizenship ceremony.[64]

Joan Hamilton took up US citizenship, much to her 'mother's horror!' This was essentially to support her husband's application for consular duty, which required him to have an American citizen as a wife. She comments:

I really was very sad about it, because I still call myself an
Australian. I really didn't want to give it up, but I knew
that Charles wanted this assignment very badly. He just
desperately wanted it…so that I could go with him overseas.[65]

Joan Hamilton, Annaheim, CA, September, 2001.

In some cases, taking up US citizenship involved complications. For
example, Australian war bride Kathleen Heeren, an American citizen since
1956, broke her US residency by going to Britain, and had to get a re-
entry permit and re-apply when she returned to America. She took out
US citizenship mainly because of her husband and children. Her older
daughter was born in England and her husband had to return to America
before the rest of the family. Knowing that he would 'desperately' want
his baby daughter to be an American citizen, Kathleen took the child's

English birth certificate to the American
embassy in London and waited hours with the
infant for her to be issued with an American
passport. Also, planning to live permanently
in America, Kathleen was aware that there was
very little work to be found in her capacity
without being a US citizen, and government
work was almost impossible to get.[66]

Kathleen Heeren, Denver,
Colorado, 2001.

Factors such as marriage, the birth of children, and the war brides' roles of 'mother' and 'wife' all reflected significantly on the meaning of citizenship for these women, and influenced their decision to become US citizens, despite the consequential loss of the citizenship of their country of origin.

Interest in politics, and a desire to vote in the country where they now lived and raised their children, also seems to have been a common theme which motivated many war brides to take up US citizenship. Dorothy Hammon, from a 'Labor union background', had worked as a secretary for the Bread-Carters' Union in Australia in the days when the bread was delivered with 'horses and carts'. She remembers that it was considered to be 'a very good job – 35 hours a week – and good money, too'.[67] Demonstrating an early interest in industrial relations, she was keen to vote. Dorothy did not go to night school to study, but borrowed all the books she needed from the library and proudly passed the test.[68]

Nancy Lankard, who became a US citizen in 1958, had worked as a volunteer for the elections in the US for ten years and wanted to have her say. She attended school two nights a week for several months with others from Canada, Japan and England, also studying to become American citizens. She recalls passing the test:

> There were questions about government, city, etc. and I was asked 'Would you take up arms against Australia?'... and...'Would you defend America against any country?' So I said 'yes', but in my mind I knew I would always be an Aussie, no matter what![69]

It was because of her involvement with her husband in local politics in America that Ivy Diers took out citizenship in 1953. She recalls:

> I felt kind of funny telling people 'Vote for Eisenhower' when I couldn't vote myself! So that was when I decided, if I'm going to live here I should become a citizen. I feel pretty strongly about that really.[70]

Colleen Halter, who became a US citizen in 1952, similarly 'wanted to vote for Eisenhower', but she says 'I always felt Australian in my heart'.[71]

Taking up US citizenship was a memorable event in the life of Peggy Dunmore Blackman, who did so in order to vote. She says:

> *I felt I did not have a right to even speak up on any issue until and unless I was an American citizen.*[72]

She recalls:

> *It was an emotional moment giving up being an Australian, standing up in court with the tears streaming down my face, and my daughter saying 'Why is Mummy crying?' It was a renunciation, but I needed no urging to be married and, bottom line, no urging to become a citizen. It was just the renunciation of loyalty to Australia as number one.*[73]

However, she comments:

> *I was now an American and if I was indeed in that category, I was going to be a good one. But it was a significant moment in my life.*[74]

Simply the notion that it seemed to be 'the right thing to do' motivated some war brides to be come American citizens. Teddy Pickerel took out US citizenship in 1949, not long after she came to America. She says:

> *It had nothing to do with my feelings for Australia, but I knew that I liked this country and I felt that if I was going to stay here and accept the protection of its flag, then it was the only honourable thing one could do. Of course, I do love America…and I still love Australia! There was no reason*

for leaving Australia except that I married an American.
There was nothing detrimental about Australia, and so I
made that transition and felt that I wanted to be a part of
it. I was very interested in politics and that sort of thing.[75]

It was in March 1975 that Jean Vallero decided to become an American citizen, 26 years after her arrival in America. She remembers the gist of her father's words when she left Australia in 1949: 'I don't want to hear you criticise America in any way, because your life will be there and anything you get will come through that country.'[76] So, she made the decision that she was 'not going to say anything bad about the country, even about the things she didn't like'. Eventually, she remembers, that right after John Kennedy was elected President there was a point where she thought she would like to have a say in the government but she says: 'I figured I couldn't criticise if I didn't vote!'[77]

It was not compulsory to vote in America, and Jean's husband never had voted. However, at one time when there was a local issue that needed to be settled, Jean finally persuaded him to register to vote, and she herself worked on the polls several times. Jean says she is 'not greatly interested' in politics, but admits that she does like to know that she can 'make a little bit of a difference'. Jean, like others, was unhappy to have to give up her Australian citizenship.[78]

Irene Perruci became an American citizen on 18 August 1961, because 'I figured that if I was going to live in this country, then I'd better abide by the laws' of that country.[79] She agreed with the sentiments of her husband's Italian/American family who never taught their children to speak much Italian, as they believed that 'when you are in America, you will speak American (sic)!' Irene went to school for six weeks before it was time for her naturalisation which she remembers:

Oh, how we studied, about this war and that war...I
couldn't remember everything. So it came to my turn and

> *the judge asked 'Who makes the laws of the land?' and*
> *I said 'Congress'. He asked 'Are the laws the same in each*
> *State?' and I said 'No, each State has its own laws'. The*
> *judge said 'Next please!' And I went for six weeks to study!*
> *And that's all he asked me!* [80]

Many of the war brides' accounts suggest that the required 'test', although requiring weeks of preparatory study, was itself not at all onerous. This raises the question of whether test questions varied in difficulty for 'aliens' from other nations, and whether Australians were preferred and looked upon favourably as new countrymen.

Australian WWII war brides in America took pride in studying and passing the naturalisation test. Helen Leirer was living in Utah in the early 1950s when she became a US citizen. Interested to learn about America, she recalls with pride:

> *I took a correspondence course through the University of Salt*
> *Lake City – a course on citizenship by mail. I was alone, I*
> *wasn't in a class and when I did the exam I was the only*
> *one in an office with a supervisor. I probably studied lots of*
> *things that I didn't have to study. It didn't matter, I didn't*
> *mind. Then I took the test and passed!* [81]

Some war brides' narratives convey a hint of scepticism regarding the citizenship process, suggesting that it was undertaken simply for convenience. For instance, Gladys Borger, born in the small Queensland country town of Howard, became a US citizen in 1949, because it made it easier for her to travel on an American passport when her husband was in the service. However, she says: 'I took the oath with my fingers crossed behind my back![82]

From the above examples told in their own words, it is clear that these Australian women were reluctant to give up their Australian citizenship as a consequence of taking up US citizenship, and most tended to wait some years before doing so. Perhaps the prospect and formality of having to study for a test was a little daunting for some. From all accounts they were prepared to thoroughly inform themselves about America, and found the test questions quite easy.

More than reluctant to give up her Australian citizenship, Hazel Walker says, 'I have never felt "American"'.[83] She did not even consider becoming an American citizen until her husband was about to be transferred from Texas to the Japanese city of Okinawa, eleven years after her arrival in the US. The Commander of her husband's Squadron advised her to take out American citizenship to avoid running into problems on arrival in Japan, and being separated from her husband and family by the Japanese. He said that in Japan 'things were made fast and easy for the US citizens, but not for others'. So Hazel 'took the required exam and was awarded US citizenship in April 1956'.[84] In 1989, however, after reading a book about citizenship acts in various countries, she contacted the Australian Consulate in Los Angeles to enquire whether she could get her Australian citizenship back. She recalls:

> *They gave me forms to fill out where I had to explain that I had taken out US citizenship, not voluntarily, but because I was told by a representative of the United States Government to take out US citizenship...Shortly thereafter I received a certificate, Evidence of Australian Citizenship, from Canberra. I was so happy to be officially Australian again, and went again to the Australian Consulate in Los Angeles and got my Australian passport.*[85]

Some women, such as Jean Wilk, were completely unwilling to forfeit their Australian citizenship. It took Jean 60 years to become a US citizen. In March, 2006 at the age of 82 when visiting Australia on an Australian passport, she enquired whether she needed a visa to return to America. The Australian immigration officers were very surprised to know that it was 60 years since she first left Australia to live in the US. Jean went to the US consulate who informed her that as she had never forfeited her Australian citizenship, more recent changes to citizenship legislation (discussed later in this chapter) now enabled her to obtain dual citizenship. She admits that she had 'felt a little guilty' for not having taken out US citizenship in all those years and tells how some people used to be critical:

> *A neighbour of my sister once commented on the fact that I had lived in the US so long and had never taken out US citizenship! She asked me if I felt like an American. I said 'No, I still feel like I'm Australian!' People used to ask me about voting and I'd just say 'I can't vote'. It didn't really worry me.*[86]

Now, as a dual Australian/American citizen, Jean is happy to hold both Australian and US passports and also to be able to vote.

The reasons that these women gave for taking up US citizenship were diverse. They were concerned with family security, especially with regard to children; employment opportunities with the government; helping to secure employment for their husbands; avoiding estate tax duty if their husband died and they were not US citizens; simply doing the 'right' or 'honourable' thing; or sometimes a combination of these reasons. An interest in politics and having the right to vote were also important factors in becoming US citizens, indicating a strong desire of these women to take their place as useful citizens in their adopted country.

Australian citizenship legislation reform

In August 1998, almost fifty years after the *Australian Citizenship Act 1948* was implemented, the Australian Citizenship Council was established as an independent body to advise the Minister for Immigration & Multicultural Affairs on contemporary issues relating to Australian citizenship. The subsequent review of citizenship policy and law led to amendments being made to the *Australian Citizenship Act 1948* in 2002. Section 17 was repealed, allowing adult Australian citizens to acquire another citizenship without losing their Australian citizenship.[87]

However, this applied only to those Australians who acquired another citizenship from the date the legislation came into effect on 4 April, 2002, and it was not proposed that this amendment apply retrospectively.[88] While this change in legislation brought Australia into line with the citizenship law of many other comparable countries, including the UK, Canada, New Zealand, USA, France and Italy,[89] it was of no benefit at all to Australian war brides in America who had mostly taken up US citizenship approximately 50 years earlier.

Further amendments to citizenship legislation provided for the resumption of prior Australian citizenship, however, this required the applicant to guarantee their intention to become a permanent resident of Australia within three years of the application. This of course could not be guaranteed by Australian war brides who have lived in America for 50 or 60 years, and who now are most unlikely to want to leave their children, grandchildren and great-grandchildren to return to Australia permanently.[90]

Reforms to Australian citizenship law announced on 7 July, 2004, were expected to pass through parliament in 2005 and offered promise that Australian WWII war brides who lost their Australian citizenship under Section 17 would soon enjoy simplified access to Australian citizenship. This would allow not only the war brides, but also their war babies and children born overseas to obtain dual Australian/American citizenship.[91] Under these reforms, the only criterion for resumption of Australian citizenship was that the person be of good character. Now there was to be no requirement for the applicant to have the intention to live in Australia permanently within three years.[92] The passage of this forthcoming legislation through parliament was happily anticipated by some Australian war brides in America, who had already indicated their excitement to be able to resume their Australian citizenship, which was to give them dual Australian-American citizenship and restore their 'lost citizenship' of many years. Some indicated that their children born in Australia and overseas were also very interested to apply for Australian citizenship.[93]

However, these expected reforms were slow to arrive. Again the Australian WWII war brides, now mostly in their eighties, had to exercise patience and once again found that they were 'ladies in waiting'. The Southern Cross Group (SCG), acting in the interests of Australians living abroad, had lobbied intently for this legislation, and in a media release welcomed the news that finally the *Australian Citizenship Act 2007* had received Royal Assent on 15 March 2007. The Act was passed by Parliament in Canberra on 1 March, but did not come into force until July 1, 2007.[94]

Just two months earlier, in recognition of Australian WWII war brides, the Australian Embassy in Washington DC hosted a special event giving tribute to these women and their courageous spirit, in a historic gathering on 24 and 25 April 2007. Ninety-five Australian war brides, despite most being in their 80s, and some in their 90s, travelled various distances from cities across the vast United States, accompanied by spouses, children and grandchildren, to participate in this special occasion. The Australian Ambassador, Dennis Richardson, and the Australian Embassy Staff gave tribute to the Australian WWII war brides with an evening devoted to them, in conjunction with events the following day to commemorate ANZAC Day. Most of the war brides had not attended an ANZAC Day ceremony since leaving Australia in the 1940s and were so proud to be invited to attend.

Tribute to Australian WWII War Brides, at Australian Embassy, Washington D.C., 24th April, 2007 [Photographer: Paul Morigi].

In a letter of thanks to the Australian Ambassador, Erin Craig, President of the WWII War Brides Association, and daughter of a war bride, writes:

> My mother, Australian war bride Iris Craig, was overwhelmed at being asked to lay the War Brides' wreath at the Korean War Memorial. A lot of the other war brides there told her how proud they were of her. You should have seen her beam![95]

Iris Craig - Placing wreath on Korean War Memorial, Washington DC, April, 2007 [Source: Amy Drake].

On behalf of the Australian WWII war brides, Erin Craig conveyed their thanks to the Ambassador, stating that 'it was an honor to participate in the commemorations for this most important of Australian dates'. The letter expressed appreciation for 'recognizing [sic] our Australian war brides' who 'felt that they were treated like royalty by their homeland' at this 'once-in-a-lifetime gathering in the United States of America...on Australian soil. It was like being home again.'[96]

Left: Lola Atkins at the Australian Embassy, Washington DC, April, 2007.

Bottom: Edna (Teddy) Pickerel at the tribute to Australian WWII War Brides at the Australian Embassy, Washington DC, April, 2007 [Photographer: Paul Morigi].

Media coverage of this historic event was widespread in America and in Australia. Soon after their tribute at the Embassy, Australian WWII war brides became eligible to become dual Australian-American citizens. One war bride, Joy Shaddle, who was the subject of TV and press coverage, says:

> *Of all the nice write-ups, this one is my favourite! When Jamie read it to me at his store, I was so touched I couldn't utter a word!* [97]

She refers to a small piece in the advertising newsletter 'July 4th Spectacular' from the only grocery store in her small home town in Illinois which reads:

Dear Friends & Amigos,

A World War II bride, Joy Shaddle, ever proud of her Forrest home, has put Forrest on the international stage. She has been given dual citizenship from the United States and her beloved Australia. Her beauty and charm captivated the TV and newspapers in both countries. A great very true love story that transcends time is genuine and true, like her accent. Always cheerful and elegant. Just thinking of her brings a smile.

Happy 4th,
Jamie

P.S. Just one of the things that make Forrest a great place!
P.P.S. Thanks to all our servicemen for our freedoms![98]

At almost 89 years of age, Joy was 'ecstatic' when a package with her Australian citizenship papers arrived on the porch at her home in Forrest, Illinois, where she has lived since 1947. She describes the moment:

I was laughing and crying. I was bursting at the seams... I never thought it would take so long – I have come full circle! [99]

Joy, like other Australian WWII war brides, was very proud to reclaim her Australian citizenship which meant much to her even after such a long period of time.

Joy Shaddle in her Forrest, Illinois home in 2007, reading
treasured love-letters from her late husband Lloyd.

The war brides' first-hand accounts offer understanding and
give insight into their experiences as 'aliens' in their adopted
country and reveal the reasons behind their motivation to
become US citizens, despite having to forfeit their Australian
citizenship. Their stories contribute to a broader understanding
of how the law regarding citizenship, its interpretation,
implementation and eventual reform, affected a generation of
Australian women and their children.

Initially, the implementation of the citizenship legislation
added to their sense of uncertainty and insecurity in a new
country; it then allowed them gradually to feel that they
belonged and could take part in American community activities;
and finally, decades later, gave them the opportunity to reclaim
their 'lost' identity as Australian citizens. For some war brides,
unfortunately, this legislative reform came too late, but can be
utilised by their children.

The strong bonds that continue to connect these women to the country of their birth can be seen in their reluctance to give up their Australian citizenship and in their eagerness to resume it, in the form of dual Australian/US citizenship, 60 years later — not only for themselves, but also for their children and in some cases, their grandchildren.

EPILOGUE

It is more than twelve years since I first interviewed an Australian WWII war bride. Sadly, at the time of writing, it is known that 14 of these women have died in recent years. Among this aging group, where most women are now in the vicinity of 90, this news is not surprising. This means, however, that the oral testimony collected during this period of research is a precious resource which records their experiences and reveals their valuable contribution to women's history.

Over this time, during six visits to the USA to meet with these women and record their memories, personal relationships and great friendships have developed. The war brides' interest in contributing has been enthusiastic from the start and has been sustained over the years by contact during these visits to America, as well as by telephone conversations and correspondence. Several war brides and some of their families have visited me in Australia, and it has been an honour to be able to repay some of their generosity and kindness shown to me when travelling in the US. My interaction with them for this project has formed another of their links to Australia, which are so important to them.

This is a generation of women who are very proud of their Australian heritage and of their lives in their adopted country of America, which they have fully embraced. It is remarkable that although as many as up to 15,000 Australian war brides joined their husbands in America, and represented the largest contingent of Australian women ever to migrate, that their stories are only now being published.

Their recorded experiences show that once Australian women decided to marry American servicemen, they were specifically affected by the arbitrary nature of some decision-making over which they had no control, which had a huge impact on these women's decisions and plans for their future lives.

During recent years, there has been a growing interest in the subject of war brides, and the topic has attracted more researchers. There has been a burgeoning of memoirs as war brides themselves have begun to chronicle their individual experiences in books and unpublished journals. In the absence of any scholarly in-depth analysis of the experiences of the Australian brides of US servicemen, this book is designed to fill this gap in historical studies.

Partly due to lack of record-keeping during the war and partly due to the marginalisation of women on the homefront, there has been little statistical or archival record-keeping regarding the Australian WWII war brides of American GIs. The archive of taped interviews with this group of women addresses this omission, and results in a unique resource recorded in their own words and from their own perspectives, adding to existing knowledge and enabling their stories to be chronicled for future generations.

The Australian women who married American GIs experienced the wartime years quite differently from the 'good-time girls' and the 'gold-diggers' whose images loom large in wartime mythology. The following extract from a recent Sydney newspaper clearly shows the importance of refuting the gendered myths and stereotypes of wartime which still linger on. Its opening words read:

> In World War II US servicemen were serviced by a grateful nation of Australian women in exchange for protection, hosiery and chocolate. Sydney has always opened its arms – and legs – to visiting Americans in times of war.[1]

This offensive text appeared in the mainstream press in 2010, as long as 65 years after the end of WWII, and confirms the need to challenge the power of false perceptions, which perpetuate the stereotypical images of women during wartime.

The Australian women who married US servicemen were loyal and committed to their husbands, and determined to make a good life for their families in a new country. Some found themselves in devastating situations after migrating to America, but they displayed courage and developed great strength of character due to circumstances over which they had no control.

When Shirley Norton's husband Robert was killed in Korea in 1951, just five years after her arrival in America, she was left a widow with four young children - the eldest was six – and Shirley's family in Australia wanted her to go home right away. She said: 'But I waited. I remembered what my father had said, so I wanted to prove I could make it on my own, which I did. I went back to work for the US Army.' With help from her mother-in-law who came to live with the family in 1956, she was able to work full-time for the Federal Government and to provide for her young family.

Shirley is proud that her four children were all able to have a good college education. She is also very proud of her late husband's war service record. She tells me:

> *My husband is buried in Arlington National Cemetery. He was very highly decorated, and had the Distinguished Service Cross, Silver Star, Bronze Star, and the Purple Heart of course. Until recently there was never any national recognition of the Korean War, but now there is, in Washington DC, with a very impressive memorial to the Korean Veterans. There are statues of all the combat, radio, infantry, and medics. It just gives you goose-bumps they are so lifelike. My husband was one of them.*

She adds:

> *Back when he was killed, for each medal that he got, I
> did get a letter from the President and the Army General
> of the time and several letters regarding his bravery and a
> description for each medal of the action. For the Silver
> Medal he had saved so many lives; for the Distinguished
> Service Cross he had brought attention to himself as Platoon
> Leader. Her put himself in the line of fire. So ... his head
> was shot off. So he brought all attention to himself while his
> Platoon took cover.*

Shirley went to Arlington Memorial Cemetery any time she was in the
vicinity, as do her children and grandchildren, to visit his grave.

Shirley Norton died five years ago and I attended the moving
ceremony at Arlington where her ashes are now resting beside those
of her beloved husband. I have happy memories of time spent with
Shirley when she visited Australia and when I stayed with her in her
summer cabin on the lake in Naples, Maine in 2004. This strong,
stoic, but kind, Australian war bride who migrated to the US for the
love of a soldier – like all the war brides – seemed to be from a special
generation of women who set a wonderful example of fortitude and
courage, and are great role models for young women of the future.

In April, 2007, ninety-five Australian war brides and their
families came from all parts of the US to attend the special tribute
given in their honour by the Australian Ambassador, Dennis
Richardson, in Washington, DC. It was an honour for me to be
invited to speak about my research on this occasion, and I did so in
the auditorium of the National Geographic building as part of this
event. This official acknowledgment of their valued contribution to
American society as good ambassadors, coming after so many years,
was timely. Almost simultaneously, legislation reform at last was
provided for the war brides, and their war babies, to be able to apply

for dual Australian-American citizenship. For these women who found it so heart-wrenching to forfeit their Australian citizenship 60 years ago, the opportunity to reinstate it means much to them and to their children. In one or two cases, the required FBI checks and fingerprinting, necessary as part of the application for dual citizenship, upset the war brides, who felt that they should not be subjected to such scrutiny after being law-abiding American citizens for so many years. One war bride felt strongly about this and decided not to go ahead with the application for this reason.

The memorable public commemoration and acknowledgment of the Australian WII war brides, as well as their participation in my research, clearly confirms to these women the importance of their memories of the past. As historian Kate Darian-Smith suggests:

> The private and public forms of commemoration of the experiences…reveal much about memory as a form of healing in old age: the tying up loose ends and offering comfort through the reflection on and need to give a meaning and sense of purpose to their lives'.[2]

In her study of US Marine veterans who spent time in Australia during WWII, Darian-Smith concludes that for some men, communal reminiscing about their wartime youth in Australia proved to be one of the most positive and empowering experiences of old age.

In the same way, the Australian Ambassador's tribute to the Australian WWII war brides in 2007, allowed them to share their experiences and to be honoured in an official capacity, which was an inspiring and empowering experience for these older women, most of whom were accompanied at this event by their children and grandchildren – the future generations – who can reflect on and learn from the war brides' recorded memories, adding a new dimension to women's history in both Australia and America.

ENDNOTES

INTRODUCTION

[1] Elfrieda Shukert and Barbara Scibetta, *War Brides of World War II,* Presidio Press, Novato, California, 1988, pp. 1, 2, and 7, also see Appendix A, p. 265; Marion F. Houstoun, et al, 'Female Predominance in Immigration to the United States Since 1930: A First Look' in *International Migration Review,* Vol. 18, No. 4, Special Issue: Women in Migration (Winter, 1984) p. 920.

[2] Estimates vary as follows: Geoffrey Bolton, *The Oxford History of Australia,* Vol. 5 (Oxford University Press) Melbourne, 1991, p. 17, states 'more than 10,000 Australian brides were seeking admission to the United States'; John Hammond Moore, *Over-sexed, over-paid and over here: Americans in Australia, 1941-1945* University of Queensland Press, St. Lucia, 1981, p. 161, states: '15 000 Australian women married US servicemen' Potts, E. Daniel & Annette Potts, *Yanks Down Under 1941-45: the American impact on Australia,* Oxford University Press, Melbourne, 1985, p. 362 states it was 'the generally accepted figure of 12,000'. Annette Potts and Lucinda Strauss, *For the Love of a Soldier. Australian war-brides and their GIs,* ABC Enterprises for the Australian Broadcasting Commission, Crows Nest, NSW, 1987, p. 47 state 'up to 12,000 girls married…and probably a further two or three thousand travelled to the US as *fiancées*', and on p. 14 they state the figure of '12,000-15,000, Australian girls married Americans'. This variation in numbers is due to the fact that no complete records were kept in Australia which clearly identified women travellers as 'war brides'. The main archival resources on this subject were incomplete copies of outgoing shipping lists for the American 'bride ships' which sailed between February 1946 and January 1947. Shipping lists for other vessels which transported war brides did not identify them separately from other passengers. Search of the National American Research Archives (NARA) in Maryland, USA, with the assistance of Naval and Army specialist researchers, did not uncover any record of arrivals in America which identified passengers as Australian war brides, who in any case, quickly dispersed across the country upon arrival, making this a challenging if not impossible research task.

[3] Patsy Adam-Smith, Australian Women at War, Nelson, Melbourne, 1984; Kate Darian-Smith, *On the Home Front: Melbourne in Wartime 1939-1945,* Oxford University Press, Melbourne, 1990; Kate Darian-Smith, 'War Stories: Remembering the Australian Home Front During the Second World War' in Kate Darian-Smith and Paula Hamilton (Eds), *Memory and History in Twentieth-Century Australia,* Oxford University Press, Melbourne, 1994; Darian-Smith, Kate, 'War and Australian Society', in Joan Beaumont (Ed), Australia's War,1939-45, Allen & Unwin, 1996.

[4] Detailed statistics regarding the war brides interviewed for this study can be found in the Appendices at the end of the thesis.

[5] Appendix 2 (1), Profile of War Brides – Ages; also see Campbell, Rosemary, *Heroes and Lovers. A question of national identity*, Allen & Unwin, Sydney, 1989, pp. 58, 64; Beaumont, *loc. cit.*, p. 72.

[6] See Appendix 2 (1), Profile of War Brides – Ages.

[7] Australian Bureau of Statistics, *4102.0 - Australian Social Trends, 1997*, [ABS Online http://www.abs.gov.au Accessed 4 May, 2008.] See Appendix 6, Marriage & Divorce Rates & Ex-nuptial Births.

[8] See Appendix 2, (2) Profile of War Brides–Socio-Economic Background.

[9] See Appendix 2, (3) Profile of War Brides–Size of Australian Family; and Appendix 6, Marriage and Divorce Rates & Ex-Nuptial Births. Also see Australian Bureau of Statistics – *4102.0 Australian Social Trends, 1997, op. cit.*

[10] Interviews with Marge Andreatta, Denver, CO, 7 September, 2001, and Helen Leirer, Garden Grove, CA, 19 September, 2001; also see Judy Mackinolty, 'Woman's place…' in *The Wasted Years,* George Allen & Unwin Australia Pty. Ltd., North Sydney, 1981, p. 107.

[11] See Appendix 2, (6) Profile of War Brides – Education.

[12] Interview with Patricia Law, Denver, CO, 8 September, 2001.

[13] Houstoun, *op. cit.*, p. 920.

[14] David Reynolds, Rich Relations. *The American Occupation of Britain 1942-1945*, Harper Collins, London, 1995, p. 419. Note: The figure of 40,000 is a conservative estimate by Reynolds, based on unpublished US Immigration and Naturalization Service (INS) figures for those entering America as alien wives of US citizens. (p. 420).

[15] Hilary Kaiser, *French war brides in America: an oral history*, Praeger Publishers, Westport, CT, 2008, pp. 150, 151.

[16] Astid Hastak, "'I Was *Never* One of Those *Frauleins': The Impact of Cultural Image on German War Brides in America"*, PhD Thesis, Purdue University, Indiana, May 2005.

[17] *ibid*; also see Mathilde Morris, *Dreams and Nightmares of a German War Bride,* Morris Publishing Company, Aurora, Colorado, 1998.

[18] Elena Russo LeMaster, *Memoirs of a War Bride,* Authorhouse, Bloomington, Illinois, 2006.

[19] Robert Perks and Alistair Thomson (Eds), *The Oral History Reader,* (2nd ed), Rutledge, London, 2006, p. ix.

[20] Paul Thompson, 'The Voice of the Past. Oral History', in Robert Perks and Alistair Thomson (Eds), The Oral History Reader, (2nd ed), Rutledge, London, 2006, pp. ix, x.

[21] Letter from US President, Ronald Reagan, dated April 5, 1985, quoted in Shukert and Scibetta, *op. cit.*, p. 260.

[22] See Shukert and Scibetta, *op. cit.*, pp. 260-61.

CHAPTER ONE

[1]Betty Kane, 'The War Bride', in *Albany Writers' Circle* No. 19. *A Collection of Short Stories and Poetry by the Writers of Albany,* November Issue, Denmark Printers, Albany, WA, 2001, p. 36. Also see List of Abbreviations.

[2,3,4] Interview with Irene Franck, San Diego, CA, 25 September, 2001.

[5,6,7] Interview with Dorothy (Mary) Bourne, Sacramento, CA, 29 September, 2001.

[8,9,10,11] Correspondence from Hazel Walker, Phoenix, AZ, 28 January, 2008.

[12] National Archives of Australia, 'Fact sheet 234 – United States forces in Queensland, 1941–45' http://www.naa.gov.au/about-us/publications/fact-sheets/fs234.aspx

[13] The "Brisbane line" was an alleged plan to abandon Northern Australia in the event of a Japanese invasion. The allegations created much public controversy and led to a Royal Commission of Inquiry in June 1943, which found that no such plan had been official policy under the Menzies government. See Paul Hasluck, *The government and the people, Australia in the war of 1939-1945,* vol.II, Australian War Memorial, 1970, Canberra, pp. 711-717

[14] Correspondence from Hazel Walker, Phoenix, AZ, 28 January, 2008.

[15] The term 'GI' originated in the 1930s denoting equipment supplied to US forces, and is an abbreviation of 'government (or general) issue'. In WWII it came also to be applied to the personnel, especially enlisted men. See Potts, E Daniel & Annette Potts, *Yanks Down Under 1941-45: the American impact on Australia,* Oxford University Press, Melbourne, 1985, p. xvi; and Catherine Soanes & Angus Stevenson, (Eds), Concise Oxford English Dictionary, 11th Ed., Revised, Oxford University Press, New York, 2006; also see List of Abbreviations.

[16] Annette Potts and Lucinda Strauss, *For the Love of a Soldier. Australian War-Brides and Their GIs,* ABC, 1987, p. 18.

[17] Allie Rudy, 'The Story of My Life', 13 November, 2006. (Unpublished journal, excerpts supplied to author in May 2007 in Washington D.C.)

[18] Interview with Nancy Lankard, 14 November, 2004, by telephone.

[19] Interview with Jean Fargo, Reno, NV, 30 September 1999.

[20] *ibid*; Potts, *Yanks Down Under, op. cit.,* p. 116.

[21,22,23,24,25] Interview with Jean Fargo, Reno, NE, 30 September 1999.

[26,27] Interview with Iris Craig, Sydney, 15 November, 2003.

[28,29] Campbell, Rosemary, *Heroes and Lovers. A question of national identity,* Allen & Unwin, Sydney, p. 73, 9.5

[30] Potts, *Yanks Down Under,* op.cit., p 331; Patsy Adam-Smith, Australian Women at War, Nelson, Melbourne, 1984, p. 294. (An Australian Army Private received 6s.0d.a day, or £9.15s.0d. a month. The American Private received £17.0s.0d. a month.)

[31] 'Disturbances Between Australian and American Troops'. Appendix 'E' to Advanced HQ Allied Land Forces Weekly Intelligence Summary No. 18, 4 December 1942, NAA Series BG121/3 Item 282M [NAA, Melbourne]

[32] Campbell, *Heroes*, p. 5.

[33] John Hammond. *Over sexed, over-paid and over here: Americans in Australia, 1941-1945*: University of Queensland Press, St. Lucia, Brisbane, 1981; also see David Reynolds, *Rich Relations. The American Occupation of Britain 1942-1945*, Harper Collins, London, 1995.

[34] Campbell, *Heroes, op. cit.*, p. 5.

[35] Marilyn Lake, *Getting Equal. The history of Australian feminism*, Allen & Unwin, St. Leonards, 1999, p. 199.

[36] Correspondence from Hazel Walker, Phoenix, AZ, 19 September, 2008.

[37] Survey conducted by Dr Lotte Fink, cited in Lake, 'Female Desire', p. 74; Lotte Fink, 'Premarital Sex Experience of girls in Sydney', in *The International Journal of Sexology*, Vol. 8, Issue 1, 1954, pp. 9-11. Also see Josephine May, 'Secrets and lies: sex education and gendered memories of childhood's end in an Australian provincial city, 1930s-1950s', Sex Education, Volume 6, No 1, February 2006, p1-15.

[38,39] Correspondence from Hazel Walker, Phoenix, Arizona, 8 February, 2009.

[40,41,42] Interview with Nancy Lankard, by telephone, 13 November, 2004.

[43] See Dymphna Cusack and Florence James, *Come in Spinner. The Lives and Loves of Women in Wartime*, Heinemann, Melbourne, 1954 (first published 1951); also Xavier Herbert, Soldiers' Women: Panther, London, 1963.

[44,45,46,47] Correspondence with Hazel Walker, 'My Romantic Marriage Proposal', Phoenix, AZ, 2008.

[48] Interview with Betty McIntire, Reno, NE, 30 September, 1999.

[49] Interview with Shirley Norton, Reno, NE, 30 September, 1999.

[50] Interview with Betty McIntire, Reno, NE, 29 September, 1999.

[51,52,53,54,55] Interview with Sunny Sansing, Reno, NE, 28 September, 1999.

[56,57] Interview with Joan Byer, at Vista, CA, 24 September, 2001.

[58] Joan Byer, 'The Dance That Changed My Life', 'Reminiscences', Unpublished journal, c.1996, p. 53

[59,60,61] Interview with Joan Byer, at Vista, CA, 24 September, 2001.

[62,63] Joan Byer, 'The Dance That Changed My Life', *op.cit.*, p. 59, 60.

[64] Campbell, *Heroes, op. cit.*, p. 73.

[65,66] Interview with Merle Archer, by phone, 27 September, 2007.

[67] *ibid*: Note:An article in a Queensland newspaper tells a similar story about 15 Brisbane women who were quietly flown to Manila, Philippines (without passports) by the American Army in 1946, which started a political incident that went on for two years. (See 'Strange saga of secret US jobs' by Terry Sweetman, in 'Agenda', *The Sunday Mail*, October 28, 2012, p.51)

[68] Interview with Merle Archer, *op.cit.*

[69,70] Interview with Joann Patterson, Reno NE, 1 October, 1999.

[71] Interview with Dorothy Thompson, Garden Grove, CA, 19 September, 2001.

[72] Interview with Betty Paukovitz, *San Diego, CA, 23 September, 2001.*

[73] Campbell, *Heroes, op. cit.*, p. 68.

[74] Letter from Rhona Jones to her mother, dated 1 December, 1943.

[75] Bruce and Chris Moore, 'US soldier finds Australian love on the back of a gum wrapper!' in *Sydney Morning Herald,* 24 April, 2009.

[76,77,78] Interview with Betty Kane, Albany, Western Australia, 21 August, 2007, by telephone.

[79] *ibid;* Pattie Simpson,'Love in a time of war', Obituaries, *The West Australian,* Thursday May 3, 2012.

CHAPTER TWO

[1] Betty Kane, 'The War Bride', in *Albany Writers' Circle No. 19. A Collection of Short Stories and Poetry by the Writers of Albany,* Denmark Printers, November, 2001, pp. 36.

[2,3,4] Interview with Cynthia Peter, Sacramento, CA, 29 September, 2001.

[5] Peter F. McDonald, *Marriage in Australia. Age at first Marriage and Proportions Marrying, 1860-1971,* Department of Demography, Institute of Advanced Studies, ANU, Canberra, 1975, p. 203; Patricia Grimshaw *et al, Creating a Nation 1788-1990,* McPhee Gribble, Ringwood, Vic., 1994, p. 265; also See Appendix 6, Marriages and Divorces and Ex-Nuptial Births, Figures 1 and 2.

[6] Potts, *Yanks Down Under, op. cit.,* p. 331.

[7,8] Joan Byer, 'The Dance That Changed My Life', op.cit., p. 61

[9,10,11] Interview with Dorothy Pence Berry, Denver, CO, 6 September 2001.

[12] Interview with Dorothy Thompson, Garden Grove, CA, 19 September 2001.

[13] Interview with Mary Bourne, Sacramento, CA, 29 September, 2001.

[14] Interview with Rita Hopkins, Salem, OR, 11 September, 2001.

[15] Chrys Ingraham, *White Weddings: romancing heterosexuality in popular culture,* Routledge, New York, 1999, p. 34.

[16] Harker, 'This Radiant Day', *RSSS Annual Report, op. cit.*

[17] Interview with Dorothy Thompson, Garden Grove, CA, 19 September, 2001.

[18] Interview with Joan Hamilton, *op.cit.*

[19,20,21] Interview with Joan Hamilton, Annaheim, CA, 19 September, 2001

[22] Interview with Joyce Olguin, Garden Grove, CA, 19 September, 2001.

[23] *ibid.* Note: Coupons issued during wartime austerity campaign were to ensure that everyone had fair access to food, clothing and other scarce goods. Coupons had to be handed over along with money in order to buy rationed goods. Source: John Curtin Prime Ministerial Library, John Curtin University, http://john.curtin.edu.au/manofpeace/homefront.html [Accessed 13 December, 2009.]

[24] Interview with Lola Atkins, San Diego, CA, 22 September, 2001; Atkins, 'A Mystic Journey', (unpublished, undated journal).

[25,26,27] Dawne Alison Balester, 'Dawne's Story', (unpublished, undated family history) [Source: The American War Brides Experience, http://www.geocities.com/US_warbrides/bride_stories/dawne.html [Accessed 4 December, 2007.] (Permission received from Dawne Alison Balester, 22 August, 2008).

[28] See Appendix 2 (7), Profile of War Brides – How long was the average wait to get married?

[29] Kate Darian-Smith, 'Remembering Romance: Memory, Gender and World War II' in Joy Damousi and Marilyn Lake (eds) *Gender and War: Australians at war in the twentieth century,* Cambridge University Press, Melbourne, 1995, pp. 125, 126.

[30] See Anne Atkinson et al, (eds), *Macquarie Dictionary,* The Macquarie Library Pty. Ltd., North Ryde, 2006: Red tape: excessive attention to formality and routine; official procedures.

[31,32] John Hilvert, *Blue Pencil Warriors. Censorship and Propaganda in World War II,* University of Queensland Press, St Lucia, 1984, p. 31.

[33,34] Letter from Lieutenant George B Gierhart to Mr & Mrs Harry S. Gierhart in Yonkers, New York, dated 7 September, 1943. (Sent by daughter of war bride in 2004, copy in possession of author.)

[35] Interview with Peggy Dunbar Blackman, Sacramento, CA, 29 September 2001.

[36,37,38,39,40] Interview with Joy Shaddle, Forestville, Sydney, 4 October, 2002.

[41] *ibid.*; also Mark Coultan, 'After 54 years, Australia reclaims its lost Joy', *The Age,* June 5, 2007.

[42] Teo, Hsu Ming, 'Love Writes: Gender and Romantic Love in Australian Love Letters, 1860-1960', *Australian Feminist Studies,* Vol. 20, No. 48, November 2005, p. 346; A fetished object is something, especially an inanimate object, that is revered or worshipped because it is believed to have magical powers or be animated by a spirit.

[43,44,45] Interview with Jean Wilk, 1 July, 2007.

[46] Interview with Dorothy Hammond, Garden Grove, CA, 19 September, 2001.

[47] Interview with Joann Patterson, Portland, OR, 14 June, 2004.

[48] Holmes, Katie. *Spaces in Her Day: Australian Women's Diaries of the 1920s and 1930s:* Allen & Unwin, St Leonards, NSW, 1995, pp. 9, 13.

[49,50,51] Dawne Alison Balester, 'Dawne's Story', (unpublished, undated family history) [Source: The American War Brides Experience, http://www.geocities.com/US_warbrides/bride_stories/dawne.html [Accessed 4 December, 2007.] (Permission to use received from Dawne Alison Balester, 22 August, 2008.)

[52] Naval Order 144, dated July 7 1942 [NARA, RG38, Chief of Naval Operations, CNO Index 1942-43 (Box 73) ALNAV 144-42].

[53] Letter from Headquarters, United States Army Services of Supply, Southwest Pacific Area, Base Section 7, A.P.O. 927 dated 10 August 1942. [National Archives of Australia, Series MP508/1, Item 115/701/352]

[54] E Daniel Potts & Annette Potts, *Yanks Down Under 1941-45:* the American impact on Australia, Oxford University Press, Melbourne, 1985, p.332

[55] Jessie Street, Truth or Repose, Australasia Book Society, Sydney, 1966, pp. 229-230

[56] *ibid.*

[57] Campbell, *Heroes, op. cit,* pp. 64-5; Michael McKernan, All In! Fighting the War at Home, Alan & Unwin, St Leonards, 1995, p. 198; Interview with Gladys Borger, Sacramento, 29 September 2001.

[58] Borger, Sacramento, *op.cit.*

[59] Potts, *Yanks Down Under, op. cit.,* p. 332.

[60,61] Lola Atkins, 'A Mystic Journey', op.cit., p. 39

[62] Interview with Allie Rudy, Denver, CO, 7 September 2001; also Rudy, Allie, 'The Story of My Life',
November 13, 2006. (Excerpts copied from unpublished manuscript supplied to author in May 2007 in
Washington D.C.)

[63,64] Interview with Colleen Halter, San Jose, CA, 27 September 2001.

[65,66] Interview with Valda Hertzberg, Darling Point, Sydney, 30 May, 2007.

[67,68,69] Interview with Patricia Law, Denver, CO, 8 September, 2001.

[70] Interview with Joy Shaddle, *op. cit.*

[71] Interview with Sunny Sansing, Reno, NV, 28 September, 1999.

CHAPTER THREE

[1]The music and lyrics of 'The Bride Train' were written by The Waifs, an Australian musical group consisting of the grandchildren of an Australian WWII war bride, Betty Kane, who married an American sailor and crossed the Nullarbor on the 'bridal train' to sail to America. When the song was released in 2004 she was 83-years-old and living in Albany, Western Australia.

[2,3,4,5,6,7,8] Interview with Barbara Gleason, Annaheim, 20 September, 2001.

[9] Telegram to Betty Kane, dated 7 February, 1946.

[10,11,12] *The Sydney Morning Herald*, January 4, 1945, p. 4.

[13,14] Pix, March 18, 1944, p. 3.

[15] Potts, *Yanks Down Under, op. cit.*, p. 365; Note: Senator Tangney was served in the Australian Senate from 1943 to 1968. See Ann Millar, *Trust the Women: women in the Federal Parliament,* Canberra, Australian Parliament, 1993.

[16] Telephone conversation with Nell Rassmussen, Florida, USA, 6 November, 2007.

[17] Potts, *Yanks Down Under, op. cit.*, p. 365.

[18] '"School" for Wives of US Servicemen' *The Sydney Morning Herald*, 23 March 1946, p. 9.

[19] Millicent Fanny Vaughan (nee Preston Stanley) 1883-1955, politician and women's activist, wife of former South Australian Premier, Crawford Vaughan. See Heather Radi, 'Preston Stanley, Millicent Fanny (1883 - 1955)', *Australian Dictionary of Biography,* Volume 11, Melbourne University Press, 1988, pp. 285-286.20 'Questions about America', *The Sydney Morning Herald*, January 25, l945, p. 5.

[21] Potts, *Yanks Down Under, op. cit.*, p. 365

[22,23] 'Australian Brides' Club in USA', The Sydney Morning Herald, 15 February, 1946, p.3.

[24,25] Potts, *Yanks Down Under, op. cit.*, p. 372

[26] *ibid.*, p. 365; "Girls' Long Wait for Ships", *The Sydney Morning Herald*, 11 September, 1946, p. 3; Potts and Strauss, For the Love of a Soldier, op.cit, p.71.

[27,28] *The Sydney Morning Herald*, January 3, 1945, p. 1.

[29] *The Sydney Morning Herald*, January 4, 1945, p. 4.

[30] Letter to author from Audrey Capuano; Penny Cuthbert, Dictionary of Australian Artists Online, www.daao.org.au/main [Accessed 4 December, 2007].

[31] Leon Stubbings, *A History of the Australian Red Cross 1914-1991. Look what you started Henry!*, Australian Red Cross, 1992, p. 29. [ARCS Archives]

[32] Melanie Oppenheimer, *Volunteering. Why we can't survive without it.* UNSW Press, Sydney, NSW, 2008, p. 45.

[33] Memories of Gwen Cadd, cited in Patsy Adam-Smith, *Australian Women at War*, Penguin, Melbourne, 1996, pp. 233, 234.

[34] Potts, Annette & Lucinda Strauss, *For the love of a soldier: Australian war-brides and their GIs*, ABC Enterprises for the Australian Broadcasting Commission, Crows Nest, NSW, 1987, p. 69.

[35] Interview with Barbara Gleason, *op .cit.*

[36,37] Stubbings, *op. cit.*, p. 29; also E.M. Webb, The Australian Red Cross at War, unpublished manuscript, p. 509. [ARCNA].

[38,39] Webb, *The Australian Red Cross, op.cit.*, , p. 509.

[40] Stubbings, *op. cit.*,

[41,42] Webb, *The Australian Red Cross, op. cit.*, p.509.

[43] Interview with Barbara Gleason, *op. cit.*

[44] Webb, The Australian Red Cross, *op. cit.*, p. 510.

[45] Gleason, *op. cit.*

[46] Webb, *The Australian Red Cross, op. cit.*, p. 510; also Stubbings, *op. cit.*, p. 29.

[47,48,49] Stubbings, op.cit.

[50,51] Gleason, *op. cit.*; also Webb, *The Australian Red Cross at War, op. cit.*, p. 510.

[52] 'Brides and Babies Leave for USA', *Argus,* September 8, 1945, p. 16.

[53] 'Hysterical mothers chase US. Bride train', *The Sydney Sunday Telegraph,* 9 September, 1945.

[54,55] 'Brides and Babies Leave for USA', *op. cit.*

[56] Webb, *The Australian Red Cross, op. cit.*, p. 511.

[57,58] 'Brides and Babies Leave for USA', *op. cit.*

[59,60] Webb, *The Australian Red Cross, op. cit.*, p. 511, 512.

[61,62] Gleason, *op. cit.*

[63,64] Webb, *The Australian Red Cross, op. cit.*, p. 512.

[65] Interview with Barbara Gleason, op.cit.

[66] Webb, *The Australian Red Cross, op. cit.*, p. 512.

[67.68.69] Jackie Hansen, email dated 16 January, 2004.

[70] US Citizenship & Immigration Service, http://uscis.gov/graphics/index.htm [Accessed 18 April 2004]

[71,72] Interview with Dorothy Hammon, Garden Grove, CA, 19 September, 2001

[73] Interview with Patricia Law, Denver, CO, 8 September, 2001.

[74] US Citizenship & Immigration Service, *op. cit.*

CHAPTER FOUR

[1] Betty Kane, 'The War Bride', in *Albany Writers' Circle No.19. A Collection of Short Stories and Poetry by the Writers of Albany,* November Issue, Denmark Printers, Albany, WA, 2001, p. 36.

[2,3,4,5] Interview with Joy Shaddle, Forestville, Sydney, NSW, 4 October, 2002

[6] See Susan Magarey *Unbridling the tongues of women: a biography of Catherine Helen Spence,* Introduction, Hale & Iremonger, 1985; Susan Eade, 'Spence, Catherine Helen (1825-1910)', *Australian Dictionary of Biography,* Volume 6, Melbourne University Press, 1976, pp. 167-168; Goldstein, Vida, *To America & Back January-July 1902. A Lecture by Vida Goldstein,* Prepared for publication by Jill Roe, Australian History Museum, Macquarie University, 2002; Janice N. Brownfoot, 'Goldstein, Vida Jane Mary (1869-1949)', *Australian Dictionary of Biography,* Volume 9, Melbourne University Press, 1983, pp. 43-45; Jill Roe, *Stella Miles Franklin. A Biography,* Harper Collins Publishers, Sydney, 2008, pp. 11-196; and 'Franklin, Stella Maria Sarah Miles (1879-1954)', *Australian Dictionary of Biography*, Volume 8, Melbourne University Press, 1981, pp. 574-576; and 'Australian Women in America, from Miles Franklin to Jill Kerr Conway' in *Approaching Australia. Papers from the Harvard Australian Studies Symposium,* Harold Bolitho & Chris Wallace-Crabbe (eds), Harvard University Committee on Australian Studies, Massachusetts, 1997, pp. 142, 150; Heather Radi, 'Street, Jessie Mary Grey (1889-1970)', Australian Dictionary of Biography, Volume 16, Melbourne University Press, 2002, pp. 328-332.

[7] Jill Roe, 'Australian Women in America, from Miles Franklin to Jill Kerr Conway' in Approaching Australia. op.cit., p. 152; also see Angela Woollacott, *To Try Her Fortune in London. Australian Women, Colonials, and Modernity,* Oxford University Press, New York, 2001: 'By the beginning of the twentieth century some Australian women had come to identify the United States as a locus of political progressivism and of career opportunities for women', (p. 199).

[8] Ros Pesman, David Walker, Richard White (Eds.), *The Oxford Book of Australian Travel Writing,* Oxford University Press, Melbourne, 1996, Introduction pp. xxii, and 104, 166.

[9] Ros Pesman, *Duty Free, Australian Women Abroad,* Oxford University Press, Melbourne, 1996, p.198.

[10] See Appendix 2, Profile of War Brides.

[11] 'Liberty ship' [Source, Wikipedia online http://en.wikipedia.org/wiki/Liberty_ ship - Accessed 27.06.2008]

[12] Melanie Oppenheimer, *All Work No Pay, Australian Civilian Volunteers in War,* Ohio Productions, Walcha, 2002, p. 202.

[13] Memories of Gwen Cadd, cited in Patsy Adam-Smith, *op. cit.,* pp. 233, 234; also Potts, Annette and Lucinda Strauss, *For the love of a soldier: Australian war-brides and their GIs,* ABC Enterprises for the Australian Broadcasting Commission,

Crows Nest, NSW, 1987, p. 69.

[14,15] Letter from Betty Kane dated 26th February, 1946.

[16] Interview with Sunny Sansing, Reno. NE, 28 September, 2001.

[17] Interview with Barbara Gleason, Annaheim, CA, 20 September, 2001.

[18] Dorothy Berry, *op. cit.*

[19] Patricia Page, *Across the Magic Line. Growing up in Fiji,* Pandanus Books, ANU, Canberra, 2004, pp.182-3.

[20,21] Interview with Rosemary Smith, Garden Grove, California, 19 September, 2001.

[22] Interview with Iris Craig, Sydney, 15 November 2003.

[23,24] Interview with June Carver, Denver, Colorado, 8 September, 2001.

[25,26] *The Sydney Morning Herald,* April 3, 1946, p.1, 3.

[27] Interview with Iris Craig, *op. cit.*

[28] Interview with Joy Shaddle, *op. cit.*; Interview with Dorothy Pence Berry, *op. cit.*

[29] Daniel Connell, *The War at Home. 1939-1949, Australian Broadcasting Commission,* Crows Nest, 1988, p. 137; Interview with Colleen Halter, San Jose, CA, 27 September 2001; Potts, *Yanks Down Under, op.cit.*, p. 373.

[30] Potts and Strauss, *op. cit.*, p. 68; Note: Eight of the sixty women interviewed sailed to America before the War had ended, Betty Stites being the first of this cohort to migrate to the US in 1943. (See Interview with Betty Stites Denver, CO, 8 September, 2001.)

[31] David Reynolds, *Rich Relations. The American Occupation of Britain 1942-1945,* Harper Collins, London, 1995, p.420; also Shukert, Elfrieda and Barbara Scibetta, *War Brides of World War II,* Presidio Press, Novato, CA,1988, pp.49, 57-64.

[32] '900 Brides Wait for Passage to America', *The Sydney Morning Herald,* January 4, 1945, p. 4.

[33] Potts and Strauss, *op. cit.,* pp. 66, 72.

[34] Enloe, Cynthia H., *Does khaki become you?: the militarization of women's lives,* London : Pandora, 1988, p. 20.

[35] Robin Lucas and Clare Forster, (eds) Wilder Shores. Women's travel stories of Australia and Beyond, UQP, 1992, p. viii (Preface).

[36] See Interview with Allie Rudy, Denver, CO, 7 September, 2001; also Interview with Dorothy Pence Berry, *op .cit.*

[37] Interview with Betty McIntire in Reno, Nevada, 30 September, 1999.

[38,39,40] Interview with Dorothy Pence Berry, *op. cit.*

[41] Theatre on July 4, 1942. The show toured the US as well as the combat areas of Europe and the Pacific and was made into a movie in 1943 starring a young Ronald Reagan. For his contributions to war charities and the uplifting of homefront morale, Berlin received the Medal of Merit from General George C. Marshall. Source: Parlor Songs, http://parlorsongs.com/bios/berlin/iberlin.php [Accessed 16 July, 2008]

[42] Interview with Dorothy Pence Berry, *op. cit.*

[43,44,45,46,47,48] Correspondence with Hazel Walker, 31 August, 2007

[49,50,51,52] Interview with Allie Rudy, *op. cit.*

[53] Interview with Joan Moran, Garden Grove, CA, 19 September, 2001.

[54,55,56,57,58] Lola Atkins, 'A Mystic Journey', (unpublished, undated journal), p. 42.

[59] Interview with Gladys Borger, Sacramento, CA, USA, 29 September, 2001.

[60] Telephone conversation with Doris Harburt, Torrens Park, SA, 12 April, 2004

[61] Correspondence from Jackie Hansen, 16 January, 2004.

[62] Harburt, *loc. cit.*

[63,64,65,66] Ruth Frost, *Pavlovas to Popcorn*, Community Books, Darling Heights, Qld., 2007, pp. 1, 2.

[67] *The Sydney Morning Herald*, April 8, 1946, p. 3.

[68]Interview with Shirley Norton, *op. cit.*

[69,70] Interview with Margaret Fosmo, Seattle, WA, 13 September, 2001.

[71] Interview with Marge Andreatta, Lakewood, Denver, CO, 8 September, 2001

[72] Interview with Iris Craig, Sydney, 15 November, 2003. The island in Sydney Harbour was most likely Cockatoo Island where there were many naval apprentices and workers employed.

[73] '2 War Brides Walk Off Ship for U.S.A.', *The Sydney Morning Herald*, April 13, 1946, p. 4.

[74] *ibid.* Note: It is not known whether or not she did in fact go back on board the ship.

[75] Interview with Dorothy (Mary) Bourne, Sacramento, CA, 29 September, 2001.

[76] Frost, *op. cit.*

[77] Michael Dugan and Josef Szwarc, *Australia's Migrant Experience*, Edward Arnold Australia, Caulfield East, 1987, p. 135.

[78] A. James Hammerton and Alistair Thomson, *Ten pound Poms. Australia's invisible migrants*, Manchester University Press, Manchester, UK, 2005, p. 99.

[79] Dugan and Szwarc, *op. cit.*, p. 136.

[80] Sean Brawley and Chris Dixon, 'Searching for Dorothy Lamour: War and Sex in the South Pacific, 1941-1945', *Australasian Journal of American Studies*, Palmerston, No. 18, July 1999, pp. 3-18.

[81]*ibid.;* Atkins, *op. cit.*

[82] Interview with Betty King, Castle Hill, 16 June, 2005.

[83,84,85,86] Ruth Frost, *op .cit.*, pp. 33, 6.

[87,88] Kathleen (Kay), Feehan Newell Bertram, Diary (unpublished) recorded aboard ship to America in June, 1945.

[89] Interview with Joyce Balogh, Tigard, OR, 10 September, 2001.

[90,91,92,93,94] Kathleen (Kay) Feehan Newell Bertram, *op. cit.*

[95,96] Interview with Barbara Gleason, *op. cit.*

[97]Interview with Joan Byer, Vista, CA, USA, 24 September, 2001.

[98] Interview with Marge Andreatta, Denver, CO, 7 September, 2007..

[99,100] Interview with Shirley Norton, *op. cit.*

[101] Erin has kept this momento of her journey to America, and it has now been donated to the National Museum of Australia and resides there with other war bride memorabilia, including her immigration tag.

[102] Interview with Dorothy Pence Berry, *op. cit.*

[103]*ibid.*; Pam Uher, 'The origin of Davy Jones' locker', *Helium*   www.helium.

com/iter [Accessed 29 August, 2008] "Davy Jones' Locker" is an idiom meaning the underwater or bottom of the sea graveyard for dead sailors, many of whom drowned at sea. It has been popularised by pirate stories and movies, where the villain makes threats to kill a victim by sending them to "Davy Jones' Locker". Reference to 'Davy Jones' in a nautical connotation can be traced to Daniel Defoe in his book *The Four Years Voyages of Capt. George Roberts* (1726) and in *The Adventures of Peregrine Pickle* by Tobias Smollett (1751).

[104,105] Interview with Dorothy Pence Berry, *op. cit.*.

[106,107,108] Shirley Tronic, Diary (unpublished), recorded on board SS *Frederick C Ainsworth*, April-May, 1946

[109,110] Kathleen (Kay) Feehan Newell Bertram, *op. cit.*

[111,112] Interview with Irene Franck, San Diego, CA, 25 September, 2001.

[113] Letter from Betty Kane to her sister, 26th September, 1946.

[114] Note: The words 'Australian Passport' first replaced 'British Passport' on the cover of an Australian passport in 1949. Source: Australian Government Department of Foreign Affairs and Trade Website, https://www.passports.gov.au/Web/PassportHistory.aspx [Accessed 2 August 2008.]

[115,116] Outgoing Ships Passenger Lists 1944 to 1947, [NAA, Series A/906/1, Canberra].

[117] See List of Abbreviations

[118] Interview with Sunny Sansing, NE, 28 September, 1999.

[119] Conversation with Joann Patterson when visiting Australia, 5 April, 2005.

[120,121,122,123] Interview with Jean Wilk, Mt. Pleasant, Chicago, 1 July, 2007 (by telephone).

[124] Outgoing Ships Passenger Lists, 1944 -1947, *op. cit.*

[125] Victor Turner, *The Ritual Process. Structure and Anti-Structure*, Cornell University Press, New York,1969, p.95; also see Kathleen Manning, *Rituals, Ceremonies, and Cultural Meaning in Higher Education*, Greenwood Publishing Group, 2000, p. 71.

[126] See Kate Darian-Smith and Rachel Jenzen, 'Memories from America: Australian War Brides and US Marines Remember the Pacific During the Second World War', in Martin Crotty (ed), *When the Soldiers Return: November 2007 Conference Proceedings*, University of Queensland with RMIT Informit, 2009, p. 13.

[127] *The Sydney Morning Herald*, April 8, 1946, p. 3.

[128] Voluntary Aid Detachments (VADs) were nursing orderlies who worked in convalescent hospitals, on hospital ships and the blood bank as well as on the homefront. [Source: Australian War Memorial website http://www.awm.gov.au/encyclopedia/vad.asp accessed 4 August 2008]

[129] Daphne Guinness, 'Mrs Beeton's house rules', *The Sydney Morning Herald*, December 13, 2007. (Note: A teaspoon of spirit of sal volatile (ammonium carbonate) in water 'swigged' during the day is recommended by Mrs Beeton for treatment of hysteria in her book *Mrs Beeton's Household Book* first published in 1861.) Also *The Sydney Morning Herald*, April 8, 1946, p. 3.

CHAPTER FIVE

[1] Betty Kane, 'The War Bride', *in Albany Writers' Circle No. 19. A Collection of Short Stories and Poetry by the Writers of Albany,* November Issue, Denmark Printers, Albany, WA, 2001, pp. 36 and 37.

[2,3,4] *The Sydney Morning Herald,* March 6, 1946, p. 3.

[5] *The Sydney Morning Herald,* March 6, 1946, p. 3.

[6] Betty King, (unpublished diary) written as Betty St Germain (nee Mott) on board SS *David C. Shanks*, April, 1946. (Copy of extract in possession of author.)

[7] Interview with Irene Franck, San Diego, CA, 25 September, 2001.

[8,9,10,11] Interview with Dorothy Pence Berry, Denver, CO, 6 September, 2001

[12] Interview with Betty McIntire, Reno, NE, 30 September, 1999.

[13,14,15] Interview with Colleen Halter, San Jose, CA, 27 September 2001.

[16] train carriage with sleeping facilities. During the day the upper berth was folded up like a modern airliner's luggage rack. At night the upper berth folded down and the two facing seats below it folded over to provide a relatively comfortable bunk for the night. Curtains provided privacy, and there were washrooms at each end of the car for men and women. Porters were usually African Americans. Source: *Wikipedia, the Free Encyclopedia,* http://en.wikipedia.org/wiki/Pullman_Company [Accessed 9 November, 2009].

[17] Correspondence with Hazel Walker, *op .cit.*

[18,19] Interview with Betty Kane, Albany, Western Australia, 21 August, 2007 (by telephone).

[20] Interview with Rosemary Smith, Garden Grove, CA, 19 September, 2001.

[21] Interview with Allie Rudy, Denver, CO, 7 September, 2001.

[22] Interview with Betty Blondon, Denver, CO, 8 September, 2001.

[23] 'Hitch-Hiked to Meet Bride', *The Sydney Morning Herald*, March 18, 1946, p. 1.

[24,25,26] 'Two divorces among U.S. brides averted', *The Northern Star,* April 15, l946, p. 1.

[27] Interview with May Webb, San Diego, CA, 25 September, 2001.

[28] Interview with Nancy Lankard, 14 November, 2004, (by telephone).

[29] Interview with Rita Hopkins, Salem, OR, 11 September, 2009.

[30,31] Interview with Patricia Law, Denver, CO, 8 September, 2001.

[32] Interview with Shirley Norton, Reno, NV, 30 September, 1999.

[33] Interview with Gladys Borger, Sacramento, CA, 29 September, 2001.

[34] Interview with Margaret Fosmo, Seattle, WA, 13 September, 2001.

[35] Interview with Ivy Diers, Seattle, WA, 13 September, 2001.

[36] Interview with Valda Hertzberg, Darling Point, Sydney, 30 May, 2007.

[37,38] Interview with Dorothy Thompson, Garden Grove, CA, 19 September, 2001.

[39,40,41] Interview with Doris Sarff, Seattle, WA, 15 September, 2001.

[42] Interview with Joy Shaddle, Forestville, Sydney, 4 October, 2002.

[43] Betty King, Interview, Castle Hill, NSW, 16 June, 2005.

[44] Interview with Patricia Law, *op. cit.*; Note: 'Pot Luck' is the term given to a

luncheon where each person brings a plate of food to contribute to the cuisine. Patricia found this was 'something new' compared to Australia where the food was supplied by the host.

[45,46] Interview with June Carver, Denver, CO, 9 September, 2001.

[47] Interview with Joann Patterson, Reno, NV, 1 October, 1999 and at Portland, OR, 14 June, 2004.

[48] Interview with Betty Blondon, *op.cit.*

[49] Interview with Dorothy (Mary) Bourne, Sacramento, CA, 29 September, 2001.

[50] Interview with Edna (Teddy) Pickerel, Salem, OR, 11 September, 2001.

[51] Interview with Iris Craig, Sydney, 15 November, 2003.

[52] Interview with Irene Perucci, Lemon Grove, San Diego, CA, 23 September, 2001.

[53] Interview with Rita Hopkins, Salem, OR, 11 September, 2001.

[54] Interview with Nancy Lankard, op.cit.

[55] Interview with Kathleen Heeren, Reno, Nevada, 30 September, 1999.

[56] Interview with Margaret Fosmo, *op. cit.*

[57] Interview with Norma Rehrer, Sacramento, CA, 29 September, 2001.

[58] Interview with Betty King,, *op. cit.*

[59,60,61,62,63] 'Thousands of American Girls Face War-Caused Spinsterhood', *The Washington Post*, July 29, 1945, p. 83.

[64] See Chapter 8, US Citizenship for Australian War Brides

[65] The White Australia Policy, framed by the Immigration Restriction Act of 1902, prohibited the immigration of Asians to Australia. It began to unravel after WWII, but was not completely dismantled until the mid-1970s. (See Andrew Jakubowicz, 'White Noise: Australia's Struggle with Multiculturalism', in *Working Through Whiteness. International perspective*, Edited by Cynthia Levine-Rasky, State University of New York Press, Albany, 2002, p. 107; also Frank G. Clarke, *Australia in a Nutshell – a Narrative History*, Rosenberg Publishing Pty. Ltd., 2003, p. 274.

[66] Interview with Joy Shaddle, *op.cit.*.

[67,68,69] Interview with Allie Rudy, *op. cit.*

[70] Interview with Shirley Norton, *op. cit.*

[71] Interview with DorothyThompson, *op. cit.*

[72] 'Housing Shortage Grows More Critical in U.S.', The Northern Star, April 3, 1946, p. 5. 'The housing shortage in major US cities continues to grow more critical as troops return from overseas'.

[73,74] Interview with Dorothy Pence Berry, *op. cit.*

[75,76] Interview with Joann Patterson, Reno, NV, 1 October, 1999 and at Portland, OR, 14 June, 2004.

[77,78] Interview with Allie Rudy, *op. cit.*

[79,80,81] Interview with Betty McIntire, *op.cit.*

[82] Interview with Cynthia Peter, Sacramento, CA, 29 September, 2001.

[83] Interview with Kathleen Heeren, *op. cit.*

[84,85,86,87,88] Interview with Irene Perucci, *op. cit.*

[89] Interview with Joan Byer, Vista, CA, 24 September, 2001.

[90,91] Interview with Joyce Balogh, Tigard, OR, 10 September, 2001

[92] Interview with Margaret Fosmo, *op. cit.*

[93] Interview with Marge Andreatta, Denver, CO, 7 September, 2001.

[94,95] Interview with Rosemary Smith, *op.cit.*

[96,97,98] Interview with Joan Hamilton, Anaheim, CA, 19 September, 2001.

[99,100] Interview with Valda Hertzberg, Darling Point, Sydney, 30 May, 2007.

[101] Interview with Norma Rehrer, *op. cit.*

[102] Interview with Jean Fargo, Reno, NV, 1 October, 1999.

[103,104,105] Interview with Peggy Dunbar Blackman, *op. cit.*

[106] Interview with Sunny Sansing, Reno, NV, 28 September, 1999.

[107] Note: See more detail regarding homesickness in Chapter 6, 'Living in America'.

CHAPTER SIX

[1] Betty Kane, 'The War Bride', *in Albany Writers' Circle No. 19. A Collection of Short Stories and Poetry by the Writers of Albany*, November Issue, Denmark Printers, Albany, WA, 2001, p. 37.

[2] Telephone conversation with Doris Harburt, Torrens Park, SA, 12 April, 2004.

[3] Barbara Edwards, 'Three Times a Migrant' in *Richmond River Historical Society Bulletin*, Richmond River Historical Society Inc., Lismore, pp. 3-7.

[4] Edwards, op. cit., pp. 3-7.

[5,6] Interview with Colleen Halter, San Jose, CA, 27 September, 2001.

[7] David Reynolds, Rich Relations. The American Occupation of Britain 1942-1945, Harper Collins, London, 1995, p. 417.

[8,9] Godfrey Hodgson, *America In Our Time: From World War II to Nixon,* Random House, New York, 1976, p. 48,19.

[10,11,12,13] Lon Jones, 'A School for Brides in LosAngeles', *The Argus,* 25 September 1945, p. 9.

[14,15] Interview with Billie Ringen at Garden Grove, CA, September, 2001.

[16,17,18] Interview with Patricia Law, Denver, CO, 8 September, 2001.

[19,20] Interview with Iris Craig, Sydney, 15 November, 2003.

[21] William H. Young with Nancy K. Young, *American Popular Culture Through History. The 1950s,* Greenwood Press, Westport, Connecticut, 2004, p. 11.

[22,23,24] Interview with Barbara Gleason, Annaheim, CA, 20 September, 2001

[25] Interview with Jean Vallero, Reno, NV, 1 October, 1999.

[26] Interview with Irene Perucci, Lemon Grove, San Diego, CA, 23 September, 2001.

[27,28,29] Interview with Betty Blondon, Denver, CO, 8 September, 2001.

[30] Blondon, *op. cit.*

[31] Interview with Irene Franck, San Diego, CA, 25 September, 2001.

[32] Interview with Valda Hertzberg, Darling Point, Sydney, 30 May, 2007; also see Hodgson, *op. cit.*, p. 54-62.

[33,34] Interview with Marge Andreatta, Denver, CO, 7 September, 2001.

[35] Karen Anderson, *Wartime Women: Sex roles, family relations, and the status of women during World War II,* Greenwood Press, Westport, Connecticult, 1981, p. 178.

[36] Young and Young, *op. cit.*, pp. xii, 10, 11.

[37] Anderson, *op. cit.*, p. 7.

[38] Interview with Norma Rehrer, Sacramento, CA, 29 September, 2001.

[39] Young and Young, *op. cit.*, p. 33.

[40] Interview with Betty Blondon, *op. cit.*

[41] Interview with Peggy Dunbar Blackman, Sacramento, CA, 29 September, 2001.

[42] Note: Proposition 13, officially titled the "People's Initiative to Limit Property Taxation," was a ballot initiative to amend the constitution of the state of California, enacted by the voters of California on June 6, 1978. Source: Wikipedia, *The Free Encyclopedia* http://en.wikipedia.org/wiki/California_Proposition_13_(1978) [Accessed 7 August 2007]

[43] Interview with Betty Blondon, *op. cit.*

[44] David Jones' News, Wednesday, 23 July, 1947.

[45,46] 'American "Chic" for Australia', *The Northern Star,* April 2, 1946, p. 2; also, see *The Sydney Morning Herald,* March 5, 1946.

[47,48] David Jones' News, *op. cit.*

[50] Interview with Joy Shaddle, Forestville, Sydney on 4 October, 2002

[51,52,53,54,55] Interview with Valda Hertzberg, *op. cit.*

[56,57,58] Interview with Teddy Pickerel, Salem, OR, 11 September, 2001. Note: The Accent Club is still active in

[59,60,61] Pickerel, *op. cit.*

[62,63,64] Interview with Norma Rehrer, *op. cit.* Note: In a Christmas card received recently in 2012, Norma, who is now 90, reports that she is now volunteering four days a month.

[65] Interview with Joann Patterson, Reno, NV, 1 October, 1999.

[66] Interview with Cynthia Peter, Sacramento, CA, 29 September, 2001.

[67,68,69] Correspondence with Hazel Walker 21 April, 2010 and 15 November, 2010,

[70] Interview with Shirley Norton, Reno, NV, 30 September, 1999.

[71] Interview with Sunny Sansing, Reno, NV, 28 September, 1999.

[72] Conversation with Sunny Sansing in Washington DC, May, 2007.

[73] Interview with Betty Paukovitz, San Diego, CA, 23 September, 2001.

[74] Interview with Rosemary Smith, Garden Grove, CA, 19 September, 2001.

[75] Telephone interview with Jean Wilk, Mt. Pleasant, IL, 1 July, 2007

[76] Interview with Joyce Olguin, Garden Grove, CA, 19 September, 2001.

[77] Interview with Billie Ringen, *op. cit.*

[78] Interview with Betty McIntire, Reno, NV, 30 September, 1999; also see Betty McIntire's unpublished journal, *op.cit.*

[79] Helen R. Lee, *Bittersweet Decision. The War Brides – 40 years later,* Roselee Publications, Lockport, New York, 1985, pp. 345, 346.

[80] Joy Damousi, *Living With The Aftermath. Trauma Nostaligia and Grief in Post-war Australia,* Cambridge University Press, Oakleigh, Vic., 2001, p. 113.

[81] NAA, Canberra, Series No.A6074, Item PO11147, Ref. Nos. 46/1/3378 – Memorandum from The Secretary, Department of Immigration, Commonwealth of Australia, Canberra, to the Secretary, Department of External Affairs, Canberra, dated 9 October, 1946; Ref. No. 46/5/2507 – Letter from Secretary, Department of Immigration, Canberra the Commonwealth Crown Solicitor, Canberra, dated 8 March, 1948;Ref. No. 48/474 – Letter re repatriation of Australian War brides from Crown Solicitor to Secretary, Department of Immigration, Canberra, dated 1 June, 1948.

[82] 'Australian wives back from USA', *The Argus,* 23 October, 1945, p.20.

[83,84] 'Australian War Brides Back', *The Sydney Morning Herald,* 28 July, 1948, p.1.

[85] Interview with Betty Kane, *op. cit.*

[86,87] Interview with Betty Stites, Denver, CO, 8 September, 2001.

[88,89] Interview with Allie Rudy at Denver, CO, on 7 September, 2001

[90] Interview with Cynthia Peter, *op. cit.*

[91] Lee, *op. cit.,* p. 349.

CHAPTER SEVEN

[1] Betty Kane, 'The War Bride', *in Albany Writers' Circle No.19. A Collection of Short Stories and Poetry by the Writers of Albany,* Denmark Printers, November, 2001, p. 38. War Bride Betty Kane published this lengthy poem, 'The War Bride', documenting her trip to America and the 1947 birth of her son. This poem was to influence her granddaughters and was the inspiration for their vocal group, 'The Waifs', to write and perform 'The Bridal Train' a top 50 hit in the Australian charts in 2004. A CD of this song was given to each of the 95 Australian WWII war brides who attended a special tribute in their honour at the Australian Embassy in Washington DC in 2007.

[2] Interview with Nancy Lankard, by telephone, 14 November, 2004.

[3] Interview with Iris Craig, *op. cit.*

[4] Interview with Dorothy (Mary) Bourne, Sacramento, CA, 29 September, 2001.

[5] Interview with Joan Hamilton, Anaheim, CA, 19 September, 2001

10 Interview with Fargo, *op. cit.*

11,12,13 *Southern Cross Club, op. cit.*

14 *Daughters of the British Empire* Idaho Chapter, http://www.dbeidaho.org/what_is_dbe.htm [Accessed 18 September, 2008]

15 Correspondence from Hazel Walker, Phoenix, AZ, received 18 September, 2008.

16 Interview with Margaret Fosmo, Seattle, WA, 13 September, 2001; also interview with Ivy Diers, Seattle, WA, 13 September, 2001.

17 Interview with Kathleen Heeren, Reno, NV, 30 September, 1999.

18 Interview with Bernice Geist, Sacramento, CA, 29 September, 2001.

19 *The Australian Women's Weekly,* February 24, 1951, p. 12.

20 Interview with Valda Hertzberg, Darling Point, Sydney, 30 May, 2007.

21 Muriel Rose Ricketts Locklear, 'My Ancestors, My Life, My Family', unpublished manuscript.

22 Interview with Billie Ringen, Garden Grove, CA, 19 September, 2001.

23 Interview with Dorothy Thompson, Golden Grove, CA, 19 September, 2001.

24.25 Interview with Allie Rudy, Denver, Colorado, 7 September, 2001.

26 Greg Berghofer, 'War bride back home', *The Chronicle,* Toowoomba, 27 April, 2004.

27 Interview with Val Smith, Paolo Alto, CA, 28 September, 2001.

28 Harry Dacre, *Daisy Bell,* J. Albert & Son, c1892. Note: This song was first sung in English music halls and was still popular in the 1940s when it was included in albums of 'Community Songs'.

29 *The Australian Women's Weekly, op. cit.*

30 Interview with Sunny Sansing, Reno, NE, 28 September 1999

31.32 The Australian-American Journal, January, 1948, The Empire Publishing Company, Louisville, Kentucky, USA.

33,34,35 *The Australian-American Journal,* January, 1948, *op. cit.*

36,37,38,39,40, *ibid.*, p. 3.

41 *ibid.*, p. 7.

42 *ibid.*, p. 8

43 *ibid.*, pp. 9-15

44 *The Australian-American Journal*, March, 1948, *op. cit.*, p. 1.

45 *The Australian-American Journal*, April, 1948, p. 1.

46 *The Australian-American Journal,* May, 1948, back cover.

47,48 Additional interview with Joann Patterson, Queens Park, Sydney, 5 April, 2005.

49,50 George McGann, 'G.I. war brides returning to visit mothers' in *The Australian Women's Weekly,* February 24, 1951, p. 12.

51,52 Interview with Barbara Gleason, Annaheim, CA, 20 September, 2001.

53,54,55,56,57 Interview with Val Smith, Paolo Alto, CA, 28 September, 2001. Note: 'pilchers' – flannel or plastic pants worn by an infant over a nappy. (Source: *Macquarie Encyclopedic Dictionary,* Macquarie University, NSW, 2006, p. 913.).

58,59,60 McGann, *op. cit.*

61 Interview with Betty McIntire, Reno, NV, 30 September, 1999.

62 Interview with Iris Craig, op.cit.

63 Interview with Joy Shaddle, Forrestville, NSW, 4 October, 2002.

64 Gleason, *op. cit.*

65 Interview with Dorothy Hammon, Garden Grove, CA, 19 September, 2001.

66 Notes taken while visiting with Joy Gustaffson, Seattle, WA, 13 September, 2001.

67,68 Interview with Joy Shaddle, *op. cit.*

69 Interview with Betty McIntire, *op. cit.*

70 Interview with Peggy Dunbar Blackman, Sacramento, CA, 29 September, 2001.

71 Interview with Betty Paukovitz, San Diego, CA, 23 September, 2001; see Sir (Ernest) Edward 'Weary' Dunlop, in *Australian War Memorial Encyclopedia online,* http://www.awm.gov.au/encyclopedia/dunlop/bio.asp [Accessed 6 September, 2008]; also 'Author Sara Henderson dead', obituary in *Sydney Morning Herald,* April 30, 2005.

72 Interview with Betty McIntire, *op. cit.*

73 Interview with Peggy Dunbar Blackman, *op. cit.*

74 Interview with Jean Vallero, Reno, NV, 1 October, 1999.

75 Interview with Patricia Law, Denver, CO, 8 September, 2001.

76,77,78,79,70,81 Interview with Dorothy Thompson, *op.cit.*

82,83 *About Rusty Walker,* http://www.walker-creative.com/index.html [Accessed 26 September, 2008.]

84 Telephone conversation with Coral Ayraud, St Lucia, Qld., 18 June, 2008.

CHAPTER EIGHT

[1,2] Mark Coultan, 'After 54 years, Australia reclaims it's lost Joy', in *The Age,* June 5, 2007.

[3,4] Lola Atkins, 'A Mystic Journey', [unpublished, undated journal] p.87

[5] Interview with Lola Atkins, 22 September, 2001; Lola Atkins, 'A Mystic Journey', *op. cit.*, p. 87

[6] Source: The Southern Cross Group http://www.southern-cross-group.org/ [Accessed 29 August, 2004]; also David Dutton, *Citizenship in Australia. A Guide to Commonwealth Government Records,* National Archives of Australia, 1999, p. 13.

[7,8,9,10] Dutton, *Citizenship in Australia, op. cit.,* pp. 9, 15, 16, 17.

[11] Department of Immigration and Multicultural and Indigenous Affairs, (DIMIA), Australian Government, http://www.citizenship.gov.au/index.htm [Accessed 3 August 2004] also Australian Government, http://www.citizenship.gov.au/current/dual_citizenship/ [Accessed 4 November, 2009] and Australian Government, http://australia.govlau/topics/immigration/ australian-citizenship [Accessed 21 January 2010].

[12] The oath of allegiance to the United States reads: 'I hereby declare, on oath, that I absolutely and entirely renounce and abjure all allegiance and fidelity to any foreign prince, potentate, state or sovereignty, of whom or which I have heretofore been a subject or citizen; that I will support and defend the Constitution and laws of the United States of America against all enemies, foreign and domestic; that I will bear arms on behalf of the United States when required by the law; that I will perform non-combatant service in the armed forces of the United States when required by the law; that I will perform work

of national importance under civilian direction when required by law; and that I take this obligation freely without any mental reservation or purpose of evasion; so help me God.' (In some cases, USCIS allows the oath to be taken without the clauses: ". . .*that I will bear arms on behalf of the United States when required by law; that I will perform noncombatant service in the Armed Forces of the United States when required by law. . .*") Source: US Citizenship and Immigration Services, http://www.uscis.gov/portal/site/uscis [Accessed 20 December 2009].

[13,14] Anne MacGregor, The Southern Cross Group, Email re: Australian War Brides, 3 September 2004; also see The Southern Cross Group website at http://www.southern-cross-group.org/ accessed 29.8.2004];

[15,16] Interview with Betty Blondon, Denver, Colorado, 8 September, 2001.

[17] Note: Women in America could not vote in federal elections until 1920, although some states had already enfranchised women by that time. See C. Sowerwine and P. Grimshaw, 'Women in Europe, the United States and Australia, 1914 to 2000', in *The Blackwell Companion to Gender History*, edited by M. Wisner-Hanks and T. Meade, Blackwell, London, 2004, p. 587.

[18] The Commonwealth Franchise Act of 1902 granted universal adult suffrage allowing most men and women over 21 to vote at federal elections, but it specifically excluded Aboriginal Australians, Torres Strait Islanders, and South Sea Islanders. Compulsory voting was introduced at federal elections in 1924. *See Australian Electoral Commission Website*, http://www.aec.gov.au/Elections/Australian_Electoral_History/Reform [Accessed 17 February, 2010].

[19,20] Marilyn Lake, 'Personality, Individuality, Nationality: Feminist Conceptions of Citizenship 1902-1940' in *Australian Feminist Studies*, 19, Autumn, 1994, pp. 28, 29.

[21] Victoria Rigney, 'For Richer or Poorer, I give Up My Citizenship, Alienation and Marriage', in *Exploring the British World: Identity, Cultural Production, Institutions*, RMIT Publishing, Kate Darian-Smith, Patricia Grimshaw, Kiera Lindsay, and Stuart Macintyre (ed), Melbourne, 2004, p. 337.

[22,23] Brian Galligan and Winsome Roberts, *Australian Citizenship*, Melbourne University Press, Melbourne, 2004, p. 97.

[24] Michael Dugan and Josef Szwarc, *Australia's Migrant Experience*, Edward Arnold Australia, Caulfield East, 1987, p. 108.

[25] See Interview with Joy Shaddle, Forestville, NSW, 4 October, 2002; and interview with Margaret Fosmo, Seattle, 13 September, 2001.

[26] Jill Roe, 'What has Nationalism Offered Australian Women?' in *Australian Women. Contemporary Feminist Thought*, Norma Grieve & Ailsa Burns (Eds), Oxford University Press, Melbourne, 1994, p. 38.

[27] Rosemary Campbell, *Heroes and Lovers. A question of national identity*, Allen & Unwin, Sydney, 1989, p. 65; also Circular letter from Director General of Manpower, Sydney. Dated 29 August, 1944. NAA,Canberra. Series B551, Item 43/61/5612.

[28] Circular letter from Director General of Man Power, *op. cit.*; Potts, E. Daniel & Annette Potts, *Yanks Down Under 1941-45: the American impact on Australia*, Oxford University Press, Melbourne, 1985, p. 332.

[29] Campbell, op.cit, p.65; Circular letter from Director General of Man Power, *op. cit.*

[30] Minute Paper, Department of the Army, Melbourne, 'Marriage of Australian Women to American Soldiers', 26 March, 1942. [National Archives of Australia, Series MP508/1, Item 115/701/352.

[31,32,33] Campbell, *op. cit,* p. 66.

[34,35,36] Interview with Dorothy Berry, Denver, CO, 6 September, 2001.

[37] Interview with Ivy Diers, Seattle, WA, 13 September 2001.

[38] U.S. Citizenship and Immigration Services, www.uscis.gov/ [Accessed 12 February, 2003.]

[39] Interview with Dorothy (Mary) Bourne, 29 September 2001

[40] Jill Roe, 'What has Nationalism Offered Australian Women?' *op. cit,* p. 38

[41] *The Immigration Act of 1924,* or *Johnson-Reed Act, including the National Origins Act, Asian Exclusion Act,* was a United States federal law that limited the number of immigrants who could be admitted from any country to 2% of the number of people from that country who were already living in the United States in 1890. This governed immigration policy until the *Immigration and Nationality Act* of 1952. However, the *War Brides Act* of 1945 and the *GI Fiancées Act* of 1946, waived these provisions and allowed the immigration of wives and fiancées of US servicemen to America. Source: Wikipedia, The Free Encyclopedia, http://en.wikipedia.org/wiki/Immigration_Act_of_1924 [Accessed 15 November, 2009; also US Department of State, http://www.state.gov/ [Accessed 6 December, 2009].

[42,43] Minute Paper, Department of the Army, *op. cit.*

[44,45] US Citizenship & Immigration Service http://uscis.gov/graphics/index.htm [Accessed 18 April 2004]

[46] Interview with Barbara Gleason, Annaheim, CA, 20 September, 2001

[47,48] Interview with Margaret Fosmo, *op. cit..*

[49] Interview with Joyce Balogh, Tigard, OR, 10 September, 2001.

[50] Interview with Joann Patterson, Reno, NV, 1 October, 1999.

[51] Interview with Joan Moran, Lemon Grove, CA, 19 September, 2001.

[52,53,54,55,56,57] Interview with Betty Stites, Denver, CO, 8 September, 2001.

[58,59] Interview with Joy Shaddle, *op. cit.*; Coultan, *op. cit.*

[61] Interview with Jean Fargo, Reno, NV, 30 September, 1999.

[62] Interview with June Carver, Denver, CO, 8 September, 2001

[63,64] Interview with Iris Craig, Sydney, 15 November, 2003

[65] Interview with Joan Hamilton, Annaheim, CA, 19 September, 2001.

[66] Interview with Kathleen Heeren, Reno, NV, 30 September, 1999.

[67.68] Interview with Dorothy Hammon, Lemon Grove, CA, 19 September, 2001.

[69] Interview with Nancy Lankard, 14 November, 2004, (by telephone).

[70] Interview with Ivy Diers, *op. cit.*

[71] Interview with Colleen Halter, San Jose, CA, 27 September, 2001.

[73,74] Interview with Peggy Dunmore Blackman, Sacramento, CA, 29 September, 2001.

[75] Interview with Edna (Teddy) Pickerel, 11 September, Salem, OR, 2001.

[76,77,78] Interview with Jean Vallero, Reno, NV, 1 October, 1999.

[79,80] Interview with Irene Perucci, Lemon Grove, San Diego, CA, 23 September, 2001.

[81] Interview with Helen Leirer, Golden Grove, CA, 19 September, 2001.

[82] Interview with Gladys Borger, Sacramento, CA, 29 September, 2001.

[83,84,85] Correspondence with Hazel Walker, 27 November, 2007.

[86] Telephone conversation with Jean Wilk, 1 July, 2007.

[87,88,89,90] Department of Immigration and Multicultural and Indigenous Affairs, (DIMIA), op. cit.

[91] The Southern Cross Group http://www.southern-cross-group.org [Accessed 29 August, 2004]. Media Release H128 2004 of 7 July 2004, former Minister for Citizenship and Multicultural Affairs, the Hon Gary Hardgrave, MP, outlined planned changes to the Australian Citizenship Act 1948.

[92,93,94] The Southern Cross Group http://www.southern-cross-group.org [Accessed 20 March, 2007]

[95,96] Letter from Erin Craig, President, World War II War Brides Association, to Ambassador Dennis Richardson, Embassy of Australia, Washington DC, dated 2 May 2007.

[97] Interview with Joy Shaddle, op.cit.

[98] Jamie's Inc., 'July 4th Spectacular' Newsletter, July, 2007.

[99] Sharon K. Wolfe, 'Forrest woman reclaims coveted dual citizenship', The Pantagraph, 18 June, 2007.

EPILOGUE

[1] Charles Waterstreet, 'G'day Mr USA', in The Sun-Herald, February 7, 2010, p. 20.

[2] Kate Darian-Smith and Rachel Jenzen, 'Memories from America: Australian War Brides and US Marines Remember Australia and the Pacific During the Second World War', Conference Paper in When the Soldiers Return: November 2007 Conference Proceedings, pp. 12-25.

LIST OF PHOTOGRAPHS
AND ILLUSTRATIONS*

Chapter One

1. Irene and Herbert Franck, Perth, WA, 15 April, 1943.
2. Hazel (left) with sister Beryl, wearing 'beach pyjamas', Redcliffe, Moreton Bay, Queensland, 1920s.
3. Hazel Walker's family home,' The Brea', 1944.
4. Hazel Mary Walker, 2 years old in 1923. Father Charles Harold, mother Mary Donald, sister Beryl Elizabeth, and brother Donald Joseph.
5. US troops in Melbourne, April 1942. [Source: Australian War Memorial AMW 012016]
6. Interior of Milk Bar, Mackay, Qld. c.1943. [Source: Australian War Memorial AMW P00561.023]
7. Dancing with an American soldier at one of the nightly socials run by staff of Australian retail organisations. [Source: Australian War Memorial AWM 012266]
8. Dancing at Melbourne Town Hall, 1944. [Source: Australian War Memorial AMW 083660]
9. 'The Dugout', Melbourne, Vic. - Volunteer clearing tables. [Source: Australian War Memorial ART 25127 – Artist: Tony Rafty.]
10. Iris Adams' US Army ID badge.
11. Jim Craig and Iris Adams, c.1943.
12. Nancy Lankard, about 18 years old.
13. *G.I. WAR BRIDES* comic, June, 1954.
14. *G.I. WAR BRIDES* comic, October, 1954.
15. Xavier Herbert - *Soldier's Women.*
16. Dymphna Cusack & Florence James - *Come in Spinner.*

17. Hazel - first job collecting mail from GPO Brisbane, 1937.

18. Hazel - dressed for church one Sunday morning, 1941. 'We wore hats and gloves in those days!'

19. Eddie Walker with Koala in Brisbane,1942.

20. Robert Norton.

21. Shirley Nicholls and Robert (Bob) Norton.

22. Aircraftwoman Nea Minna Dorienne Woolard, known as 'Sunny', in her WAAF uniform in Townsville, Qld.

23. John Goffage - better known after the war as Australian actor Chips Rafferty. [Source: Australian War Memorial OG0068]

24. Nea Woolard, AC1 WAAF and Major Richard Sansing, 5th Army Corp, Garbutt Field, Townsville, Qld.

25. Sunny's Military Service Record.

26. Joan and Raymond Byer, Vista, 2001.

27. Joann (right) and her sister Shirley in the garden of the family home.

28. Dorothy Leishman holidaying at Coolangatta, Queensland, 1943.

29. Dorothy Leishman and Leroy Thompson, shopping in Sydney, 1944.

30. Rhona Jones and Frank Osborn, St Mark's Church, Darling Point, Sydney, 3 January, 1945.

31. Betty Denton c.1943.

32. Bob Kane, US Sailor.

Chapter Two

1. Dorothy and Robert Pence on their wedding day in Brisbane, 13 August, 1943.

2. Dorothy (Mary) Cook with her mother, outside family home in Albany, W.A. on her wedding day, 24 February, 1943.

3. Rita and Franklin Hopkins married on 27 May, 1944.

4. Dorothy Leishman married Leroy Ferdinand Thompson on May 27, 1944..

5. Dawne Balester.

6. Memento Jewellery made from silver coins by Joseph Patterson in New Guinea, for his fiancé and his mother, 1944.
7. Lloyd G Shaddle, US Navy, 1945.
8. Joy Parker, c.1945.
9. Jean Reeves and Casimer Wilk on their wedding day in June 1947.
10. Alice (Allie) Drew married Lowell Robert (Bud) Rudy in Melbourne, Vic., 20 November, 1943.
11. Patricia Evans married Kenneth Law in America on 2 October, 1948.
12. Joy Isobel Parker married Lloyd G. Shaddle in New York, on 14 March, 1947.
13. Little Church Around the Corner, New York, NY.

Chapter 3
1. Barbara Faith Sheridan married Bernard James Gleason at Wesley Church, Perth, W.A. on 19 February, 1944.
2. Betty Denton, c.1944.
3. Betty Kane's 'Bridal Train' Telegram, dated 7 February, 1946.
4. Members of the Wives and Fiancées Association attend lectures at the US Information Library in Sydney.
5. Audrey Westley and Angelo (Bob) at Circular Quay Sydney, August 1944.
6. 'Stars and Stripes' hand-knitted woollen jumper.
7. Barbara Gleason (right) with baby Beverley and friends June and Peg, arriving at Melbourne after crossing the Nullarbor by train in 1945.
8. Australian Mothers of War Brides Goodwill Mission Club, 1950. [Source: NAA: A8139/1]

Chapter 4
1. Sydney Harbour Bridge, Circular Quay, Sydney, c.1945. [Source: State Records NSW 9856_a017_A017000167]
2. Australian WWII War Brides, Melbourne, leaving for the USA, 1945. [Source: Australian War Memorial, POO561036]

3. Jean Street and Lyle Morse married on 9 June, 1945.

4. A time for reflection. Joyce Street Morse on the way to the USA, 1946.

5. SS *Mariposa*, a refitted luxury cruise ship.

6. SS *Lurline*

7. SS *Monterey*

8. Hazel Walker with baby Danny (6 mths), 'fresh off the ship from Australia', Chicago, June 1945.

9. SS Fred C Ainsworth.

10. Iris Craig and her mother, Mary Josephine Adams.

11. Dorothy (Mary) Bourne (2nd from right) with 15 mths old daughter on board USAT *Fred C. Ainsworth*, 21 April, 1946.

12. Menu from SS *Lurline,* 1945.

13. Iris Craig (hand on head) and Erin at her feet holding her prize, on SS *Lurline,* 1946.

14. Erin Craig's immigration tag dated April 7, 1946, worn on arrival in San Francisco.

15. Billie Ringen wearing WAAF badge and medals, Garden Grove, CA, 19 September, 2001.

16. Jean Reeves in Perth, W.A. c.1945.

17. Passenger List SS Monterey, 1 April, 1946.

18. Mavis Salamonski (née McSweeney) 2nd back row, 4th from right,with war brides on SS *Mariposa*, April 1946.

Chapter 5

1. Betty de St Germain (née Mott) (5th from left) with other young Australian WWII war brides sailing to the USA.

2. Irene and Herb Franck with daughter April, in Chicago, Illinois, 1944.

3. Pullman sleeping car - interior - arranged for daytime use. [Source: State Historical Society of Wisconsin, Visual Archives, image 34412]

4. Shirley Norton with baby Robert, c.1946.

5. Joan Stein in the snow in Amityville, NY, c.2001.

6. Doris Saarf has kept her original Australian Passport as a memento of her journey to America in September, 1947.
7. Traffic jam in San Francisco, c.1946. [Source: San Francisco History Center, San Francisco Public Library]

Chapter 6
1. Jerry Lytle, 1945.
2. Colleen Moore, 1942.
3. Iris Craig and daughter Erin adjusting to life on Alcatraz Island, c.1947.
4. Peggy Dunbar Blackman, Sacramento, CA, 29 September, 2001.
5. Lloyd and Joy Shaddle settled in Forrest, Illinois.
6. Joy Shaddle with her children in Forrest, Illinois.
7. Valda Hertzberg, Darling Point, Sydney, 2007.
8. Edna (Teddy) Pickerel (née Love), Salem, OR, 2001.
9. Norma Rehrer, Sacramento, CA, 2001.
10. Hazel and Eddie Walker enjoyed square dancing in Danville, Illinois, 1940s.
11. Shirley Norton's children in 1954.
12. Jean Wilk (née Reeve) visiting the signal station at Rottnest Island, 2006.
13. Joyce Olguin, Garden Grove, September, 2001.
14. Betty McIntire, Denver, CO, 2001.

Chapter 7
1. *Australian Women's Weekly,* March, 1947 showing family after visiting the Royal Easter Show in Sydney.
2. Joy Gustaffson, Ivy Diers, Margaret Fosmo and Sonti the Australian Cockatoo, Seattle, 2001.
3. John Heeren.
4. Kathleen Heeren.
5. Muriel Locklear in Brisbane - 18 yrs old.
6. Muriel and Ernie Locklear.
7. Australian WWII war brides at the home of Dorothy Thompson

(front row, left). Billie Ringen (front row, right), September, 2001.

8. Australian WWII war brides Helen Lierer (left) and Joan Hammon (middle) at Dorothy Thompson's luncheon, September, 2001.

9. Dorothy Thompson's hand-stitched 'Australia' banner hung outside her home on 'reunion' days.

10. 'They Can't Beat Our Dinkum Pie', *The Advertiser*, March 19, 1970.

11. Allie Rudy in Washington DC, 2004.

12. Val Smith in her garden, Palo Alto, California, 2001.

13. Lola and Tom Atkins outside their home in San Diego, CA, 2001.

14. Norma Rehrer (right) hosting luncheon, Sacramento, September, 2001.

15. *Australian-American Journal,* April, 1948.

16. US Wives Mothers' Social Club, Victoria. This club had branches in all state capitals.[Source: Australian War Memorial, AWM REL34259]

17. Barbara and Jim Gleason, celebrating his 83rd birthday, Annaheim, CA, 2001.

18. Ben Smith, San Antonio, Texas, 1941.

19. Val Smith (née Ballard) aged 18.

20. Betty Bridges and her 'Australiana Corner', Seattle, WA, 2001.

21. Joy Gustaffson and Sonti, her Australian Cockatoo, Seattle, 2001.

22. Hazel Walker with son Rusty on her 90th birthday, Phoenix, Arizona.

23. Sunny Sansing at the official dedication of the WWII War Memorial in Washington DC, 2004.

Chapter 8

1. Lola Atkins, San Diego, CA, 2001.

2. Cover of Iris Craig's British Passport.

3. Iris Craig's British Passport - 1945.

4. Iris Craig's British Passport stamped 'British Subject'.

5. Ivy Diers, visiting Sydney, 13 November, 2006.

6. Dorothy (Mary) Bourne, Sacramento, 2001.

7. Joann Patterson, Portland, Oregon, September, 2001.

8. Joan Moran, September, 2001.

9. Joan Hamilton, Annaheim, CA, September, 2001.

10. Kathleen Heeren, Denver, Colorado, 2001.

11. Tribute to Australian WWII War Brides Washington DC 2007.

12. Iris Craig placing wreath on Korean War Memorial, Washington DC, April, 2007 [Source: Amy Drake].

13. Lola Atkins at the Australian Embassy, Washington DC, April, 2007.

14. Edna (Teddy) Pickerel at the tribute to Australian WII War Brides at the Australian Embassy,Washington, DC, 2007.

15. Joy Shaddle in her Forrest, Illinois home in 2007, reading treasured love-letters from her late husband Lloyd.

* Photographs have been taken by the author or received from war brides, with permission to reproduce images. Otherwise copyright clearance and permission for use has been obtained where possible, and the source is acknowledged in the photograph captions.

LIST OF ABBREVIATIONS

AMF	Australian Military Forces
APO	Army Post Office
ARC	American Red Cross
ARCNA	Australian Red Cross National Archives
ARCS	Australian Red Cross Society
AWAS	Australian Women's Army Service
AWM	Australian War Memorial
CPO	Chief Petty Officer
GI	General or Government Issue
NA	The National Archives, London
NAA	National Archives of Australia
NARA	National Archives and Record Administration (US)
NSW	New South Wales
US	United States
USASOS	United States Army Services of Supply
USAT	United States Army Transport
USN	United States Navy
USSO (USO)	United States Service Organization
VAD	Voluntary Aid Detachment
WAACS	Women's Auxiliary Army Corp Services
WAAFS	Women's Australian Air Force Services
WAAFS	Women's Auxiliary Air Force Services
WRANS	Women's Royal Australian Navy Services
WWIIWBA	WWII War Brides Association

APPENDIX 1 – AUSTRALIAN WWII WAR BRIDES WHO PARTICIPATED IN THIS STUDY

SURNAME	NEE	FIRST NAMES	AUSTRALIAN ORIGIN	NAME OF SHIP	PLACE AND DATE SAILED	PLACE AND DATE ARRIVED
ANDREATTA	HURLEY	Marjorie	Rockhampton Qld	Mariposa	Brisbane Apr 1946	S'Frisco 25 Apr 1946
ARCHER		Merle	Sydney NSW	President Monroe	New Caledonia Aug 1945	S'Frisco Aug 1945
ATKINS	WILKINS	Lola	Northam WA	Lurline	Sydney 5 Apr 1944	S'Frisco 20 Apr 1944
AYRAUD	WEST	Coral John Presnell	Brisbane Qld	Mariposa	1946	S'Frisco March 1946
BADER	McGUIRE	Patricia Joyce	Brisbane Qld	Air-PanAm from NZ	BrisSydNZ 28 Sept 1946	S'Frisco Oct 1946
BALESTER	McLEOD-SHARPE	Alison Garland (Dawne)	Mentone Vic	Monterey	Sydney 27 Oct 1946	S'Frisco 14 Nov 1946
BALOGH	EVERTON	Joyce		Lurline	1945	S'Frisco June 1945
BATTLE	WHITE	Doreen Mary	Subiaco WA	Fred C Ainsworth	Fremantle Apr 1946	S'Frisco April 1946
BENTSON	STAINES	Joan Bernice	Brisbane Qld	Mariposa	Brisbane 30 May 1946	S'Frisco April 1946
BERRY formerly PENCE	MILBOURNE-JACKSON	Dorothy E.	Crookwell NSW	General Mann	Brisbane 26 Dec 1944	San Pedro 13 Jan 1945
BLACKMAN	DUNBAR	Peggy	Scone NSW	Mirrabooka	August 1945	S'Frisco 27 Aug 1945
BLONDON	WINKWORTH	Betty June	Newcastle NSW	Lurline	Sydney Oct 1946	S'Frisco 1946
BORGER	KING	Gladys Irene May	Maryborough Qld	Lurline	Brisbane 14 Sept 1944	S'Frisco Sept 1944
BOURNE	COOK	Dorothy (Mary)	Meekatharra WA	Fred C Ainsworth	Fremantle April 1946	S'Frisco 1946
BRIDGES	ROADLY (k/a Betty)	Elizabeth Gwendolyn	Glen Iris Vic	Arongi	April 1947	S'Frisco 2 May 1947
BROCK		Jean Esther	Kalgoorlie WA	Fred C Ainsworth	Fremantle	
BUFFMEYER	ROBINSON	Catherine Eugene (Gene)	Sydney NSW	Monterey	Sydney Oct 1946	S'Frisco 1946
BYER	HUGHES	Joan Margaret	Perth WA	Fred C Ainsworth	Fremantle April 1946	S'Frisco May 1946
CAMPBELL	BROGDEN	Phyllis May (Maisie)	Ballarat Vic	Marine Phoenix	Sydney January 1947	1947
CAPUANO	WESTLEY	Audrey	Strathalbyn SA		1946	April 1946
CAROLLA	HILLHOUSE	Iris Ann	Perth WA	Marine Phoenix	Fremantle 17 April 1947	May 1947
CARVER	ARUNDELL	Jaynel June	Sydney NSW	Lurline	Sydney 1946	S'Frisco 1946
CASTENGERA		Eileen	Perth WA			
CHAMBERS	FRANKS	Elanor	Brisbane Qld	Mariposa	Brisbane April 1946	S'Frisco April 1946
CHERRY	MYLCHREEST	Lillian	Brisbane Ald		Brisbane 1946	S'Frisco 1946
CLARK	MATTINGLEY	Iris Joan	Springsure Qld			
CLAUSON	HURRELL	Edna (Sue)	Melbourne Vic	Lurline	Sydney March 1946	S'Frisco 1946
CONNOR	HOFER	Mavis Irene	Carlton NSW	Marine Phoenix	Sydney 10 June 1948?	S'Frisco July 1948?
COOMBS	WILSON	Betty Treherne	Sydney NSW	Mariposa	Brisbane 29 May 1946	S'Frisco June 1946
COPELAND	STEWART	Jean Isabel	Hakea WA	Marine Phoenix	Sydney 14 Feb 1947	S'Frisco March 1947
CORBIN	COOPER	Marjorie (Marge)	Katoomba NSW	Mariposa	April 1946	S'Frisco April 1946
CRAIG	ADAMS	Iris	Sydney NSW	Lurline	Sydney 21 Mar 1946	S'Frisco April 1946
CURRINGHAM	CATO	Bernice Mary	Perth WA	Monterey	May 1946	S'Frisco May 1946

SURNAME	NEE	FIRST NAMES	AUSTRALIAN ORIGIN	NAME OF SHIP	PLACE AND DATE SAILED	PLACE AND DATE ARRIVED
CURRIER	BYRNES	Daphne	Marrickville NSW	Mariposa	Brisbane 6 March 1946	S'Frisco 1946
DAHLQUIST	BARRATT	Betty Doreen	Perth WA	Marine Falcon	Sydney August 1945	S'Frisco 1945
DAKE	O'HARA	Annie Betty	Sydney NSW	Lurline	Brisbane 10 Sept 1945	S'Frisco 1945
DIERS	WILLIS	Ivy	Rockhampton Qld	Mariposa	Brisbane April 1946	S'Frisco 25 Apr 1946
DIXON	ALLEN	Nydia June	Geraldton WA	Marine Phoenix	Sydney 2 June 1947	S'Frisco 21 June 1947
DOGGETT	BRIDGE	Bernice Natalie	Brisbane Qld	Lurline	Brisbane June 1945	S'Frisco 1945
DOLE	CRITCH	Elizabeth	WA	Lurline		
DOUGAN	FALL	Joan Dorothy	Yarloop WA	Monterey	Sydney Oct 1946	S'Frisco 14 Nov 1946
DUFFY	LAWSON	Patricia	Sydney NSW	Monterey	Sydney April 1945	S'Frisco 1945 Apr 194
DVORAK	MUIRHEAD	Janet	Brisbane Qld	Mariposa	Apr 1946	S'Frisco April 1946
EVANS	LONEGAN	Joyce Helena	Sydney NSW	Aorongi	Dec 1949	January, 1950
FARGO	ROBERTSON	Jean Weir	Sea Lake VIC	David C Shanks	Sydney June 1946	S'Frisco 28 June 1946
FEUERBACH			Ballarat Vic	David C Shanks	Sydney 1946	S'Frisco 1946
FINK	WARNER	Joan	Vaucluse NSW	Monterey	Sydney 1947	S'Frisco 1947
FITTS	MONCKTON	Mena Katherine	Brisbane Qld	Lurline	Brisbane 16 Sept 1944	S'Frisco 1944
FOSMO	COOPER	Margaret	Brisbane Qld	Mariposa	Brisbane April 1946	S'Frisco 25 Apr 1946
FRANCK	VICKERS	Irene Victoria	Perth WA	Gunnawarra	Melbourne 15 Sept 1943	S'Frisco 1943
FREELAND	GOLDING	Roma Jean	Pemberton WA	Lurline	Brisbane 1944	S'Frisco 12 Aug 1944
FROST	DOWSETT	Ruth Isobelle	Melbourne Vic	David C Shanks	Sydney 28 March 1946	S'Frisco April 1946
GARDNER	MORRIS	Norma Jean	Brisbane Qld	General Butner	Brisbane 14 Dec 1945	San Pedro Dec 1944
GEIST	ANDREASSEN	Bernice	Port Douglas Qld	Lurline	Jan 1947	S'Frisco 26 Jan 1947
GERE	LE PAGE	Joan Dorothy	Perth WA	Fred C Ainsworth	Easter 1946	S'Frisco May 1946
GLEASON	SHERIDAN	Barbara Faith	Perth WA	Lurline	September 1945	S'Frisco Sept 1945
GLENN	HOUSTON	Jean Eleanor	Melbourne Vic	Mariposa	Brisbane 26 May 1946	S'Frisco 1946
GREER	FRAZER	Bett	Orange NSW	Marine Phoenix	Sydney 24 Feb 1947	S'Frisco 14 March 1947
GROSETTA	NUNN	Margaret Rose	Greenmount WA	Fred C Ainsworth	Freemantle Apr 1946	Honolulu Hawaii 1946
GUSTAFFSON	MANN	Dorothy (k/s Joy)	Rockhampton Qld	Mariposa	Brisbane 11 Apr 1946	S'Frisco 25 April 1946
HALTER	MOORE	Colleen P	Brisbane Qld	Mariposa	Brisbane June 1946	S'Frisco 14 June 1946
HAMILTON	HANDLEH	Joan Margaret Edith	Sydney NSW	Monterey	April 1946	S'Frisco April 1946
HAMMON	ZGLINICKI	Dorothea Mary	Croydon Park NSW	Marine Phoenix	February 1947	S'Frisco 1947
HANSEN	WHITE	Jaqueline S.	Perth WA	Fred C Ainsworth	Fremantle 15 May 1946	S'Frisco 1946
HARBURT	HARBURT	Doris	Adelaide SA			
HARRIS	TRUNFULL	Shirley	Bassendean WA	Fred C Ainsworth	Fremantle April 1946	S'Frisco 1946

SURNAME	NEE	FIRST NAMES	AUSTRALIAN ORIGIN	NAME OF SHIP	PLACE AND DATE SAILED	PLACE AND DATE ARRIVED
HAWKES	HOOLIHAN	Norma Mary	Townsville Qld	Marine Phoenix	14 April 1947	S'Frisco May 1947
HAWKS	MILLARD	Betty	Sydney NSW			
HAWKINS		Josine				S'Frisco 17 March 1947
HEBERT	GALVIN	Joan	Sydney NSW			S'Frisco 1946
HEEREN	McCORMACK	Kathleen Mary	Perth WA	Fred C Ainsworth	Fremantle 21 Apr 1946	S'Frisco 1946
HENRY	FULLER	Mavis	Tocumwal NSW			S'Frisco 1946
HERTZBERG (Formerly KATZ/GOLDBERG)	STEIGRAD	Valda Rebecca	Sydney NSW	Barrunduna (Swed)	Brisbane Aug 1946	S'Frisco 22 Aug 1946
HEWETT	McDONNELL	Noreen Mona	Brisbane Qld	Mariposa	Brisbane May 1946	S'Frisco June 1946
HOLYCROSS-HUDSON		Blanche V.				
HOPKINS	NORTH	Rita Frances	Rockhampton Qld	Lurline	Brisbane 12 Sept 1944	S'Frisco 28 Sept 1944
HOVER	LUCAS	Marjorie	Perth WA	Lurline	Brisbane 4 June 1945	S'Frisco 18 June 1945
HURLESS	MANNIX	Irene Theresa	Bartle Frere Qld	Lurline	Brisbane 11 Sept 1945	S'Frisco 25 Sept 1945
HYATT	SHOTTON	Joyce				
HYDE	MATTHEWS	Helen Elizabeth	Brisbane Qld	Mariposa	Brisbane 11 April 1946	S'Frisco 1946
JOHNSON	GRAEBNER	Ruth Dorothea	Perth WA	By air	Syd-NZ Pan-am Sep '46	
KELSEY	WRIGHT	Frances (Fran)	Tasmania		Sydney	S'Frisco
KESSELER	MASON	Shirley Berne	Randwick NSW	Monterey	Sydney May 1946	S'Frisco May 1946
KING (Formerly de ST GERMAINE)	MOTT	Betty Louise	Willoughby NSW	David C Shanks	Sydney April 1946	S'Frisco May 1946
KLOPP	ARMSTRONG	June Mary Victoria	Sans Souci NSW			
LALLEY	LAWSON	Norma Betty	Wembley Park WA	Hanry T Butner	Melbourne June 1944	San Pedro 1944
LANKARD		Nancy	Sydney NSW		Sydney 21 March 1946	April 1946
LASSITER		Margaret (Peg)	Melbourne Vic		1944	1944
LAW	EVANS	Patricia	Sydney NSW	Marine Phoenix	Sydney 1947	S'Frisco 1947
LAWTON (Formerly GWYNNE)	HARRIS	Barbara Jean	Adelaide SA	Goonawarra	Sydney January 1946	S'Frisco Feb 1946
LEDER	GATE	Joyce C	Cremorne NSW			
LEIRER	THOMSON	Helen Low	Leura NSW		Sydney March 1946	S'Frisco April 1946
LOCKLEAR		Muriel				
LOGAN	MILLS	Nancy	Bellevue Hill NSW	Lurline	Brisbane June 1945	S'Frisco 1945
McDONOUGH	CARMAN	Joan	Brisbane Qld	Mariposa	Brisbane 30 May 1946	S'Frisco 1946
McELWEE	BUTLER	Margaret Hope (Hope)	Brisbane Qld	Mariposa	Brisbane Feb 1944	S'Frisco 1944
McGREW	CONDREN	Irene Francis	Sydney NSW	Monterey	Sydney February 1946	S'Frisco 1946

SURNAME	NEE	FIRST NAMES	AUSTRALIAN ORIGIN	NAME OF SHIP	PLACE AND DATE SAILED	PLACE AND DATE ARRIVED
McINTIRE	WADDELL	Bette Jean	Melbourne Vic	Monterey	Sydney 1 April 1946	S'Frisco 1946
MALONE	TREDEA	Ruby	Charters Towers Qld			N York Mar 1945
MASON	WARNER	Betty	Sorrento Vic	Monterey	Sydney Feb 1945	S'FriscoApr 1946
MASTERS	HODGSON-BROWN	Betty Aileen	Harden NSW	Monterey	Sydney March 1946	
MATTINGLEY		Joyce Addison	Sydney NSW			
MESSERSCHMIDT	TURNER	Rae	Kempsey NSW	Marine Phoenix	Sydney 14 April 1947	S'Frisco 2 May 1947
MILDER	SKEGGS	Irene	Perth WA	Fred C Ainsworth	Fremantle 25 April 1946	S'Frisco 15 May 194
MINER	McENROE	Margery M	Melbourne Vic	Lurline	Brisbane Aug 1945	S'Frisco 1947
MOORE	ELLIS	Patricia Stella	Perth WA	Marine Phoenix	Sydney June 1947	S'Frisco 1947
MORAN	MONAGHAN	Joan M	Perth WA	General Butner	Sydney June 1944	S'Frisco 4 Jul 1944
MORRIS	PARKER	Beulah	Woollahra NSW	Mariposa	Syudney Feb 1946	S'Frisco 1946
MURRAY	SALMON	Ethel Dorothy	Waverley NSW	David C Shanks	Sydney April 1946	S'Frisco may 1946
NOGGLE	PRICE	Lurline H	Northam WA	Marine Phoenix	April 1947	S'Frisco May 1947
NORTON	NICHOLLS	Shirley June	Melbourne Vic	Monterey	Sydney 1 April 1946	S'Frisco 1946
OLGUIN	KELLY	Joyce	NSW	Lurline	Sydney May 1946	S'Frisco 1946
PACK	FERGUSON	Florence (Mabel)	Rockhampton Qld	Mariposa	Brisbane 20 Feb 1946	S'Frisco 1946
PARK	MILLAR	Ruby Elizabeth	Moe Vic	Lurline	Brisbane 1 Sept 1944	S'Frisco 28 Sep 1944
PATTERSON	NICHOLLS	Joan N (Joanne)	Melbourne Vic	Monterey	Sydney Feb 1946	S'Frisco 1946
PAUKOVITZ	LYON	Betty Harvey	Fremantle WA	Lurline	Brisbane Sept 1945	S'Frisco 1945
PERUCCI	COWIE	Irene Alice	Northam WA	Lurline	Sydney 4 April 1944	S'Frisco April 1944
PETER	ROBERTS	Cynthia	Mosman NSW	David C Shanks	Sydney June 1946	S'Frisco 23 Jun 1946
PICKEREL	LOVE	Edna Muriel (Teddy)	Boonah Qld	Mariposa	Brisbane 11 April 1946	S'Frisco 25 Apr 1946
PORTER	BARRITT	Joan Evelyn Marie	Qld	Mariposa	Brisbane 2 April 1946	S'Frisco April 1946
RASSMUSSEN		Nell	Sydney NSW	Sunderland F/boat	Sydney 3 Sept 1946	
REED	BALLINGER	Mona Kathleen	Ballarat Vic	Monterey	Sydney 6 April 1946	S'Frisco April 1946
REEDY	BERCOVE	Rae Passie	Perth WA	Lurline	15 September 1944	S'Frisco 28 Sep 1946
REEDY	LUCAS	Mavis	Perth WA	Fred C Ainsworth	F'mantle April 1946	S'Frisco 20 Apr 1946
REHRER	COX	Norma Lawrence	Winton Qld	Lurline	Brisbane June 1945	S'Frisco 1945
RICHARD	IRONS	Elsie Olive	Clermont Qld	Mariposa	Brisbne 9 April 1945	S'Frisco 25 Apr 1946
RICHARDSON (F'merly STEELE)	CREER	Margaret Bromley	Newcastle NSW	Mariposa	Sydney June 1946	S'Frisco June 1946
RINGEN	BRAUER	Viola Evelyn (Billie)	Tenterfield NSW	Mariposa	Brisbane 20 Feb 1946	S'Frisco 6 Mar 1946
RIOPELLE	HIGGINS	Kathleen Patricia	Maroubra NSW	Lurline	Brisbane 1 Sept 1945	S'Frisco 24 Sep 1945
RUDY	DREW	Alice Kathleen (Allie)	Ballarat Vic	Lurline	June 1945	S'Frisco 18 Jun 1945
RYCYK	IRVINE	Barbara Cecilia	Wynnum Qld	Mariposa	Brisbane March 1946	S'Frisco March 1946

SURNAME	NEE	FIRST NAMES	AUSTRALIAN ORIGIN	NAME OF SHIP	PLACE AND DATE SAILED	PLACE AND DATE ARRIVED
SALAMONSKI	MCSWEENEY	Mavis Jean	Rockhampton Qld	Mariposa	Bris. 3rd April 1946	S'Frisco 25 Apr 1946
SANSING (F'merly WOOLARD)	POTTS	Dorienne Minna (Sunny)	Chatswood NSW	Sunderland F/Boat	Rose Bay–NZ–Pan Am	S'Frisco 1946
SARFF	MAY	Doris Gwendoline	Pelaw Main NSW	Marine Phoenix	Sydney May 1947	S'Frisco 1947
SCANTLING	RATCLIFFE	Nonee (Doreen)	Ballarat Vic	Lurline	Brisbane Oct 1946	S'Frisco Sept 1946
SEYFRIED	JAMES	Joy Bernice	Brisbne Qld	Air BCPA	Sydney 10 Nov 1948	NYork 14 Nov 1948
SHADDLE	PARKER	Joy Isabella	Sydney NSW	Lowlander	Sydney 10 Jan 1947	NYork 5 May 1947
SHIPPLER	HERE	Joy Anne	Balmoral NSW	Marine Phoenix	Sydney June 1947	S'Frisco 1947
SIMPSON	LELIEVRE	Verna Joyce	Northan WA	Lurline	Brisbane Aug 1945	S'Frisco 1945
SINKOVITCH	TOMSON	Margory	Cormiston Tas			
SKILLMAN	COX	Winifred Nelva	Melbourne Vic	Davic C Shanks	Sydney April 1946	S'Frisco 1946
SLATTUM	SHEPHERD	Isobel M (Bel)	Mackay Qld	Lurline	14 September 1944	S'Frisco 28 Sep 1944
SMITH	FORBES	Rosemary Dorothea	Sydney NSW	Lurline	Sydney	S'Frisco Apr 1946
SMITH	BALLARD	Val June	NSW	Monterey	June 1946	S'Frisco 1946
SPERRY	MARTIN	Avis	Sydney NSW	Romance of the Sky	Pan Am, Sydney	S'Frisco–New York
ST JEAN		Peggy	Brisbane Qld	Mariposa	Brisbane April 1946	S'Frisco 1946
ST ONGE		Olive	Yarraville Vic		Melbourne Feb 1945	1945
STERN	MORGAN	Joan (Bette)	Newcastle NSW	Monterey	1 April 1946	S'Frisco 22 Apr 1946
STITES	BOYLE	Betty	Coburg Vic		1945	1945
STORK (F'merly WALKER)	SMITH	Marian	Sydney NSW	Monterey	Brisbane April 1946	S'Frisco Apr 1946
THOMAS	FELL	Irene	Gardenvale Vic	Lurline	September 1945	S'Frisco Sep 1945
THOMPSON	LEISHMAN	Dorothy	Lutwyche Qld	Mariposa	Brisbane 20 Feb 1946	S'Frisco 6 Mar 1946
TODD		Eileen W	Perth WA			
TOTH	DUNCAN	Joan	Brisbane Qld	Mariposa	Brisbane 24 May 1946	S'Frisco June 1946
TRAVERS	THOMPSON	Pat	Perth WA	Lurline	Brisbane June 1945	S'Frisco Jun 1945
TRONIC	ANDREW	Lorraine (Shirley)	Subiaco WA	Fred C Ainsworth	Fremantle Apr 1946	S'Frisco May 1946
UNREIN		Gloria	Perth WA			
VALLERO	ANDERSON	Lavinia (Jean)	Wilston Qld	Arongi	Sydney 28 Nov 1949	Vancouver 1949
WALKER	CASTLEDINE	Hazel Mary	Red Hill Qld	Lurline	28 May 1945	S'Frisco 18 Jue 1945
WARD	PARNELL	Elaine Florence	Buckworth Vic	Air – ANA	Sydney January 1947	Seattle WA 1947
WATKINS	BEACH	Josephine Olive	NSW		Brisbane June 1945	S'Frisco 1945
WEBB	CAMPBELL	May	Subiaco WA	Mariposa	Brisbane 19 Feb 1946	S'Frisco March 1946
WILK	REEVES	Jean Constance	Subiaco WA	Marine Phoenix	Sydney May/Jun 1947	S'Frisco June 1947
WIMBERLEY	LISSON	Merle Constance	Sydney NSW	Monterey	Sydney July 1946	S'Frisco Aug 1946

APPENDIX 2 - PROFILE OF WAR BRIDES

1. AGES
At outbreak of war in 1939 – ages ranged from **12–25**, the majority being around age of **16.**

By August 1942, when there was a very visible American presence, ages ranged from **15-29**, the majority being around age of **19.**

Ages when married – ranged from **17-32**, the majority being between **19 and 23,** with most aged **20.**

2. SOCIO-ECONOMIC BACKGROUND
Based on fathers' occupations:

Shearer, chamber magistrate, journalist, building contractor, tram conductor, thoroughbred horse trainer, hosiery business owner, gold miner, building contractor, WW1 veteran, master grocer, railway clerk, banker, photographer, fireman/farmer, carpenter/farmer, telephone mechanic at PO, railway engineer/mine manager, master plasterer, mechanical engineer, railway engineer, wool industry, cattle & dairy farmer/butcher, bank manager, sailor/fisherman, school teacher/funeral parlour manager, soldier in Indian Army/WWII veteran, upholsterer, grazier, council worker, railway engineer, train driver, tire salesman, bush carpenter/tree logger, butcher, building contractor, RAME engineer/WW1 veteran, store owner, farmer, chief engineer in the Navy, railway mechanic, farmer/produce merchant, store manager, blacksmith striker, electrical engineer, mounted policeman, painter.

The war brides' family backgrounds are diverse, and include a range of socio-economic levels which cross working-, middle- and upper-middle-class boundaries.

3. SIZE OF AUSTRALIAN FAMILY

No. of children in family: **% of 60 families**

(Range from 1 – 11 children)

No. of children	% of 60 families
1	8.3
2	13.3
3	13.3
4	13.3
* 5	16.8
6	8.3
7	5.0
8	5.0
10	1.7
11	1.7
	100.0

*Despite falling marriage rates in the 1920s (see Appendix 5) when the war brides were born, the biggest group of families (16.8% of 60) had 5 children.

4. AUS. STATE OF ORIGIN OF ALL WAR BRIDE PARTICIPANTS

	QLD	NSW	VIC	WA	SA	TAS	NT	TOTAL
# War Brides	39	54	24	40	3	1	-	161

5. RELIGION WHEN GROWING UP

Anglican

C of E	Catholic	Presbyterian	Baptist	Methodist	*Other	N/A	Unknown	TOTAL
18	8	5	2	5	2	6	14	60

*Other - 1 Jewish, 1 Congregationalist,
Note: 4 war brides had Catholic/Protestant parents.

6. EDUCATION

Only 3 of 60 (5%) war brides interviewed went to University in Australia (courses were interrupted by the war); 1 graduated from Music College; **2** attended Technical College; 14 attended Business/Commercial Colleges; 5 studied Fashion/Dressmaking/Design; 1 trained as a Nurse (unfinished); 1 completed a 5-year apprenticeship and graduated in Draughting; **33** of 60 (55%) interviewed did not disclose any tertiary college or university education in Australia after leaving school.

7. THE AVERAGE WAIT TO GET MARRIED

No of War Brides	Interval between meeting and marriage		
	Years	months	weeks
1*		3	-
3**		4	-
3		5	-
5		6	-
4		9	-
2		10	-
3		11	-
3	1	0	-
1	1	1	-
3	1	3	-
1	1	4	-
6	1	6	-
1	1	7	-
1	1	10	-
4	2	0	-
1	2	4	-
1	2	5	-
2	2	6	-
2	3	0	-
1	3	6	-
1	4	0	-
1	5	0	-
8	unknown	unknown	unknown
60			

* (Proposed on first night)
** (2 Married without first obtaining US Army permission)
Note: 2 months and 3 months, are shortest intervals between first meeting and marriage; 4 and 5 years are the longest intervals.

8. HOW MANY AUSTRALIAN/ AMERICAN COUPLES DIVORCED?

6 of 60 women interviewed (10%) were divorced – but not for some years and not before children were teenagers or older.

9. HOW MANY BECAME AMERICAN CITIZENS?

57 of 60 (95%) became US citizens

10. HOW MANY RETURNED PERMANENTLY TO AUSTRALIA TO LIVE?

3 of 60 women interviewed (5%) returned, accompanied by their husbands, to live permanently in Australia.

APPENDIX 3 – MAP OF AUSTRALIA showing original locations
of WWII War Bride Participants (including those who participated in this study by
questionnaire, interview, telephone and/or correspondence.)

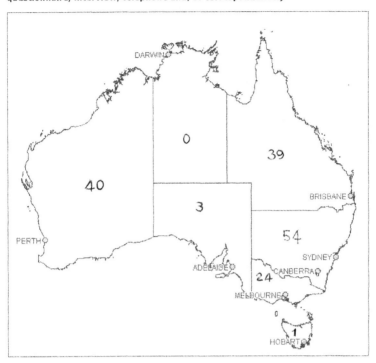

NEW SOUTH WALES	Sydney and suburbs	41
	Rural	13
	TOTAL	**54**
QUEENSLAND	Brisbane and suburbs	24
	Rockhampton	5
	Townsville	1
	Mackay	1
	Rural	8
	TOTAL	**39**
SOUTH AUSTRALIA	**TOTAL**	**3**
VICTORIA	Melbourne & suburbs	13
	Rural	11
	TOTAL	**24**
TASMANIA	**TOTAL**	**1**
WESTERN AUSTRALIA	Perth and suburbs:	27
	Rural	13
	TOTAL	**40**
		161

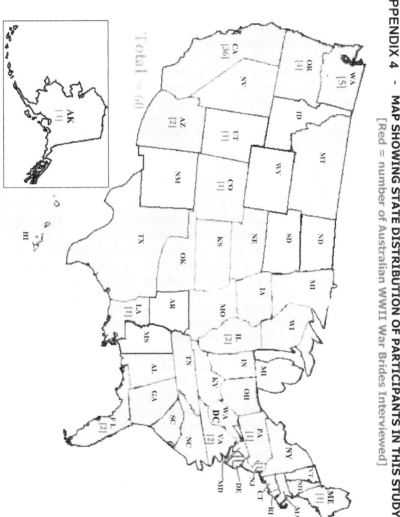

APPENDIX 4 - MAP SHOWING STATE DISTRIBUTION OF PARTICIPANTS IN THIS STUDY

[Red = number of Australian WWII War Brides Interviewed]

APPENDIX 5: LIST OF US STATES, ABBREVIATIONS AND CAPITALS

1. Alabama - AL - Montgomery
2. Alaska - AK - Juneau
3. Arizona - AZ - Phoenix
4. Arkansas - AR - Little Rock
5. California - CA - Sacramento
6. Colorado - CO - Denver
7. Connecticut - CT - Hartford
8. Delaware - DE - Dover
9. Florida - FL - Tallahassee
10. Georgia - GA - Atlanta
11. Hawaii - HI - Honolulu
12. Idaho - ID - Boise
13. Illinois - IL - Springfield
14. Indiana - IN - Indianapolis
15. Iowa - IA - Des Moines
16. Kansas - KS - Topeka
17. Kentucky - KY - Frankfort
18. Louisiana - LA - Baton Rouge
19. Maine - ME - Augusta
20. Maryland - MD - Annapolis
21. Massachusetts - MA - Boston
22. Michigan - MI - Lansing
23. Minnesota - MN - Saint Paul
24. Mississippi - MS - Jackson
25. Missouri - MO - Jefferson City
26. Montana - MT - Helena
27. Nebraska - NE - Lincoln
28. Nevada - NV - Carson City
29. New Hampshire - NH - Concord
30. New Jersey - NJ - Trenton
31. New Mexico - NM - Santa Fe

32. New York - NY - Albany
33. North Carolina - NC - Raleigh
34. North Dakota - ND - Bismarck
35. Ohio - OH - Columbus
36. Oklahoma - OK - Oklahoma City
37. Oregon - OR - Salem
38. Pennsylvania - PA - Harrisburg
39. Rhode Island - RI - Providence
40. South Carolina - SC - Columbia
41. South Dakota - SD - Pierre
42. Tennessee - TN - Nashville
43. Texas - TX - Austin
44. Utah - UT - Salt Lake City
45. Vermont - VT - Montpelier
46. Virginia - VA - Richmond
47. Washington - WA - Olympia
48. West Virginia - WV - Charleston
49. Wisconsin - WI - Madison
50. Wyoming - WY - Cheyenne

APPENDIX 6 – MARRIAGE AND DIVORCE RATES & EX-NUPTIAL BIRTHS

Figure 1

C6.16   CRUDE MARRIAGE AND DIVORCE RATES, Australia(a)—1901 to 1998

(a) Excludes full-blood Aborigines prior to 1966. (b) Rate per 1,000 population.
(c) The peak is due to the introduction of the Family Law Act in 1976.
Source: Marriage registrations; divorce registrations

The marriage rate reflects the prevailing economic and social conditions. It increased in times of prosperity such as the early 1900s, rose before each world war, fell during it and rose again after it, and fell in times of adversity such as in the 1930s during the Depression. It rose again around the time of the Vietnam war. Over the last 20 years marriage rates have fallen, and age at first marriage and age at first birth have increased dramatically. In contrast divorce rates rose in the 1970s, stabilised in the 1980s and have increased slightly through the 1990s. Coincident with the fall in marriage rates, there has been an increase in de facto relationships, which have become more socially acceptable in the last 20 years, even if children are involved. The proportion of births which are ex-nuptial has risen from around 6% in 1901 to 29% in 1998 (graph C6.17); at least half of these births are to women in de facto relationships.
[Source: ABS 1301.0 – Births, Year Book Australia, 2001] [1]

Figure 2

C6.17   EX-NUPTIAL BIRTHS—1902–1998

Source: Birth registrations

The median age at first marriage was around 27 years for males and 24 for females in the 1920s, remained high during the 1930s Depression years and fell dramatically after 1940. It continued to fall until around 1975 when, associated with marked changes in the professional and social development of women, age at marriage increased again to levels similar or even higher than those seen in 1920s.
[Source: ABS 1301.0 – Births, Year Book Australia, 2001] [2]

---

[1] Australian Bureau of Statistics – 'Trends in marriage and divorce', Australian Social Trends 1995, Canberra.
[Source: Marriage Registrations]
[2] *ibid.*

BIBLIOGRAPHY

PRIMARY SOURCES

OFFICIAL RECORDS

Australian Red Cross National Archives

Stubbings, Leon G., *"Look what you started Henry!"*: a history of the Australian Red Cross 1914-1991, Australian Red Cross Society, East Melbourne,1992.

Webb, E. M., *The Australian Red Cross at War,* unpublished manuscript.

Australian War Memorial Archives, Canberra ACT

Items 1-21, PR00 385 Australian War Memorial, Canberra. Letter from Jim Disken dated 17 August, 1982, in Papers of Tessa Greeley.

Items 1-21, PR00 385 Australian War Memorial, Canberra. Letter from Bill Leech dated 26 September 1982, in Papers of Tessa Greeley.

AWM Ref. No. F04021 Roy Parker (for 'When the War Came to Australia'), Australian War Memorial collection.

National American Research Archives (NARA), Maryland, USA

NARA, RG38, Chief of Naval Operations, CNO Index 1942-43 (Box 73) ALNAV 144-42. Naval Order 144, dated July 7, 1942.

National Archives of Australia (NAA), Canberra,

NAA, Canberra. Series A/906/1, Outgoing Ships Passenger Lists 1944 to 1947.

NAA, Canberra. Series MP508/1, Item 115/701/352. Minute

Paper, Department of the Army, Melbourne, 'Marriage of Australian Women to American Soldiers', 26 March, 1942.

NAA, Canberra. Series MP508/1, Item 115/701/352.Letter from Headquarters, United States Army Services of Supply, Southwest Pacific Area, Base Section 7, APO 927 dated 10 August, 1942.

NAA, Melbourne. Series BG121/3 Item 282M. 'Disturbances Between Australian and American Troops'. Appendix 'E' to Advanced HQ Allied Land Forces Weekly Intelligence Summary No.18, 4 December, 1942.

NAA, Canberra. Series B551, Item 43/61/5612. Circular letter from Director General of Man Power, Sydney, dated 29 August, 1944.

NAA, Canberra, Series No.A6074, Item PO11147, Ref. No. 46/1/3378 – Memorandum from The Secretary, Department of Immigration, Commonwealth of Australia, Canberra to the Secretary, Department of External Affairs, Canberra, dated 9 October, 1946.

NAA, Canberra. Series No.A6704, Item PO11147, Ref. No. 46/5/2507 – Letter from Secretary, Department of Immigration, Commonwealth of Australia to The Commonwealth Crown Solicitor, Canberra, dated 8 March, 1948.

NAA, Canberra, Series No.A6074, Item PO11147, Ref/ No. 48/474 – Letter re repatriation of Australian War brides from Crown Solicitor to Secretary, Department of Immigration, Commonwealth of Australia, Canberra, dated 1 June, 1948.

NAA, Canberra. 'Fact Sheet 234 – United States forces in Queensland, 1941-45', National Archives of Australia.

National Archives, London

NA, Ref: FO371/44657 297185 – '50,000 Brides Wait for Ships', *Stars and Stripes,* 10 September, 1945.

NA, Ref. FO 371/44567 297185 – 'GI Brides are told they must wait', *News Chronicle,* October 12, 1945.

CORRESPONDENCE

Anne MacGregor, The Southern Cross Group, Email re: Australian War Brides, 3 September, 2004.
Erin Craig, President, World War II War Brides Association, Letter to Australian Ambassador Dennis Richardson, Embassy of Australia, Washington DC, dated 2 May, 2007.

UNPUBLISHED JOURNALS, PAPERS, AND DIARIES OF WAR BRIDES

Atkins, Lola, 'A Mystic Journey', (unpublished, undated journal).
Balester, Dawne, 'Dawne's Story', (unpublished, undated family history) [Source: The American War Brides Experience, http://www.geocities.com/US_warbrides/bride_stories/dawne.html [Accessed 4 December, 2007.] (Permission to use received from Dawne Alison Balester, 22 August, 2008.)
Byer, Joan, 'The Dance That Changed My Life', 'Reminiscences' (unpublished journal), c.1996.
Craig, Iris, 'Presentation of an Australian War Bride' (unpublished), to the World War II War Brides Association, 9 March, 2006.
Feehan Newell Bertram, Kathleen (Kay), Diary (unpublished) recorded aboard ship on her trip to America in June, 1945.
King, Betty, Diary (unpublished) written as Betty de St Germain (nee Mott) on board SS *David C. Shanks,* April, 1946.
Rudy, Allie, 'The Story of My Life', November 13, 2006. (unpublished manuscript).
Tronic, Shirley, Diary (unpublished), recorded on board SS *Frederick C. Ainsworth,* April-May, 1946.

NEWSPAPERS AND MAGAZINES

The Age (Melbourne)
The Argus (Melbourne)
The Australian
Australian Financial Review
The Australian-American Journal, January, March, May, 1948, The
    Empire Publishing Company, Louisville, Kentucky, USA.
The Australian Women's Weekly
'Bride Lines' Vol. 1, No. 8,"SS *Lurline*", 3 April, 1946.
Courier Mail (Brisbane)
Daily Telegraph
David Jones' News, Wednesday, 23 July, 1947. (Sydney)
GI War Brides, June 1954.
The Good Weekend (Sydney)
Jamie's Inc., *'July 4th Spectacular',* Newsletter, July, 2007. (Forrest,
    Illinois, USA)
The Northern Star (Lismore)
The Pantagraph (Illinois, USA)
Pix
The Sydney Morning Herald

SECONDARY SOURCES

BOOKS

Australian Dictionary of Biography, Volumes 6 (1976), 8 (1981),
    9 (1983), 13 (1993), 16 (2002), Melbourne University Press,
    Melbourne.
------- AWAS: *women making history,* Boolarang Publications,
    Chevron Island, Qld, 1989.
Adam-Smith, Patsy, *Australian Women at War,* Nelson, Melbourne,
    1984.
Alison Alexander, *A Wealth of Women. Australian women's lives*

from 1788 to the present, Duffy and Snellgrove, Potts Point, NSW, 2001.

Anderson, Karen, *Wartime Women: Sex roles, family relations, and the status of women during World War II,* Greenwood Press, Westport, CT, 1981.

Andrews, Michael, Australia Year by Year. *A concise history of Australia since 1770,* Trocadero Publishing, Sydney, 1984.

Atkinson, Ann and Alison Moore, (Senior Eds), *Macquarie Australian Encyclopedic Dictionary,* Macquarie University, North Ryde, NSW, 2006.

Ashton, Paul, On the Record. *A Practical Guide to Oral History,* North Sydney Municipal Council, North Sydney 1991.

Banner, Lois W., *Women in Modern America A Brief History,* Harcourt Brace Jovanovich, Inc., New York, 1974.

Barker, Anthony J., *Fleeting Attraction: a social history of American servicemen in Western Australia during the Second World War,* University of Western Australia Press, Nedlands, WA, 1996.

Bartlett, Norman, *1776-1976 Australia and America Through 200 years,* Ure Smith, Sydney, 1976.

Battle, Lois, *War Brides,* St. Martin's Press, New York, NY, 1982.

Beaumont, Joan, *Australia's War 1939-45,* Allen & Unwin, Sydney, 1996.

Bell, Roger J., *Unequal Allies: Australian-American Relations and the Pacific War,* Melbourne University Press, Carlton, Vic., 1977.

Bell, Phillip and Roger Bell, *Implicated: The United States In Australia,* Oxford University Press, Melbourne, 1993.

Bell, Roger J., and Ian J. Bickerton, (eds), *American studies: new essays from Australia and New Zealand,* ANZASA, Kensington, NSW, 1981.

Bevege, M., Margaret James, Carmel Shute (eds), *Worth her salt: women at work in Australia,* Hale and Iremonger, Sydney, c1982.

Bolton, Geoffrey, *The Oxford History of Australia.* Vol. 5: Oxford University Press, Melbourne, 1991.

Brettell, Caroline B., 'Liminal Space and Liminal Time: A Woman's Narrative of a Year Abroad 1938-39', Linda Straight (ed.), Women on the Verge of Home, State University of New York Press, Albany, NY, 2005.

Brownfoot, Janice N., 'Goldstein, Vida Jane Mary (1869 - 1949)', Australian Dictionary of Biography, Volume 9, Melbourne University Press, Melbourne, 1983, pp. 43-45.

Buttsworth, Sara, 'Women Colouring the Wartime Landscape' in On the Homefront. Western Australia and World War II, Jenny Gregory (ed.), University of Western Australia Press, Nedlands, 1996.

Campbell, Rosemary, Heroes and Lovers. A question of national identity, Allen & Unwin, Sydney, 1989.

Chambers, Deborah, Representing the Family, SAGE Publications Ltd., London, 2001.

Charlton, Peter, South Queensland WWII 1941-1945, Boolarong Publications, Brisbane, 1991.

Chilla, Bullbeck, Living Feminism: The Impact of the Women's Movement on Three Generations of Australian Women: Cambridge University Press, Melbourne, 1997.

Clarke, Joan, All On One Good Dancing Leg, Hale & Remonger, Sydney, 1994.

Clarke, Frank G., Australia in a Nutshell – a Narrative History, Rosenberg Publishing Pty Ltd, Sydney, 2003.

Cooke, Miriam, 'WO-man, retelling the war myth' in Gendering War Talk, Miriam Cooke and Angela Woollacott (eds), Princeton University Press, Princeton, NJ, 1993.

Connell, Daniel, The War at Home, ABC, Crows Nest, NSW, 1988.

Costello, John, Love, Sex, and War: Changing Values 1939-45: Guild Publishing, London, UK, 1985.

Cusack, Dymphna and James, Florence, Come in Spinner. The Lives and Loves of Women in Wartime, Heinemann, Melbourne, 1954 (first published 1951).

Damousi, Joy, Living With the Aftermath. Trauma, Nostalgia and

Grief in Post-war Australia, Cambridge University Press, Oakleigh, Vic, 2001.

Damousi, Joy and Lake, Marilyn (eds), *Gender and War. Australians at war in the twentieth century,* Cambridge University Press, Melbourne, 1995.

Damousi, Joy, '*Marching to different drums: women's mobilisations 1914/1939;* in *Gender relations in Australia: domination and negotiation,* edited by Kay Saunders and Raymond Evans. Sydney, NSW: Harcourt Brace Jovanovich, 1992, pp. 350-375.

Darian-Smith, Kate, *On the Home Front: Melbourne in Wartime 1939-1945,* Oxford University Press, Melbourne, 1990.

Darian-Smith, Kate, '*War Stories: Remembering the Australian Home Front During the Second World War*' in *Memory and History in Twentieth-Century Australia,* edited by Kate Darian-Smith and Paula Hamilton, Oxford University Press, Melbourne, 1994.

Darian-Smith, Kate, 'Remembering Romance: Memory, Gender and World War II' in Joy Damousi and Marilyn Lake (eds) *Gender and War: Australians at war in the twentieth century,* Cambridge University Press, Melbourne, 1995.

Darian-Smith, Kate, 'War and Australian Society', in Joan Beaumont (ed) *Australia's War, 1939-45,* Allen & Unwin, St Leonards, NSW, 1996.

Darian-Smith, Kate, Patricia Grimshaw, Kiera Lindsay, and Stuart Macintyre (eds), *Exploring the British World: Identity, Cultural Production, Institutions,* RMIT Publishing, Melbourne, 2004.

Darian-Smith, Kate and Rachel Jenzen, 'Memories from America: Australian War Brides and US Marines Remember the Pacific During the Second World War', in Martin Crotty (ed), *When the Soldiers Return: Refereed Conference Proceedings,* University of Queensland with RMIT Informit, 2009.

Douglas, Louise, Roberts, Alan and Thompson, Ruth, Oral history: a handbook, Allen & Unwin, Sydney, 1988.

Douglas, Louise and Peter Spearritt, *Australia 1938 Oral History Handbook,* Australian National University, Canberra, 1981.

Douglas, Jeannie, 'Women's Travel Narratives of the 1950s' *in Memory and History in Twentieth-Century Australia,* edited by Kate Darian-Smith and Paula Hamilton, Oxford University Press, Melbourne, 1994.

Dutton, David, *Citizenship in Australia. A Guide to Commonwealth Government Records,* National Archives of Australia, Canberra, 1999.

Dyson, Catherine, *Swing By Sailor: True stories from the war brides of HMS Victorious,* Hachette Australia, Sydney, 2007.

Dugan, Michael and Josef Szwarc, *Australia's Migrant Experience,* Edward Arnold Australia, Caulfield East, Vic., 1987.

Eade, Susan, 'Spence, Catherine Helen (1825 - 1910)', *Australian Dictionary of Biography,* Volume 6, Melbourne University Press, Melbourne, 1976, pp. 167-168.

Enloe, Cynthia H., *Does khaki become you? : the militarization of women's lives,* Pandora, London, 1988.

Fallows, Carol, *Love & War. Stories of War Brides from the Great War to Vietnam,* Bantam Books, Sydney, 2002.

Fink, Lottie, *The Child and Sex,* Angus and Robertson Ltd, Sydney, 1944.

Fink, Lotte, 'Premarital Sex Experience of girls in Sydney', in *The International Journal of Sexology,* Vol. 8, Issue 1, 1954.

Friedman, Barbara, *From the Battlefront to the Bridal Suite. Media Coverage of British War Brides 1942-1946,* University of Missouri Press, 2007.

Frost, Ruth, *Pavlovas to Popcorn,* Community Books Australia, Darling Heights, Qld, 2007.

Gabaccia, Donna, *From the Other Side: Women, Gender, and Immigrant Life in the US, 1820-1990,* Indiana University Press, Bloomington, 1994.

Galligan, Brian and Winsome Roberts, *Australian Citizenship,* Melbourne University Press, Melbourne, 2004.

Goldsmith, Betty and Beryl Sandford, T*he Girls They Left Behind.
Life in Australia during World War II – the women
remember,* Penguin Books, Ringwood, Vic., 1990.

Goldstein, Vida, 'To America and back, January-July 1902: a lecture',
prepared for publication by Jill Roe. Australian History
Museum, Macquarie University, Sydney, 2002.

Granfield, Linda, *Brass Buttons and Silver Horseshoes. Stories
from Canada's British War Brides,* McClelland & Stewart,
Toronto, Canada, 2002.

Grattan, C. Hartley, *Introducing Australia*, 1944.

Greenwood, G., *Early American/Australian Relations,* 1944.

Gregory, Jenny (ed.) *On the Homefront. Western Australia and
World War II,* UWA Press, Nedlands, WA, 1996.

Grimshaw, Patricia, et al, *Creating a Nation 1788-1990,* McPhee
Gribble, Ringwood, Vic., 1994.

Hall, Robert, *The Black Diggers: Aborigines and Torres Strait
Islanders in the Second World War,* Aboriginal Studies Press,
Canberra, 1997.

Hamilton, Paula, 'The Knife Edge' in *Memory and History
in Twentieth-Century Australia,* Kate Darian-Smith and Paula
Hamilton (eds), Melbourne University Press, Melbourne,
1994.

Hamilton, Paula and Linda Shopes (eds), *Oral History and Public
Memories,* Temple University Press, Philadelphia, PA, 2008.

Hammerton, A. James and Alistair Thomson, *Ten pound Poms.
Australia's invisible migrants,* Manchester University Press,
Manchester, UK, 2005.

Handlin, Oscar, *The Uprooted: The Epic Story of the Great
Migration that made the American People,* Little Brown,
Boston, MA, 1951.

Hanke, Lewis (ed.), *Guide to the Study of United States History
Outside the US, 1945 –1980*, Kraus International
Publications, White Plains, NY, 1985.

Harper, Norman, *A great and powerful friend: a study of Australian*

American relations between 1900 and 1975, University of Queensland Press, St. Lucia, Brisbane, 1987.

Hartmann, Susan M., *The home front and beyond: American women in the 1940s,* Twayne Publishers, Boston, MA, c.1982.

Hasluck, Paul, *The Government and the People, 1939-1945,* Vol. 11, Australian War Memorial, Canberra, 1996.

Hasluck, Paul, *The Government and the People, 1942-1945,* Vol. 12, Australian War Memorial, Canberra, [1956-70].

Hassam, Andrew, *Sailing to Australia. Shipboard Diaries by Nineteenth-Century British Emigrants,* Melbourne University Press, Melbourne, 1995.

Herbert, Xavier. *Soldiers' Women:* Panther, London, 1963.

Hergenhan, Laurie, *No Casual Traveller: Harley Grattan and Australia – US connections,* University of Queensland Press, St. Lucia, 1995.

Hibbert, Joyce (Ed) *The War Brides.* Peter Martin Associates, Ltd. Toronto, Canada, 1978.

Hodgson, Godfrey, *America In Our Time: From World War II to Nixon,* Random House, New York, 1976.

Hogan, Susan, 'Dawn, Gloria (1929 - 1978)', in *Australian Dictionary of Biography,* Volume 13, Melbourne University Press, Melbourne, 1993.

Holmes, Katie. *Spaces in Her Day: Australian Women's Diaries of the 1920s and 1930s:* Allen & Unwin, St Leonards, NSW, 1995.

Howard, Ann, *You'll be sorry,* Tarka, Sydney, 1990.

Inglis, K., 'At War' in *Australians 1939-88,* Sydney, 1988.

Ingraham, Chrys. *White Weddings: romancing heterosexuality in popular culture,* Routledge, New York, 1999.

Jakubowicz, Andrew, 'White Noise: Australia's Struggle with Multiculturalism', in *Working Through Whiteness: international perspectives,* (ed.) Cynthia Levine-Rasky, State University of New York Press, Albany, NY, 2002.

James, Daniel, 'Listening in the Cold. The practice of oral history in an Argentine meatpacking community', in Robert Perks and

Alistair Thomson (eds), *The Oral History Reader,* (2nd Edition), Routledge, London, 2006.

Jarratt, Melynda, C*aptured Hearts. New Brunswick's War Brides,* Gooselane Editions, New Brunswick, Canada, 2008.

Johnson, Lesley. *The Modern Girl: Childhood and Growing Up:* Allen & Unwin, Sydney, 1989.

Kaiser, Hilary, *French War Brides in America. An Oral History,* Greenwood, London, 2007.

Kane, Betty, 'The War Bride', in *Albany Writers' Circle No.19. A Collection of Short Stories and Poetry by the Writers of Albany,* November issue, Denmark Printers, Albany, WA, 2001.

Keene, Judith, *Fighting for Franco : international volunteers in nationalist Spain during the Spanish Civil War, 1936-1939,* Leicester University Press, New York, 2001.

Keene, Judith, *The last mile to Huesca: an Australian nurse in the Spanish Civil War,* UNSW Press, Kensington, c.1988.

Kelson, Gregory A. and Debra L. De Laet (eds), *Gender and immigration,* New York University Press, NY, c.1999.

Kingston, Beverley. *My Wife, My Daughter and Poor Mary Ann: Women and Work in Australia,* Thomas Nelson Australia Pty Ltd, West Melbourne, Vic., 1975.

Lake, Marilyn and Damousi, Joy (eds), *Gender and War: Australians at war in the twentieth century,* Cambridge University Press, Melbourne, 1995.

Lake, Marilyn, 'Female desires: the meaning of World War II' in Joy Damousi and Marilyn Lake (eds) *Gender and War: Australians at war in the twentieth century,* Cambridge University Press, Melbourne, 1995.

Lake, Marilyn & Katie Homes (eds), *Freedom Bound; Documents on women in modern Australia,* Allen & Unwin, St Leonards, NSW, 1995.

Lee, Helene R., *Bittersweet Decision. The War Brides 40 years later,* Roselee Publications, Lockport, NY, 1985.

Leder, Jane, *Thanks For The Memories: Love, Sex, And World War II*, Praeger Publishers, London, 2006.

Leonardi-Lamorte, Maria, *Maria: The Life Story of a World War II Italian Bride*, iUniverse, Lincoln, NE, 2006.

Lewis, Robert, *A Nation At War. The Australian Home Front in the Second World War. Documents & Commentary*, Longman Cheshire, Melbourne, 1984.

Long, Vera Audrey Cracknell, From Britain With Love: World War II Pilgrim Brides Sail to America, Vienna, VA. 1988.

Longmate, Norman, *How We Lived Then. A history of everyday life during the Second World War*, Arrow Books, London, 1977 (first published 1971).

Lucas, Robin and Clare Forster, (eds), *Wilder Shores. Women's travel stories of Australia and Beyond*, University of Queensland Press, St Lucia, 1992.

Mack, Louise, *An Australian Girl in London*, T. Fisher Unwin, 1902.

Magarey, Susan, *Unbridling the tongues of women: a biography of Catherine Helen Spence*, Introduction, Hale & Iremonger, Sydney, c.1985.

Manning, Kathleen, *Rituals, Ceremonies, and Cultural Meaning in Higher Education*, Bergin & Garvey, Westport, CT, 2000.

Martin, Allan William, 'At war: women in the war' in *Australians from 1939*, Vol 5, Ann Curthoys, A W Martin and Tim Rowse (eds), Fairfax, Syme & Weldon Associates, Broadway, NSW, 1988, pp. 26-28.

Matthews, Jill Julius, Good and Mad Women: *The Historical Construction of Femininity in Twentieth-Century Australia:* George Allen & Unwin, Sydney, 1984.

Mackinolty , Judy, 'Woman's place…' in *The Wasted Years,* George Allen & Unwin Australia Pty Ltd, North Sydney, 1981.

McIntyre, Darryl, *Townsville at war 1942: life in a garrison city*, Townsville City Council, Townsville, c.1992.

McKernan, Michael, *All In! Fighting the War at Home*, Allen & Unwin, St Leonards, NSW, 1995.

Meadows, Maureen, *I Loved Those Yanks,* George M. Dash, Sydney, 1948.

Millar, Ann, *Trust the Women: women in the Federal Parliament,* Australian Parliament, Canberra, 1993.

Moore, John Hammond (ed.), *The American Alliance? Australia, New Zealand and the United Sates: 1940-1970?* Cassell Australia, Melbourne, 1970.

Moore, John Hammond (ed.), *Australians in America 1876-1976,* University of Queensland Press, St. Lucia, Brisbane, 1977.

Moore, John Hammond, *Over sexed, over-paid and over here: Americans in Australia, 1941-1945,* University of Queensland Press, St. Lucia, Brisbane, 1981.

Morris, Mathilde, *Dreams and Nightmares of a German War Bride,* Cambridge Writers Press, Auroro, Colorado, 1998.

Mosler, David and Bob Catley, *America and Americans in Australia,* Praeger, Westport, CT, 1998.

O'Hara, Peggy. *From Romance to Reality: Stories of Canadian War Brides.* Highway Book Shop, Cobalt, Ontario, 1985.

Oppenheimer, Melanie. *All Work No Pay. Australian Civilian Volunteers in War:* Ohio Productions, Walcha, NSW, 2002.

Oppenheimer, Melanie. *Volunteering. Why we can't survive without it.* UNSW Press, Sydney, NSW, 2008.

Page, Patricia, *Across the Magic Line. Growing up in Fiji,* Pandanus Books, ANU, Canberra, 2004.

Pelz Grant, Susie, T*he True Story of a German War Bride*, Publish America, Frederick, MD, 2008.

Perks, Robert and Alistair Thomson (eds), *The Oral History Reader,* (2nd Edition), Routledge, London, 2006.

Pesman, Ros, David Walker, and Richard White (eds). *The Oxford Book of Australian Travel Writing,* Oxford University Press, Melbourne, 1996.

Pesman, Ros, *Duty Free, Australian Women Abroad,* Oxford University Press, Melbourne, 1996.

Peter F McDonald, *Marriage in Australia: age at first marriage and proportions marrying, 1860-1971,* Department of Demography, Institute of Advanced Studies, ANU, Canberra, 1975.

Portelli, Alessandro, 'What makes Oral History Different', in Robert Perks and Alistair Thomson (eds), *The Oral History Reader,* (2nd Edition), Routledge, London, 2006.

Potts, Annette & Lucinda Strauss, *For the love of a soldier: Australian war-brides and their GIs,* ABC Enterprises for the Australian Broadcasting Commission, Crows Nest, NSW, 1987.

Potts, E Daniel & Annette Potts, *Yanks Down Under 1941-45: the American impact on Australia,* Oxford University Press, Melbourne, 1985.

Radi, Heather, 'Street, Jessie Mary Grey (1889 - 1970)', *Australian Dictionary of Biography,* Volume 16, Melbourne University Press, 2002, pp. 328-332.

Ralph, Barry, *They passed this way: the United States of America, the states of Australia and World War II,* Kangaroo Press, East Roseville, 2000.

Reiger, Kerreen M, *The Disenchantment of the Home. Modernizing the Australian Family 1880-1940,* Oxford University Press, Melbourne, 1985.

Reynolds, David, *Rich Relations. The American Occupation of Britain 1942-1945,* Harper Collins, London, 1995.

Ricou-Allunis, Jeannine, *Memoir of a French War Bride,* Authorhouse, 2004.

Rickard, John and Peter Spearritt, (eds), *Packaging the Past: public histories,* Melbourne University Press, Carlton, Vic., 1991.

Robertson, John, *Australia at War 1939-1945,* Heinemann, Melbourne, 1981.

Roe, Jill, 'What has Nationalism Offered Australian Women?' in Norma Grieve & Ailsa Burns (eds), *Australian Women. Contemporary Feminist Thought,* Oxford University Press, Melbourne, 1994.

Roe, Jill, 'Australian Women in America' in Harold Bolitho and Chris Wallace-Crabbe (eds), *Approaching Australia: papers from the Harvard Australian Studies Symposium,* (Harvard University Press) Cambridge, MA, 1999.

Roe, Jill, *Stella Miles Franklin. A Biography,* Harper Collins Publishers, Sydney, 2008.

Saunders, Kay, and Geoffrey Bolton, 'Girdled for war: women's mobilisations in World War Two', in Kay Saunders and Raymond Evans, (eds) *Gender relations in Australia: domination and negotiation,* Harcourt Brace Jovanovich, Sydney, NSW, 1992, pp. 376-397.

Saunders, Kay, *War on the homefront: State intervention in Queensland, 1938-48,* University of Queensland Press, St. Lucia, Brisbane, 1993.

Saunders, Kay, 'In a cloud of lust: Black GIs and sex in World War II', in Joy Damousi and Marilyn Lake, (eds) *Gender and war: Australians at war in the twentieth century,* Cambridge University Press, Melbourne, 1995.

Sheridan, Susan et al, (eds) *Who Was That Woman? The Australian Women's Weekly in the Postwar Years,* UNSW Press, Sydney, 2002.

Sheiner, Robin, *Smile the War is Over,* MacMillan, South Melbourne, 1983.

Schick-Grehl, Leni, *Love, War and Curling Irons,* Trafford Publishing, Victoria, BC, 2008.

Shukert, Elfrieda and Barbara Scibetta, War Brides of World War II, Presidio Press, Novato, CA,1988.

Shute, Carmel, 'Heroines and heroes: Sexual mythology in Australia 1914-1918' in Joy Damousi and Marilyn Lake (eds), *Gender and War. Australians at War in the Twentieth Century,* Cambridge University Press, Melbourne, 1995, pp.117-29.

Soanes, Catherine & Angus Stevenson, (eds), *Concise Oxford English Dictionary,* 11th Ed., Revised, Oxford University Press, New York, 2006.

Sowerwine C and P Grimshaw, 'Women in Europe, the United States and Australia, 1914 to 2000', in (eds) M. Wiesner-Hanks and T. Meade, *The Blackwell Companion to Gender History*, Blackwell, London, 2004, pp. 586-610.

Spearritt, Peter and David Walker, *Australian Popular Culture,* Allen & Unwin, Sydney, 1979.

Straight, Linda (ed.), *Women on the Verge of Home*, State University of New York Press, Albany, NY, 2005.

Street, Jessie M. G., *Truth or Repose,* Australasian Book Society, Sydney, 1966

Summerfield, Penny, *Reconstructing Women's Wartime Lives,* Manchester University Press, Manchester, UK, 1998.

Tamura, Keiko, *Michi's Memories: The story of a Japanese war bride,* Pandanus Books Research School of Pacific and Asian Studies, ANU, Canberra, 2003.

Thomson, Alistair, *Anzac Memories: Living with the Legend,* Oxford University Press, Melbourne, 1995.

Thomson, Joyce A., *The WAAAF in Wartime Australia,* Melbourne University Press, 1991.

Thompson, Paul, 'The Voice of the Past. Oral History', in Robert Perks and Alistair Thomson (eds), *The Oral History Reader,* (2nd Edition), Routledge, London, 2006.

Thompson, Paul, *The Voice of the Past. Oral History,* (3rd Edition), Oxford University Press, New York, 2000 (first published 1978).

Torngren, Maya, Maya. *The Story of a German War Bride,* iUniverse Inc., Lincoln, NE, 2007.

Townsend, Colin and Eileen, *War Wives. A Second World War* Anthology, Grafton Books, London 1989.

Turner, Victor, *The Ritual Process. Structure and Anti-Structure,* Cornell University Press, New York, NY, 1969.

Van Gennep, Arnold, *The Rites of Passage,* (translated by Monica B. Vizedom and Gabrielle L. Caffee), Routledge & Kegan Paul, London, 1960.

Virden, Jenel, *Goodbye Piccadilly: British war brides in America,* University of Illinois Press, Urbana, IL, c.1996.

Walker, David, 'The Getting of Manhood' in Peter Spearritt & David Walker (eds) *Australian Popular Culture,* Sydney, 1979.

Walker, David *Anxious Nation: Australia and the Rise of Asia, 1850-1939,* University of Queensland Press, St. Lucia, Qld, 1999.

White, Richard, 'War and Australian Society' in Michael McKernan & Margaret Browne (eds) *Australia: Two Centuries of War and Peace,* Canberra, 1988.

Winfield Pamela, with Brenda W Hasty, *Sentimental Journal: The Story of the GI,* Constable and Co., London, 1985.

Winfield, Pamela, *Melancholy Baby: The Unplanned Consequences of the GIs' Arrival in Europe for World War II,* Bergin & Garvey, Westport, CT, 2000.

Wood, Val, *War brides: they followed their hearts to New Zealand,* Random Century, Auckland, NZ, 1991.

Woollacott, Angela, *To Try Her Fortune in London. Australian Women, Colonialism and Modernity,* Oxford University Press, 2001.

Young, William H with Nancy K Young, T*he 1950s. American Popular Culture Through History,* Greenwood Press, Westport, CT, 2004.

Yow, Valerie, '"Do I Like Them Too Much?" Effects of the oral history interview on the interviewer and vice-versa', in Robert Perks and Alistair Thomson (eds), *The Oral History Reader, (2nd Edition), Routledge, London, 2006.*

ARTICLES, CONFERENCE PAPERS, REPORTS AND PROCEEDINGS

—— 'G.I. War Brides', *Monthly Film Bulletin,* Vol. 13, pp. 145-56, 1946, p. 124.

Barrowclough, Nikki, 'Talking about my generation', *Good Weekend,* May 3, 2008, p. 38.

Barrett, J, 'Living in Australia 1939-45', *Journal of Australian Studies* Vol. 1, No. 2, November, 1977.

Brawley, Sean and Chris Dixon, 'Searching for Dorothy Lamour: War and Sex in the South Pacific, 1941-45, *Australasian Journal of American Studies,* Vol. 18, No. 1, July 1999, pp. 3-20.

Brawley, Sean and Chris Dixon, 'Jim Crow Downunder? African American Encounters with White Australia, 1942-1945', *The Pacific Historical Review,* Vol. 71, No. 4 (Nov., 2002), pp. 607-632.

Buttsworth, Sara, 'Women Colouring the Wartime Landscape' in *On the Homefront. Western Australia and World War II,* Jenny Gregory (ed.), University of Western Australia Press, Nedlands, 1996.

Coates, Donna, 'Reality Bites: the Impact of the Second World War on the Australian Home Front in Maria Gardner's *Blood Stained Wattle* and Robin Sheiner's "Smile the War is Over"', *Antipodes,* June, 2009, pp. 49-55.

Coates, Donna, 'Damn(Ed) Yankees: The American "Invasion" and Its Impact on Australian Women's Second World War Fictions'. Paper presented at the ANZSANA Conference, University of Texas, Austin, TX, 1996. (Unpublished.)

Coates, Donna, 'Damn(Ed) Yankees: The Pacific's Not Pacific Anymore', *Antipodes,* December, 2001, pp.123-29.

Coultan, Mark, 'After 54 years, Australia reclaims its lost Joy', *The Age,* June 5, 2007.

Crabbe, C. Wallace and H. Bolitho (eds), *Approaching Australia. Papers from the Harvard Australian Studies Symposium,* Harvard University Press, Cambridge, MA, c.1998.

Darian-Smith, Kate and Jenzen, Rachel, 'Memories from America: Australian War Brides and US Marines Remember Australia and the Pacific during the Second World War' [online], in *When the Soldiers Return,* Conference Proceedings, November 2007, Martin Crotty (ed.), School of History,

Philosophy, Religion and Classics, University of Queensland, Brisbane, 2009, pp.12-25.

Davis, Joan, '"Women's Work" and the Women's Services in the Second World War as Presented in Salt', *Hecate: an Interdisciplinary Journal of Women's Liberation,* Vol. 18, No. 1 (1992), pp. 64-87.

Dixon, Chris and Sean Brawley, 'Searching for Dorothy Lamour: War and Sex in the South Pacific 1941-45', *Australasian Journal of American Studies,* Vol. 18, 1999.

Dux, Monica, '"Discharging the Truth": Venereal Disease, the Amateur and the Print Media, 1942-1945', *Lilith,* Vol. 10, 2001.

Edwards, Barbara 'Three Times a Migrant', *Richmond River Historical Society Bulletin,* Richmond River Historical Society Inc., Lismore, NSW, pp. 3-7.

Featherstone, L., 'Sexy Mamas? Women, Sexuality and Reproduction in Australia in the 1940s', *Australian Historical Studies,* 2005.

Fortune, Gabrielle "Mr Jones' Wives": war brides, marriage, immigration and identity formation' in *Women's History Review,* Vol. 15, No. 4, September 2006.

Freame, Jessica, *'Woman of the Year:* Katharine Hepburn and the American Nation During World War II', *Lilith,* 12, 2003, History Dept., University of Melbourne, Vic.

Graham, Don. 'Koka-Kola Kulture: Reflections Upon Things American Down Under', *Southwest Review,* Vol. 78, No. 2, 1993, pp. 231-44.

Grayzel, Susan R, 'Fighting for Their Rights: A Comparative Perspective on Twentieth-Century Women's Movements in Australia, Great Britain, and the United States', *Journal of Women's History,* Vol. 11, No. 1, 1999, pp. 210-18.

Harker, Margot, 'This Radiant Day', *RSSS Annual Report*, ANU, Canberra, 1998.

Hartmann, Susan M, 'Prescriptions for Penelope: Literature on

Women's Obligations to Returning World War II Veterans', *Women Studies,* Vol. 5, 1978, pp. 223-239.

Houstoun, Marion F *et al*, 'Female Predominance in Immigration to the United States Since 1930: A First Look', *International Migration Review,* Vol. 18, No. 4, Special Issue: Women in Migration, Winter, 1984.

Kunek, Srebrenk, 'Brides, Wives and Single Women: Gender and Immigration', *Lilith,* Vol. 8, 1993, pp. 82-113.

Lake, Marilyn, 'The Desire for a Yank: Sexual Relations between Australian Women and American Servicemen During World War II', *Journal of the History of Sexuality,* Vol. 2, No. 4, 1992, pp. 621-33.

Lake, Marilyn, 'Personality, Individuality, Nationality: Feminist Conceptions of Citizenship 1902-1940', *Australian Feminist Studies,* Vol. 19, Autumn, 1994.

Lange, Cheryl, 'Introduction', 'Immigration and Citizenship', *Studies in Western Australian History,* Vol. 21, 2000.

Matt, Susan J., 'A Hunger for Home: Homesickness and Food in a Global Consumer Society', *The Journal of American Culture,* Vol. 30, No. 1, March 2007.

May, Josephine 'Secrets and lies: sex education and gendered memories of childhood's end in an Australian provincial city, 1930s-1950s', *Sex Education,* Vol. 6, No. 1, February 2006, pp. 1-15.

Potts, E. Daniel & Annette Potts, 'Australian Wartime Propaganda and Censorship', *Historical Studies,* Vol. 21, No. 85, October, 1985.

Prisk, Max, 'Picture This When the Jitterbug Came to Town. 100 Years of Herald Photography', *Sydney Morning Herald, Weekend Edition,* July 26-27, 2008, 'News', p. 12.

Reed, Liz, 'Narrating Women's Wartime Lives: Australia, New Zealand and Canada Remember', *Journal of Australian Studies,* March 1999.

Reekie, G., 'Women's responses to war work in WA 1942-46', *Studies in WA History,* Vol. 7, 1983.

Reekie, G., 'War, sexuality and feminism: Perth women's organisations 1938-45', *Historical Studies,* Vol. 21, No. 85, October, 1985, pp. 576-591.

Roe, Jill, 'Cut in Half? Australian war brides in the US since World War II', Schlesinger Library Visiting Scholar Project: Progress Report, 13 December, 1999. (unpublished transcript in possession of author.)

Rose, Sonya O., 'Girls and GIs: Race, Sex and Diplomacy in Second World War Britain', *International Review of Social History,* Vol. 19, 1997.

Saunders, Kay, 'Not for them battle fatigues: the Australian Women's Land Army in the Second World War', *Journal of Australian Studies,* 1997.

Saunders, Kay, 'Conflict between the Australian and American Governments over the introduction of Black American servicemen into Australia during the Second World War', *Australian Journal of Politics and History,* Vol. 2, No. 33, pp. 39-46, 1987.

Saunders, Kay & Helen Taylor, 'To combat the plague': the construction of moral alarm and state intervention in Queensland during World War II', *Hecate,* Vol. 14, 1988.

Saunders, Kay 'The Dark Shadow of White Australia: Racial Anxieties in Australia in World War II', *Ethnic and Racial Studies,* Vol. 17, No. 2, pp. 325-341.

Saunders, Kay 'The reception of Black American Servicemen in Australia during World War II: The Resistence of "White Australia"', *Journal of Black Studies,* 1995, Vol. 25, pp. 331-348.

Shute, Carmel 'From Balaclavas to Bayonets: women's voluntary war work, 1939-41', *Hecate,* Vol. 6, No.1, 1980, pp. 5-26.

Sturma, Michael, 'Loving the alien: the underside of relations between American Servicemen and Australian women in Queensland 1942-1945', *Journal of Australian Studies,* Vol. 24, 1989.

Summerfield, Penny, 'Culture and Composure: Creating Narratives of the Gendered Self in Oral History Interviews', *Culture and Social History,* Vol. 1, No. 1, 2004, p. 90.

Teo, Hsu Ming, 'Love Writes: Gender and Romantic Love in Australian Love Letters, 1860-1960', *Australian Feminist Studies,* Vol. 20, No. 48, November 2005.

ORAL HISTORY PROJECTS

Liston, Carol and Robyn Arrowsmith, 'From Farms to Freeways', UWS, Werrington, 1993. (Unpublished.)

Liston, Carol, Deborah Chambers, and Robyn Arrowsmith, 'Private and Public Images of Women', Women's Research Centre, UWS, 1993. (Research published in Deborah Chambers, Representing the Family, SAGE Publications Ltd., London, 2001, p. xi, and pp. 75-91.)

Wieneke, Christine and Robyn Arrowsmith, *When I'm 65 or 70 or 75: women and the abolition of the retirement age for women,* School of Ecology, UWS, Hawkesbury, Sydney, 1993. (Published in-house by UWS, Hawkesbury.)

FILM

Potts, Annette & Lucinda Strauss, *For the love of a soldier:* Australian war-brides and their GIs, ABC-TV Documentary Film, DVD-Pathfinder Productions Pty. Ltd., Bronte, NSW, c.1986.

ON-LINE SOURCES

About Rusty Walker, http://www.walker-creative.com/index.html [Accessed 26 September, 2008.]

The American War Bride Experience, http://www.geocities.com/us_warbrides/ [Accessed 7 June, 2009, 29 July, 2009.]

Australian Dictionary of Bibliography Online Edition, http://www. adbonline.anu.edu.au/adbonline.htm [Accessed 3 March, 2009, 17 January, 2010.]

Australian Government, http://australia.gov.au/topics/immigration/ australian-citizenship [Accessed 21 January 2010].

Australian Government, http://www.citizenship.gov.au/current/dual_ citizenship/ [Accessed 4 November, 2009]

Australian Government Department of Foreign Affairs and Trade, https://www.passports.gov.au/Web/PassportHistory.aspx accessed 2 August, 2008.]

Australian National Dictionary Centre – ANDC – on-line: www. anu/edu/au [Accessed 30 September, 2008.]

Australian War Memorial http://www.awm.gov.au/encyclopedia/vad. asp [Accessed 4 August, 2008.]

Australian War Memorial Encyclopedia online, [see Sir (Ernest) Edward 'Weary' Dunlop] http://www.awm.gov.au/ encyclopedia/dunlop/bio.asp [Accessed 6 September, 2008.]

Daughters of the British Empire Idaho Chapter, http://www. dbeidaho.org/what_is_dbe.htm [Accessed 18 September, 2008.]

Department of Immigration and Multicultural and Indigenous Affairs, (DIMIA), Australian Government, http://www. citizenship.gov.au/index.htm [Accessed 3 August, 2004.]

John Curtin Prime Ministerial Library, John Curtin University, http://john.curtin.edu.au/manofpeace/homefront.html [Accessed 13 December, 2009.]

Schneider, Dorothea *The Literature on Women Immigrants to the United States,* Dept. of Sociology, University of Illinois, March 2003, http://barthes.enssib.fr/clio/revues/AHI/articles/ volumes/schneid.html [Accessed 12 September, 2007.]

Southern Cross Club, Washington DC's History, http://www. southerncrossclubdc.com/History/History.htm [Accessed 1 September, 2008.]

The Southern Cross Group, http://www.southern-cross-group.
org/ [Accessed 29.August 2004, 20 March, 20 December,
2007, 11 September, 2008.]

US Citizenship and Immigration Services, http://www.uscis.gov/
portal/site/uscis [Accessed 20 January, 2008.]

Uher, Pam 'The origin of Davy Jones' locker', *Helium,* www.helium.
com/iter [Accessed 29 August, 2008.]

Waller, Ken, 'Growing Up During the War', August 1988. *Moreton
Bay College,* http://www.mbc.qld.edu.au [Accessed 5 June,
2003.]

Wikipedia, The Free Encyclopedia, http://en.wikipedia.org/wiki/
California_Proposition 13 (1978) [Accessed 7 August,
2007.]

Wikipedia, The Free Encyclopedia, http://en.wikipedia.org/wiki/
Immigration_Act_of_1924 [Accessed 15 November, 2009.]

Wikipedia, the Free Encyclopedia, http://en.wikipedia.org/wiki/
Pullman_Company [Accessed 9 November, 2009.]

THESES

Brake, Sandra, 'United States armed forces in the Rockhampton
district', BA Thesis, Central Queensland University, 1980.

Campbell, Rosemary, 'The Americans in Brisbane 1942-45', PhD
Thesis, University of Sydney, 1987.

Featherstone, Lisa, 'Breeding and Feeding: social history of mothers
and medicine in Australia 1880-1925', PhD thesis,
Macquarie University, Sydney, 2004.

Fortune, Gabrielle Ann, '"Mr Jones' Wives": World War II War
Brides of New Zealand Servicemen', PhD, Department of
History, The University of Auckland, 2005.

Gentle, Janice Larson, 'American Women Migrants in Sydney:
Similarity and Difference', MA (Hons) Thesis, Macquarie
University, Sydney,1994.

Harker, Margot, "This Radiant Day": A history of the Australian

Wedding, 1788-1960', unpublished PhD thesis, ANU, Canberra, 1998.

Hastak, Astrid, "I was never one of those Fräuleins": the impact of cultural image on German war brides in America', PhD Thesis, Purdue University, West Lafayette, IN, May 2005.

Jarrett, Melynda, 'The War Brides of New Brunswick', Master of Arts Thesis, University New Brunswick, Canada, 1995.

Lark, Regina Frances, 'They challenged two nations: Marriages between Japanese women and American GIs, 1945 to present', PhD Thesis, University of Southern California, 1999.

Mercer, Martha Jones, 'British Brides, American Wives: The Immigration and Acculturation of War Brides in Mobile, Alabama, 1945-1993, Master of Arts Thesis, University of South Alabama, 1993, UMI Dissertation Publishing, Ann Arbor, Michigan.

Index

Lightning Source UK Ltd.
Milton Keynes UK
UKOW05f0352081216

289396UK00001B/350/P